AN EMPIRE   MILLION

JEAN THIRIART

EUROPE

AN EMPIRE OF 400 MILLION

✯ ✯ ✯

TRANSLATED WITH AN
INTRODUCTION BY ALEXANDER JACOB

ARKTOS
LONDON 2021

Copyright © 2021 by Arktos Media Ltd.

All rights reserved. No part of this book may be reproduced or utilised in any form or by any means (whether electronic or mechanical), including photocopying, recording or by any information storage and retrieval system, without permission in writing from the publisher.

ISBN	978-1-914208-03-4 (Paperback)
	978-1-914208-04-1 (Hardback)
	978-1-914208-05-8 (Ebook)
TRANSLATION	Alexander Jacob
EDITING	Constantin von Hoffmeister
COVER & LAYOUT	Tor Westman

Arktos.com | fb.com/Arktos | @arktosmedia | arktosmedia

CONTENTS

Introduction by Alexander Jacob ◆ vii

Dedication ◆ xxiii

Acknowledgements ◆ xxiv

CHAPTER I
The Dimensions of the European State ◆ 1

CHAPTER II
The Style of the Unitarian European State ◆ 19

CHAPTER III
The Friends and Enemies of Unitarian Europe ◆ 47

CHAPTER IV
Legal Europe Against Combatant Europe ◆ 63

CHAPTER V
The Place And the Role of Man in the
European Communitarian Society ◆ 73

CHAPTER VI
The Universal Mission of Europeanism,
Our Natural Right to Hegemony ◆ 117

CHAPTER VII
How Unitarian Europe Will Be Formed ◆ 141

CHAPTER VIII
Those Who Will Constitute Europe or the Modern Party,
That Is to Say, Organisation Introduced into Politics ◆ 193

CHAPTER IX
For a Lucid Morality and against a Debilitating Morality ◆ 237

INTRODUCTION

BY ALEXANDER JACOB

JEAN-FRANÇOIS THIRIART (1922–92) was, without doubt, one of the most significant pioneers of the project of a united Europe, which has been espoused by several contemporary European geopolitical thinkers, such as Robert Steuckers, Claudio Mutti and Aleksandr Dugin. Rather like the American political thinker Francis Parker Yockey (1917–60) before him, Thiriart was one of the first to pivot his entire political project on the precondition of a liberation of Europe from the control of America, which he considered the principal enemy of Europe. And his major book on a united, or unitarian, Europe, published in 1964, is an important manual for all European national revolutionaries who wish to continue to fight for the independence of Europe — which remains to this day a vassal state of America.

Thiriart was born in Brussels and participated in socialist movements in Belgium, such as the *Jeune Garde Socialiste* and the *Union Socialiste Anti-Fasciste*. During the Second World War, Thiriart joined the *Fichte Bund* (part of the Hamburg National-Bolshevik movement of the 1920s) and then the *Amis du Grand Reich Allemand*, an association composed of elements of the extreme left in Wallonia who were favorable to European collaboration with the Reich. Thiriart's association with this group led to imprisonment in 1944 and a deprivation of civic rights in Belgium until 1959.

Thiriart re-emerged in 1960, during the decolonization of the Congo, by participating in the foundation of the *Comité d'Action* and the *Défense des Belges d'Afrique,* which later became the *Mouvement d'Action Civique.*

On March 4th 1962, a meeting was organised in Venice whose participants included, besides Thiriart, who represented the MAC and Belgium, the Italian Social Movement from Italy, the Socialist Reich Party from Germany, and the Union Movement of Oswald Mosley from Great Britain. In a common declaration, these organizations proclaimed that they wanted to found a "National European Party, centred on the idea of European unity, which does not accept satellitisation of Western Europe by the USA and does not reject reunification with the territories of the east, from Poland to Bulgaria, through Hungary."

However, the narrow nationalism of the Italians and Germans rapidly broke up the project of a European National Party. The failure of this attempt at a party organization coincided with the defeat of the OAS (*Organisation Armée Secrète*), which fought for French Algeria during the Algerian War and which Thiriart sympathised with. Thiriart concluded that the only solution was the creation of a Revolutionary European Party, in a common front with parties or countries opposed to the order of Yalta. The MAC was thus transformed in January 1963 into *Jeune Europe*, a European organization that had members in Austria, Germany, Spain, France, Great Britain, Italy, the Netherlands, Portugal, and Switzerland. The new movement was rather different from the customary nationalist movements in Europe. It was very strongly structured, insisted on ideological formation in true schools of leadership and it tried to implement a central syndicate, the *Syndicat Communautaire Européen*. While *Jeune Europe* was banned in France on account of its ties to the OAS, it succeeded in recruiting many members in Italy.

The journals of the organisation, first *Jeune Europe* (1963–66), then *La Nation Européenne* (1966–68), also had a considerable audience. There were Italian counterparts, *Europa Combattente* and *La Nazione Europea* (which was edited by Claudio Mutti, the present editor of the journal *Eurasia*), as well. General Perón, in exile in Madrid, declared "I regularly read *La Nation Européenne* and I entirely share its ideas. Not only as regards Europe but also the world."[1]

Apart from numerous articles related to his Europeanist ideas, Thiriart had, already in 1961, written a 'Manifeste à la nation européene', in which he proclaimed his concept of a Communitarian Europe united against the American and Soviet blocs. This manifesto was followed by the present work, *Un empire de 400 million d'hommes*, published in 1964, and a further booklet entitled *La Grande Nation: L'Europe unitaire de Brest à Bucarest*, published in 1965.

Jeune Europe also aimed at forming European Revolutionary Brigades to start the armed struggle against the American occupier, and searched for external support in Europe as well as among Third World revolutionaries. Thus contacts were made with Yugoslavia and Romania, Communist China, as well as Iraq, Egypt, and the Palestinian Resistance.

In April 1968, the publisher of the journal of *Jeune Europe, La Nation Européene*, Gérard Bordes, went to Algeria with a *Mémorandum à l'intention du gouvernement de la République Algérienne*, signed by himself and Thiriart, which proposed that "European revolutionary patriots support the formation of special fighters for the future struggle against Israel; technical training of the future action aimed at a struggle against the Americans in Europe; building of an anti-American and anti-Zionist information service for a simultaneous utilization in the Arabian countries and in Europe". However, this Algerian effort proved to be unsuccessful. Nonetheless, the military support of his militants in the Anti-Zionist combat is incontestable

---

[1] The February 1969 issue of *Nation Européene* contained the text of a long interview that Thiriart conducted with Juan Perón.

since the first European who fell in the struggle against Zionism, in June 1968, Roger Coudroy, was a member of *Jeune Europe*.

In autumn 1968, Thiriart travelled to the Middle East at the invitation of the governments of Iraq and Egypt and the Ba'ath Party. He met Nasser during this visit but, under Soviet pressure, the Iraqi government refused to support the idea of a cooperation between Arab nationalists, including the nascent Palestinian ones, and Thiriart's European Revolutionary Brigades.

The lack of the desired financial and material aid to *Jeune Europe* and its failure to find a firm base for its pan-European operations — as Piedmont had been for the unification of Italy in the middle of the 19th century — was a severe blow to Thiriart's revolutionary ambitions. Further, the fact that, after the crises of decolonisation, Europe benefited from a decade of economic prosperity reduced the prospects of any revolutionary movement. In 1969, disappointed by the relative failure of his movement and the weakness of his external support, Thiriart renounced militant combat.

In the early 1980s, Thiriart worked on a book that was never finished: *The Euro-Soviet Empire From Vladivostok to Dublin*. As the title of this book shows, Thiriart's view of the Soviet Union had completely changed. Discarding the old motto "Neither Washington, nor Moscow", Thiriart assumed a new slogan: "With Moscow, against Washington". Thiriart had already expressed his satisfaction with the Soviet military intervention in Prague, denouncing the Zionist plots in the so called "Prague Spring", in an article entitled *'Prague, l'URSS et l'Europe'*,[2] where he maintained that

> [a] Western Europe free from US influence would permit the Soviet Union to assume a role almost antagonistic to the USA. A Western Europe allied, or a Western Europe aggregated to the USSR, would be the end of the American imperialism [...] If Russians want to separate Europeans from America — and they necessarily have to work for this aim in the

---

2   *La Nation Européenne*, n. 29, November 1968.

long-term — it's necessary that they offer us the chance to create a European political organization against the American golden slavery.

At the time of the collapse of the Soviet Union, in 1991, he supported the creation of the European National Liberation Front, which was the successor of *Jeune Europe*. It was with a delegation of the EFL that he went to Moscow, in 1992, to meet some of the members of the Russian opposition to Boris Yeltsin. Unfortunately, shortly after his return to Belgium. Jean Thiriart died of a heart attack.

*

Thiriart left unfinished many theoretical works, in which he analysed the necessary evolution of the anti-American combat in the light of the disappearance of the USSR. Of all Thiriart's writings, however, *Un Empire* is clearly the most elaborate exposition of his political vision, even if some of its political references are now outdated.

The essential basis of Thiriart's political doctrine is his conviction of the supremacy of the European peoples on account of their great historical maturity, the unrivalled influence of their culture and the international potential of their technological and industrial resources.

Thiriart's elevation of the Europeans to the first place among the different races of the world derives from his classification of these races into three major types:

> One can summarily divide the human races into three categories: the creative races, the races capable of rapid adaptation, the sterile races. Within each group also there exist levels.
>
> We shall place notably the Indo-Europeans among the creative races, the Japanese race among the races capable of adaptation, and the black among the races that are especially sterile.[3]

Thiriart also pauses to compare the advancement of Europe to that of India, which shares in an Indo-European heritage. Most people

---

3 All quotations from *Un Empire* are from the present edition.

are aware of the relative deficiency of India in its scientific and economic development, but few notice the fact that even in the intellectual realm its characteristic excellence has been limited to the field of metaphysics:

> The East has never been creative except in the domains of metaphysics or mysticism, activities that are particularly little constructive. If one excepts the rare historical accidents, Alexander or the men come from the steppes through the North, India has been a region remarkably isolated from the big international confrontations. What emerged from this? A sort of life with a torpid rhythm. Geographically, demographically, historically, a great nation should have emerged from this peninsula blessed by climate and protected by the Himalayas. However, nothing of the sort emerged from it.

Similarly, China, which

> [w]e notice ... under the Mings, later under the Manchu emperors, as already having lost its speed, ALREADY IN AN IMPASSE. This China of the 17th century and 18th had produced remarkable painters and poets and, already 2000 years earlier, a well-known philosopher, Lao Tzu, and a military moralist, Confucius; but it had to call to its aid Portuguese and Flemish Jesuits to construct its artillery and to calculate its calendar.

However, Thiriart is not unaware of the rapid rise of China under the Communists, so that, already in 1964, the world had to deal with not two great powers, the USA and the USSR, as at the Yalta Conference at the end of the Second World War, but with four—the USA, the USSR, China and, finally, the Europe that Thiriart himself was fighting for, and that he wanted his readers to fight for too.

The excellence of Europe, however, is not merely one that emerges in relation to the imitative capacity of the Japanese or the lack of that capacity among the blacks but also, more crucially, in relation to the qualities of its quasi-European rivals, the USA and the USSR (now Russia). Both of these powers are derivatives of Europe, lacking historical maturity and also, significantly, the necessary individualistic development of its peoples, which Europe alone has. Both the USA and the USSR have a capacity to produce only collectivist men, the former marked by conformism to capitalistic fashions imposed by commercial interests and the latter by obligatory adherence to the collectivist social models imposed on them by the state. The mission of Europe is thus nothing less than the rescue of humanity from the grip of the 'mass men' of the two superpowers, America and Russia.

Even though Europe is a highly developed nation culturally and industrially, what is lacking to Europe as an integral continent is political unity, and the achievement of the latter is the principal task that Thiriart focuses on in this work. One step forward to the creation of the united Europe that Thiriart envisaged was the Common Market that was born of the Treaty of Rome in 1957. Though many of the so-called European nationalist groupings of his time mocked this union as a technocratic one with no potential for the unification of the continent, Thiriart saw in it the same potential for a prospective unification of the continent that the Prussian *Zollverein* of 1834 had had for the unification of Germany in 1871. The 'economic child' that was given birth to in Rome would, in the near future, grow into a political colossus — once the puppet politicians installed by Washington were swept aside.

The hidden danger that Thiriart detected in Soviet Communism was that, behind its collectivist totalitarian system, there lurked the real threat of a typical Russian imperialism, which was only masked during the Soviet period. However, the rebellions of East Germany, Czechoslovakia, Poland and Hungary between 1953 and 1964 had shown that the Soviet system could never succeed in absorbing the peoples of Eastern and Central Europe since their historical traditions had moulded them differently from the Russians.[4] Also, Russia will have to face a constant threat from the Chinese, whom Thiriart even

---

4   When one considers the 'Eurasian' movement of today, which is centred in Russia, one must remember that the distrust that Thiriart felt of the Russian imperialist ambitions continues in the hearts of many Eastern and Central Europeans, who cannot suffer the expansion of the Russian Federation any

considers as a short-term ally in the fight against the European ambitions of the Soviets.

In any case, as Thiriart rightly pointed out, the only solid basis for any future cooperation between Europe and Russia would be one that begins with the indispensable condition for such a cooperation — namely, the eviction of America from the continent. In this regard, the reader must pay special attention to the passages in which Thiriart excoriates the 'extreme right-wing' groups of his time for their willingness to squabble among themselves about existing borders between, say Austria and Italy in South Tyrol, while all the while silently submitting to the totally foreign colonialism represented by the American occupation of Europe, and more particularly by the strong arm of this colonialism, NATO. The so-called right-wing groups are also dangerous since they only tend to break up, balkanise, the union of Europe through petty nationalist chauvinism. Secessionist movements, like those of the Bretons or Catalonians, are even worse since they are designed to splinter Europe into ever smaller units that will be more vulnerable to the supranational power of the Americans and the Soviets/Russians. Just as the German princes of the 17th century had damaged the cause of German union through their internal quarrels and recourse to France and Austria in such a way as to benefit only the latter great powers, so

> [t]oday, with regard to Europe, all the petty nationalists who in the final analysis practise Atlanticism, that is to say, the subjection to Washington, more than they could suffer the yoke of the Soviet Union before the collapse of Communism.

While Thiriart himself hoped that the end of the Communist regime in Russia would usher in an era of cooperation between Russia and Europe, the recent resurgence of Russian power under its popular president Vladimir Putin shows us that not only is the imperialistic impulse of Russia undiminished in its non-Communist condition but its capitalistic framework also happens to be a plutocratic oligarchic one that exhibits the worst tendencies of capitalist inequity disguised by a veneer of Orthodox Russian 'traditionalism' that seeks to present the 'Russian soul' as the opposite of the soulless materialistic West.

not being able to agree among themselves, are as criminal as the little German princes of the 17th century with regard to Germany.[5]

Thiriart considers federalism as being preferable to a confederate 'Europe of nations' since the latter attempts to bind the different nations together only legally and not socially. However, federalism too must be considered only a transitional stage to Thiriart's form of Communitarian Europe, which will also be a unitarian one, or one that considers all of Europe as a single nation. As an example of a successful Communitarian political entity Thiriart points to the United Kingdom, which contains Anglo-Saxons and Celts in a more or less homogeneous nation:

> The loyalty that Celts, Anglo-Saxons and Scots have shown for four centuries to the Crown will tomorrow be an example for the peoples of Europe when they will have to vow a total loyalty to the UNITARIAN EUROPEAN STATE without, for that reason, renouncing anything of their origins and cultures.

In spite of the apparent strength of the American empire, Thiriart considers the necessary collapse of the American power to be evident already in the various problems that America already faced in the sixties, such as the racial conflicts that showed no sign of a permanent resolution, and the resistance of Latin countries to the American imperialism. Thiriart believes that both Latin America and Africa must be encouraged by Europe to debilitate the American control of their affairs, just as China too in the East must initially be helped to fight Russian imperialistic tendencies (even though China must be combated eventually when Russia is aligned with Europe).

---

5   The right-wing groups of present-day Europe that not only fail to attack the Americans on their continent but also seek to establish ties with so-called 'Alternative Right' groups in America in a so-called fight against an Islamic bogeyman thus do not represent an advance from the right-wing groups of Thiriart's time but rather a sinister transformation of the Right into an ideological arm of American and Zionist imperialism.

Thiriart, as a champion of Belgium's colonies in Africa as well as of France's in Algeria, firmly believes that Africa must be considered a 'prolongation' of Europe and a protectorate of the latter. America and Soviet Russia must be strenuously kept out of Africa at all costs. For only the control over North Africa, as well as of the interior of the continent, could ensure that the Mediterranean Sea would once again become Europe's *Mare Nostrum*, as the Romans used to call it.

Indeed, Thiriart's vision is one of Europe as a renewed Roman Empire, a vision that however learns from the mistakes of the two earlier attempts to establish such a European empire under Bonaparte and Hitler. He does not believe that unitarian Europe should be dominated by either the French or the Germans but wishes for a remoulding of the entire continent under strong leaders who will consider themselves and their citizens as primarily Europeans.

This task of forming a European nation Thiriart delegates to what he calls an 'avant-garde' elite, which will be constituted of the first freedom fighters in the fight against the two evils of American capitalism and Soviet Communism. From this initial team will emerge the 'heroic' members, who, along with the men of vision who impelled the new European Party, will constitute a new aristocracy — such as was consolidated nine centuries ago by William the Conqueror in England with the help of his barons.

The elite will be totally authoritarian in its character and formation, with power necessarily being channelled to the masses from the top. The first task of the new Party will be to de-proletarianise the masses and render them responsible 'adults' after their years of stultification through the various forms of collectivist propaganda dispensed by the Americans and Russians. The strengthening of society is a condition of its resistance to enemy forces and this can only be accomplished through the reinforcement of moral values in it. Indeed, the Communists often benefit from the misfits and 'victims' of Western society, whose resentment and discontent in the decadence of the West make them easy recruits into the Communist ranks.

The European Party, designated as an 'avant-garde' party, is in many ways a party of guerrilla warfare against the two major enemies on the continent, for only through subterfuge can these enemies be brought down. The guerrilla warfare of the new Party must seek to undermine the nerve-centres of the reigning powers:

> The political life of a nation is concentrated in some nerve-centres of information, trade unionism, youth movements. To introduce oneself into these nerve-centres progressively, silently, allows one to organise short-circuits there. A regime can seem strong and have muscle, that is to say, many policemen, many newspapers of its own: but what can these muscles serve if the nerve-centres which determine its movements by giving them impulses are attacked, disconnected?

Recruitment to the Party should be careful and cool-headed rather than impulsive so that reckless types are excluded, or at least included only when they are needed in times of crisis. What the Party seeks are people 'committed' to its dogma rather than mere 'members'. In this, the European Party will resemble the Jesuit Order or even the Masons, or the Communist Party itself, since all these are ubiquitous organisations with members who are wholly committed to their cause. The European Party should also have, in the initial stages, a mobile militia that will be capable of rendering speedy aid to any of its members in times of threats from the occupying foreign forces.

As for the leaders, they will, through their clarity of political vision and devotion to the cause, meet dangers without hesitation. Just as military commanders are privately resisted by their troops on account of their harsh discipline but admired in times of crisis by the same troops on account of their experience and judgement, so too will the new leaders be easily distinguished by their ability to command — as opposed to the democratic leaders of popularity, who are in reality weaker even than the people who vote them into power.

The real elite will be directed by a concern for the general welfare of the entire community. As a corollary, not every citizen will be granted equal rights, and no rights will be granted to those who are not willing to defend these rights. The selfless and the heroic will naturally possess superior ranks within the new hierarchy. Similarly, the European nation itself will not seek refuge in a foolish pacifism but will show itself capable of defending its freedom through armed force. This means necessarily the establishment of an independent European Army and the acquisition of nuclear arms.

The socio-economic pattern of the European Communitarian nation will be one that is essentially idealistic and not materialistic, as the Communist and American societies are. That is, it will be focused on the Promethean possibilities of the European individual and support this individualism in such a way that economic independence is guaranteed to it at the same time that licentiousness is curtailed. It will be egalitarian in the opportunities it offers its citizens but hierarchical in its organisation of society, according to the relative merits and capacities of the citizens.

Free enterprise will be encouraged, for state ownership leads to the incompetence of a social welfare state:

> The ownership of all the means of production in the hands of the state leads to the substitution of the reign of anonymous capitalist companies with the reign of irresponsible economico-humanitarian societies; one passes from selfishness and pure profit to incompetence and chaos.

Capitalist enterprise will be adopted only as a means and not as an end, as it is in the USA. No monopolies will be tolerated and economic organisation will be based on considerations of the dimension and nature of the enterprise so that, for example,

1. in the case of hydro-electric energy, there will be state property and state management;
2. in the case of an oil-producing territory, there will be state property and private management in the form of the state leasing to an industrial group,

3. and in almost all the rest of industry, there will be only private property and private management.

The socialism of Communitarian Europe will neither be a parasitical financial plutocracy nor a bureaucratic and bourgeois state socialism. It will 'subject itself to the natural criteria of competition, responsibility, competence, initiative.' Both managers and workers will be equally considered producers according to their contribution to the work involved in an enterprise. Trade unions will be depoliticised and Europeanised. Ownership of property will be transferred from speculators and politicians to producers. Wealth will no longer be a criterion of classes, only individual capacity will be that. Social mobility will be encouraged, since the elites may be found in any stratum of society and must be impelled upwards.

In terms of international trade, Europe will be protectionist and interventionist. It will not allow the USA to rob it further of the raw materials that are present in its own former colonies. It will establish its own 'Monroe Doctrine', which will make the Mediterranean a European 'lake'. It will not pay American capitalists, and their European partners, for resources that once belonged to Europe and will no longer suffer a further depletion of its financial resources by having to donate aid to Third World countries — whose corruption is sustained by the international capitalist investors and whose resulting poverty is supposed to be alleviated by Europe. Europe will strive to be autarkic as far as possible, since the industrial character of the Western European economy will be satisfactorily complemented by the agrarian character of the Eastern European one. Europe's future priorities will thus be continental ones, after centuries of maritime adventures abroad.

*

Influenced by the geopolitics of Karl Haushofer (1869–1946), Ernst Niekisch (1889–1967) and Jordis von Lohausen (1907–2002), Thiriart supported the transformation of territorial states into continental states and particularly of the European states into a single nation. That is why, in a 1987 interview with the American evangelical writer Gene H. Hogberg,[6] Thiriart admitted to his admiration of Hitler and Stalin as geopoliticians, if not as politicians:

> Hitler and Stalin appear somewhat as "means to an end," the tools, the potential obstetricians of history, we could say of History, with a capital "H" … The historical unification of Europe is inevitable: in the long run it is "statistically" obligatory — dictated by geopolitics.

The need for a union between Europe and Russia is reinforced by the fact that, in its cold war with America, Russia is exposed on its western flank between Lübeck and Sofia, and it is imperative that it seek an alliance with Europe to prevent America from slowly strangling it through its control of the European coastal countries that constitute the 'Rimland' of Eurasia.

However, Thiriart believed that the 'thalassic' empire of the Americans was by its very nature doomed:

> In my work 'The Euro-Soviet Empire', which is coming out this summer, I contrast the temporal stability of states whose territory is contiguous, with the historical fragility of states whose territory is dispersed and scattered over the surface of the planet. From a military point of view, a sea-going power remains more effective than a continental power …
>
> … But when we consider it from a historical point of view, in historical perspective, the reverse is true. A continental state is better able to weather a crisis than a maritime power. When you're out of breath on land, you sit down for 10 minutes. When you're out of breath at sea, you drown. Think of the British Empire in 1938 and what remained of it in 1958. The work of four centuries disappeared in less than a quarter of a century.
>
> In the long run, your links with Asia are doomed. They are doomed strategically. Under no circumstances will 21st century China tolerate you in Manila or Singapore. Your present control of the China Sea is undisputed,

---

6   Reproduced online at alphalink.com.au (translation by David Wainwright).

but it belongs to the current perspective, not to the historical perspective. It's just a concept (devised by) bankers, financiers, merchants and journalists. Venice made the same mistake in the past. Yet, as soon as a continental power such as the Ottoman Empire emerged, Venice rapidly collapsed. An imperialist China of the 21st or 22nd century will never tolerate you in the Philippines, any more than the Turkish empire could tolerate the Venetians in Crete.

America's current economic military expansion in Japan and the Philippines is the result of circumstances rather than of geopolitical or geostrategic realities. Vietnam was a warning shot. Don't delude yourselves: The Japanese do not like you and they will not soon forget Hiroshima … What remains today of those French, English, Belgian, Dutch, Portuguese and Italian empires? In less than 50 years all has changed; all has been lost. What will remain of the American empire by 2035?

Thiriart believed that America's geopolitical domain will have to be restricted to the two Americas, just as Europe's will be expanded to Siberia and Africa:

For stability, a state needs both contiguity and continuity. That is the lesson of geopolitics. If I were American, I would write in favour of economic and historical integration from Alaska to the Argentine, just as I write, as a European, in favour of total integration from Vladivostok to Dublin. I do not see history through economic glasses (as American financiers or bankers look at profits from Tokyo and Singapore). I do not look at history with glasses coloured by ideology like those who wage an anti-Communist battle — when Communism is already spent, at least in its Marxist form.

A forward-looking historical policy would have Europe develop Africa and Siberia and would have the United States develop the whole of Latin America. That is where you must initially seek your economic partners, but it must be done fairly. Then make them your friends. Finally, bring about a type of integration through a common culture. By going to South America you will find European roots. It is remarkable what colonial Spain achieved. The old capitals from Mexico City to Buenos Aires, built between the 16th century and the end of the 18th century, are architectural miracles in stone.

Bury the era of the WASPs, and try to love the Latin Americans instead of looking down on them. In Manila you have a precarious foothold. Here in Europe, also from a historical point of view, your foothold is precarious. Sooner or later you will be driven both from Asia and Europe.

If America does not modulate its geopolitical ambitions to a peaceful cooperation with Latin America, Europe will be forced to support Latin America in its struggle against American imperialism. As he put it, 'The revolutionary solution would be for Europe to unify in a death struggle with the United States.' Indeed, Europe may even attempt to make Spanish its own *lingua franca* so that 'a Europe officially speaking Spanish would immediately be in the suburbs of Los Angeles and Miami.'

DEDICATION

I DEDICATE this work to all the people of Europe who do not accept servitude. My thoughts are directed to those who have fought, who fight and who will fight the grossest and most brutal form of oppression, that of Russian Communism.

A hundred million men of Europe have been prisoners for twenty years now. They owe this in large part to the senile megalomania of Roosevelt, whose name will remain cursed in our countries.

To these hundred million men I announce hope and tell them: you are no longer alone, you are no longer abandoned in your fight for freedom. Brothers and sons of the heroic insurgents of East Berlin, Poznan, Pilsen and Budapest, know that, much before the end of the century, you will see the foreign occupier leave, you will hear the caterpillar tracks of our tanks growling in our fields, you will see the flags of Europe flying over Warsaw, Prague, Budapest, Sofia and Bucharest.

Jean Thiriart

ACKNOWLEDGEMENTS

In gratitude,

To my comrades and friends who assisted me in diverse ways in the elaboration of the present book.

Some offered me intellectual collaboration, others material aid, or even obscure daily chores.

Among them there are some who were at the origin of this work through their moral encouragements.

In gratitude,

This book was begun in the calm of a cell of the Forest prison, where a judge of virtuous education but not familiar with revolutionary customs made me discover a definitive confirmation of my political vocation.

Among the very numerous comrades to whom my gratitude is addressed, I should particularly point out: Marie-Rose A., Frédéric Crispi, Emile Hirsch, René Dastier, Gérard Désiron, Fernand Miller, Prince David of Westdorpe, Léon Quitilier, Paul Teichmann, Alice Thiriart, Jean van den Broeck, Col. E.R. Marcel Verlinden.

JEAN THIRIART

CHAPTER I

THE DIMENSIONS OF THE EUROPEAN STATE

I should speak to you of changes, began the general, that I have observed for some time with anxiety. I am thinking of the metaphysical tendencies that are increasingly manifest among you and other members of the general staff. I would not have to repeat any of it if we wished to found a monastic order — now, such is not my intention. I am therefore going to communicate my views on the situation. He pushed the bouquet that prevented him from seeing Lucius[1] clearly, and continued:

We live in a state of affairs where the old relations have been lost for a long time, thus, to be brief, in a state of anarchy. Nobody doubts that this state demands changes. On the contrary, opinions differ on the means to reach a new stability. Let us leave aside the Mauretanians[2], who elaborate an art of prospering in and through anarchy; there remain two big schools of thought, of which one wishes to regulate life based on the inferior, the other on the superior.

The first, which is grouped at Heliopolis, around the Governor and his Central Office, is based on the ruins and hypotheses of the old popular parties, and intends to ensure the domination of an absolute bureaucracy. The doctrine is simple: it sees in man a zoological being and considers technology as the means of giving to this being form and power, and also of holding him in check.

This is an instinct elevated to a rational level. Consequently, it has as its aim the formation of intelligent termites. The doctrine is well founded, as much in its elementary aspect as in its rational one, and that is its strength.

The second school is ours; it is constructed on the ruins of the old aristocracy and of the senatorial party, and is represented by the Proconsul and the Palace. The Governor wants, outside of history, to elevate a collective being to the rank of a state; we tend to a historical order. We want the freedom of man, of his being, of his mind and of what he possesses, and the state to the extent only that these possessions demand a protection. From there results the difference between our means and methods and those of the Governor. He is obliged to level, to atomise and to flatten his human

---

[1] In Ernst Jünger's novel *Heliopolis* (1949), Lucius de Geer, commander of the Proconsul of Heliopolis, finally leaves Heliopolis when he realises he cannot reconcile himself to the political viewpoints of either his leader or the latter's opponent, the Governor. [All annotations are by the translator.]

[2] Mauretania is one of the fictional regions around Heliopolis.

material, in the midst of which there is to reign an abstract order. With us, on the contrary, it is man who should be the master. The Governor aims at the perfection of technology, we aim at the perfection of man.

From there arises then a difference in the selection. The Governor wants technological superiority. The research of specialists leads necessarily to atrophied types. This is not at all a necessary evil but a demand based on principle since its order must be founded on the obliteration of man. Thus, between two postulates that are equal in degree, that one is the more apt that brings with it the least dignity, the least conscience, the least freedom — in short, the one in which technological impulse encounters the least resistance. Practically, this is manifested in the fact that one finds in its services a mixture of automatons and confessed criminals.

On the contrary, our ambition is to form a new elite. Our task is incomparably more difficult; we swim against the current. We are in a way forced to gain some territory on the waters, to drive our piles into the river one after the other. While the levelling finds in each man matter in which to exercise, our desire must be directed towards the perfect image of man, which is revealed only rarely, and is always only an approximation. In this the Proconsul is for us a model, the bearer of excellent virtues, the aristocratic principles, but also those of democracy that subsist intact. For, in its decadence, democracy does not live any longer in the people, but resides, like germs, in the individual. Thus, situations may present themselves where one must force the people to its salvation. The enlightened mind acts then as its tutor.

We know that the Proconsul wishes to take this responsibility upon himself. To this end he seeks to bind to himself the best personalities, the Senate of the future.

Ernst Jünger, *Heliopolis*

My position is extremely simple. I am a citizen of the ancient Roman Empire. I love Europe and its civilisation, which is civilisation.

Alexis Curvers

The state begins when groups separated at birth are obliged to live as a community. This obligation is not a simple violence; it supposes a project which encourages collaboration, a common task proposed to scattered groups. Above all, the state is the project of an action and a programme of collaboration. One appeals to people in order that they may do something together. The state is not consanguinity, or linguistic unity, or territorial unity, or continuity of habitation.

José Ortega y Gasset

I wish to be great and achieve the European monument, for the greatest glory of the world. We are three hundred and sixty million people.

Pierre Drieu La Rochelle (1928)

Every people or every grouping of peoples is thus not a nation. Only those are who accomplish a historical destiny differentiated from the universal. From this it follows that it is superfluous to specify if a nation possesses qualities of geographical, racial or linguistic unity; its importance is determined if it possesses, within the universal, the unity of a historical destiny. The classical ages understood this with their customary clarity. That is why they never used the words 'fatherland' and 'nation' in the Romantic sense, nor anchored their patriotism in the obscure love of the soil. They preferred, on the contrary, expressions such as 'empire' or 'service of the king', that is to say, expressions that refer to the historical instrument.

José Antonio Primo de Rivera,
Essais sur le nationalisme, April 1934

From Brest[1] to Bucharest: Let Us Efface Yalta

IN THE CONTEXT of geopolitics and a common civilisation, as it will be demonstrated further below, unitarian[2] and Communitarian Europe extends from Brest to Bucharest.

At the moment it is still amputated of half its territory.

Millions of compatriots have been, for almost 20 years, subjugated by the Communist dictatorship and by foreign occupation. *Our goal is to liberate them.*

East Germans, Poles, Czechoslovaks, Albanians, Latvians, Estonians, Lithuanians, Hungarians, Bulgarians, Romanians and Yugoslavs are Europeans. Without them, Europe is incomplete, without them, Europe is mutilated.

One of our first objectives will thus be to efface the American betrayal of Yalta,[3] which will remain in history as the sign of the impotence and the cowardice of the capitalist plutocracy.

1　Brest is a port city in Brittany.

2　Thiriart uses the term '*unitaire*' for a Europe considered as a single political unit.

3　The Yalta Conference was held in February 1945 in the Crimea and attended by Roosevelt, Churchill and Stalin as the heads of state of the USA, the UK and the Soviet Union. The conference finalised the division of Europe into Western and Russian spheres of influence, which Churchill had negotiated with Stalin in Moscow in October 1944.

Europe, a Giant of More Than 400 Million People That Does Not Wish to Be Either a Stake or an Arena

Superficial and ill-informed minds or morbid defeatists cultivate the legend of a 'little' Europe crushed between two 'greats', namely the USA and the USSR.

A simple examination of the objective reality — within the grasp of a schoolboy of 12 — allows one to destroy this fable.

Europe of the Common Market alone counts 167 million inhabitants; Western Europe from Sweden to Portugal counts 301 million inhabitants!

Finally, Eastern Europe combines 113 million Europeans. Which brings us to 414 million people in Europe from Brest to Bucharest and from Narvik[4] to Athens.

The 414 million Europeans are to be compared to the 180 million inhabitants of the USA and 210 million inhabitants of the USSR.

Thus, by itself, Europe represents more than the USSR and the USA combined!

It may be mentioned that our 414 million Europeans belong to countries for the most part at a very high industrial development; it is not a question of millions of poor or millions of underdeveloped people, but of millions of people deriving from a rich, powerful and prosperous civilisation.

Our furnaces, our steelworks, our factories growl with intense activity; our banks contain a gold reserve superior to that of the USA. Better still, the American dollar maintains its course only thanks to the artifices of loans imposed on federal Germany by diplomatic extortion. Europe has everything to be the FIRST nation in the world: it only lacks political unity.

---

4   Narvik is a town in Norway.

Everything will be possible for Europe as soon as it realises its political unity. The key to our destiny rests in these two words: POLITICAL UNITY.

It is the only thing that we lack. If this is realised everything else will be given in addition because everything already exists. A people of 400 million must demand a destiny equal to its dimension. Europe does not wish any longer to be a stake between Moscow and Washington, or an arena of a conflict between the materialism of the rich and the materialism of the poor. Neither a stake nor an arena nor booty.

Tomorrow we shall throw the weight of our 400 million men, determined, united, disciplined, into the balance of history.

Neither Moscow nor Washington

Between the Soviet bloc and the US bloc our historic task is to build a large fatherland: unitarian, powerful, Communitarian Europe.

Europe, this MIRACLE of the history of man, this miracle which followed the Greek miracle, has, through the prodigious fecundity of its unique culture, given birth to a civilisation adopted by the whole world. In the competition begun between the great Western cultures, the Indian, the Chinese and the Japanese, it is ours that has crushed the others. *Culture is the creator of civilisation.*

Civilisation, on the contrary, never creates culture. ONLY Europe possesses culture, whence its primacy over the United States and Communist Russia, which possess only the civilisation born of our culture, as Oswald Spengler has admirably demonstrated.

This civilisation cut off from its culture is condemned to sterility, which will first be translated by a sclerosis and then by a return to barbarism. Politically dominated by Moscow or by Washington, European culture is stifled; it risks being ossified in its state of civilisation. It is to be remarked that all the discoveries in the nuclear and satellite fields are the work of Europeans. European brains are being picked.

Only a Europe that is politically united can furnish the means for the power that will guarantee the historical conditions indispensable for the survival of this culture.

No other power is, besides, capable of replacing Europe in its humanist mission.

Europe Vis-à-Vis Africa, Latin America, the Arab world, the USSR, the USA

The key elements of unitarian Europe:

- with Africa: symbiosis,
- with Latin America: alliance,
- with the Arab world: friendship,
- with the USSR: proximity,
- with the USA: relations based on equality.

Africa is the natural prolongation of Europe.

Africa must live in a symbiosis with Europe. It is its natural prolongation. Our interest is to associate ourselves with the peoples of Africa by helping them through reasonable means to attain the material and spiritual development which will free them from anarchy and permit them to acquire, thanks to us, a real economic comfort.

Modern Africa cannot do without Europe. The economies of these two continents are complementary. Europe cannot, further, in any case, tolerate that an extra-African power might instal itself in Africa and thus threaten it on its southern flank.

Latin America, quite like Europe, must fight the Yankee imperialism and against the Communist subversion. Our enemies are the same and we can declare: all of that demands an alliance.

The unity of the Arab world is of an interest parallel to that of Europe and cannot, and will never be able to, present a serious danger to it. This unity bars the route to Africa to Communism, eliminates the pretext of Yankee interventionism in the Eastern Mediterranean and, finally, forms at once a buffer and an element of union between Europe and West Asia.

With the USSR good neighbourliness will be possible only after the independence regained by all our Eastern provinces. *The peaceful proximity to the USSR will commence the day that the latter is returned to its borders of 1938. But not before; every form of coexistence supporting the division of Europe is only a fraud.*

As regards the USA, the first stage of our action will aim at decolonising Europe from the ECONOMIC and military Yankee tutelage. This action will be conducted to the point of confiscating the American properties if events demand it. An alliance of the classical type between Europe and the USA is evidently not to be rejected *a priori*. It can be accomplished only on a footing of strict equality between two sovereign states. At present Western Europe is only a satellite of the USA.

The ambition to a nuclear monopoly within NATO and the continental pressures on the Common Market are an eloquent illustration of this.

Europe Must Remain Strongly Neutral and an Army Can Guarantee It

Europe must be neutral and powerful. It must free itself from the tutelage of the USA. Its neutrality will be vigilant and armed. Between the blocs of the USA and the USSR, militarised to the teeth, the effective neutrality of Europe is conceivable only if it is in turn armed.

This neutrality can be perfectly negotiated with a Russia returned to its borders of 1938, beside which we have, as much as it, an interest in coexisting in peace.

A powerful state and a weak state cannot by any means coexist, the second becoming in one way or another the vassal of the first.

One can coexist only with an equal.

The idea of a coexistence between the USA and the USSR was able to be realised only when a balance of 'atomic terror' was established between them. This balance, it may be said in passing, is much more precarious and dangerous when two powers rather than three are involved.

Europe must by itself obtain a peaceful proximity to the USSR. Failing to do so will result in the USA negotiating an agreement with Moscow on our back.

The first goal of Europe will be its reunification. The evacuation of Eastern Europe by the Soviet Army will be one of our first objectives.

The following reciprocity must be proposed to the USSR: evacuation of Eastern Europe by the Red Army against elimination of all American military or political presence in Western Europe.

The key of European diplomacy will be the peaceful proximity to the USSR. Only a strong and united Europe will be able to force Moscow to understand that this is also the interest of the USSR.

In fact, unitarian Europe will not be, like the present Western Europe, an American military bridgehead.

The first Soviet token of good faith will be the reunification of its German 'province' with Europe and the acceptance of the presence of the European Army on the entirety of the German territory.

If Europe does not hasten to be unified, and then to peacefully become a neighbour of the USSR, the latter and the USA will divide Europe amongst themselves in a definitive manner, or Washington will even exchange its token—Eastern Europe—for some territorial advantage or other in the world.

The USA has, besides, already abandoned certain tokens in Europe. Notably during the Cuba affair, where it evacuated its Italian and Turkish rocket bases in exchange for the dismantlement of the Soviet bases in the Caribbean.[5]

No Crusades

Unitarian Europe does not intend to undertake any crusades outside its territorial limits.

The wheat fields of the Ukraine or the petrol of Baku was the last external military adventure in the form of a crusade. On the other hand, as long as a single square metre of the European territory is occupied by Soviet Russia, there cannot be any question of bartering any illusory *'peace at any cost'*.

All borders are contestable. One should nevertheless stop at one of them. We choose, between the USSR and Europe, the borders of 1938 that preceded the Stalinist conquests.[6]

The peaceful proximity to the USSR will begin when the latter has returned within its historical borders.

Unitarian Europe will not tolerate Communism within its borders under the naive and suicidal pretext that it is 'one opinion among others'.

Communism as a 'philosophy' is only an instrument in the hands of the Pan-Russian policy. It is inaccurate to pretend that the USSR supports Communism. In fact, Communism is an instrument in the service of the policy of nationalist expansion of Russia. Communism is a sort of artificial 'good conscience', designed to mask the traditional imperialistic appetites of the Kremlin. Tito understood that

---

5   See p. 248 below.
6   I.e. the borders before the Soviet occupation of Eastern Poland, Eastern Romania, Eastern Finland and the Baltic States as a result of the Molotov-Ribbentrop Non-Aggression Pact of August 1939.

well. Djilas[7] wrote about it and the Hungarian, Polish and Romanian Communist leaders have bridled against this Russian nationalism.

To the extent that we do not tolerate Communism within our borders, because we consider it as an agent of a foreign power, we do not intend to interfere in the internal politics of the USSR or, in this regard, intend to undertake a crusade in the USSR itself.

We think that, in the long term, the maintenance of Communism in our neighbour is of a nature that compromises the full blossoming of the Russian nation. To our neighbours and to our enemies we wish, for the benefit of OUR peace, that the most sterile forms of the parliamentary pseudo-democracy or those of the Communist police state subsist only among them.

Reunification of Germany Through the Reunification of Europe

The problem of the reunification of Germany, which is a part of the problem of the reunification of Europe, the second conditioning the first, must be treated within the framework of the disengagement of the American protectorate. The Communist bloc in effect will never permit the German reunification as long as Europe is under the heel of the USA.

The reunification of Germany WILL FOLLOW and not precede that of Europe.

The Germans are extremely naive in imagining that they can deal alone with Moscow.

Krushchev would immediately admit the reunification of Germany on condition that it leave Europe, that is to say, that it it be completely

---

7   Milovan Djilas (1911–95) was a Yugoslav democratic socialist dissident who supported Tito in his struggle against the Soviet domination of Yugoslavia. In 1954, however, he was dismissed from the Central Committee of the Yugoslav Communist Party on account of his criticism of the continuing one-party system in Yugoslavia.

at the mercy of the Soviet Union. This is a great snare in which certain German milieus are trapped, through blindness in the case of narrow-minded nationalists, through greed when they are mercantile.

On the contrary, Europe in a situation of strength will be able to negotiate a global solution.

The reunification of Germany will thus be, in fact, the integration of the German 'province' into the new fatherland of Europe.

Amsterdam Is to Be Defended in the Mediterranean, Lisbon Is to Be Defended on the Elbe

Berlin, Pretoria: two fronts of one and the same war! Europe is conceived and defended globally and not 'in fragments'. One of the ideological tragedies of the OBTUSE *'petty nationalist'* causes is that the 'German nationalists' are only interested in Berlin and in the reunification of Germany, that the 'French nationalists' are only interested in Algeria, that the 'Belgian nationalists' have been humiliated only by the Congo affair in 1960.

Europe, both its preoccupations and its combats, must be one and indivisible.

To defend Berlin, support Portugal in Angola, and to support the government of South Africa is to defend ALL of Europe.

The politics of 'little packets' practised for fifteen years has been catastrophic for Europe. France was alone in Algeria, Belgium was alone in the Congo, tomorrow Portugal will be alone in Angola. The Europe of today presents itself in a situation analogous to that of ancient Greece; in fact, just as the 'city states' which refused unification fell under the domination of Philip of Macedon, Europe at present will fall under the yoke of Krushchev.

This vitiated, suicidal conception of the defence of Europe is the usurious interest of the mortgage of old petty nationalisms, which have today become restrictive and inoperative.

Anybody who threatens the least fragment of Europe will in future have to expect to suffer the massive response of all of Europe.

If, in the past, we had applied this policy, the Netherlands, France, England, Belgium, Portugal would not have suffered all the defeats and humiliations accumulated since 1945, from Java to Goa.

The Algerian War lost by France alone would never have been lost by a unitarian Europe.

Our enemies would not even have dared to undertake it.

The Dimensions of the European State — Europe From Brest to Vladivostok

Let us take a brief excursion into the realm of anticipation and imagine what the stage after the unification of Europe will be: it will inevitably, from the fact of geopolitics, be registered in terms of a Brest-Vladivostok axis.

A Europe from Brest to the Urals, an idea borrowed from General de Gaulle, contains a monstrous heresy, that of the association of Europe with a reduced Russia.

A historic Europe-USA association would have been durably possible if the Americans had not imposed, as a precondition, the destruction of our colonial empires (French, English, etc.). We can prophesy, without risk, that it is due to the period of 1940–1960, when the Yankee anti-European imperialism was manifested virulently, that there will not be any possible association with the USA and that Europe will turn away from it, and even will even turn against it. The USA wished to reduce us before associating itself with us in order to dominate us in this association. That is very petty Machiavellianism and very short-sighted.

The Asiatic demographic tide should not be contained at the Urals but on the River Amur, at the present borders of the USSR in Eastern Siberia.

General de Gaulle was already deceived once in wishing to defend Europe at Marseilles rather than in Algiers; he is deceived again in fixing the stop-line at the Urals and not at the Siberian borders. Politics consists in conducting oneself with certain enemies as if they could become allies tomorrow, and vice versa. That is indeed why we should not hope for the total destruction of the USSR but only for a weakening which would oblige it to restore Eastern Europe to us; that is indeed why we cannot trust blindly in the American nuclear power, when tomorrow the US will perhaps be our adversary, since it is already today, in multiple cases, an accomplice of the Soviets!

The only true object of historical contestation between us and the USSR is Central Europe and Eastern Europe, which it holds under its yoke (I shall of course speak elsewhere of the Communist Party!).

Thus the first phase of our politics will be essentially anti-Russian and, for that reason, pro-Chinese. It will be that until the precise moment when our European fatherland will regain its border of the Dniester.[8] At the moment that Europe will have recuperated its territories without a possible later contestation, a reversal of policy will be implemented and neighbourliness will take the place of implacable battle.

In the short term, we should wish for a Chinese anti-Russian advance and, in the long term, do everything to help Russia to contain the Asiatic tide.

We should bring down the USSR but not destroy it. Bismarck had understood this game after Sadowa with regard to Austria.[9] Siberia, occupied in a striking majority by whites coming from European Russia, constitutes the glacis of Europe or, more exactly, will constitute it tomorrow.

Knowing that Russia could tomorrow be an 'allied neighbour', we are not interested in bringing it down. Let us not practise such a stupid

---

8   The Dniester runs through the Ukraine and Moldova.
9   The Battle of Sadowa in July 1866 marked the end of the Austro-Prussian War and the defeat of the Austrian Empire.

game as that which Washington conducted against Europe from 1940 to 1960. This American game will leave behind such bitternesses that it will end by splitting this alliance, which is still guaranteed only by the spinelessness of our present European politicians.

These cases of reversals of alliance dictated by interests alone abound in history: France played this game from the 17th to the 20th centuries, bringing down the House of Austria just at the moment when Prussia seemed to be extremely menacing. We could avoid the first phase, the hardest, that of the implacable fight against the USSR, if the latter had enough historical maturity to understand it. For the moment we still have to doubt it. Ideology always clouds the diplomatic and historical judgement of the leaders of the Kremlin, prisoners of their myth of the 19th century. The USSR rightly appreciates the neutrality of Sweden, which guarantees its north-western flank; one day it will be able to appreciate the same (armed) neutrality of all of Europe.

It goes without saying that it is a matter of a Europe that is free up to Bucharest. My proposal may shock but it is essentially pragmatic in inspiration, free of all ideological facts. The scheme of a probable future — I did not say certain — is translated by a USSR preoccupied with containing Asia and a Europe preoccupied with reconquering Africa. That presupposes an absolute peace from Reval[10] to Odessa.

The objection that Moscow cannot tolerate without danger a unitarian and strong Europe (up to Bucharest) has no value. Europe enjoys a great historical maturity, it knows now the vanity of crusades and wars of conquest towards the East. After Charles XII,[11] Bonaparte and Hitler, we have been able to measure the risks of such enterprises as well as their costs.

If the USSR wishes to conserve Siberia, it must make peace — with Europe from Brest to Bucharest, I repeat.

---

10   The old name of Tallinn, capital of Estonia.
11   See below p. 259.

The USSR does not and will not have in the least the strength to conserve both Warsaw and Budapest, on the one hand, Chita[12] *and Khabarovsk,*[13] *on the other hand. It will have to choose or risk losing all.*

Our politics differs from that of General de Gaulle because he has committed, or is committing, three errors:

- drawing the border of Europe at Marseilles and not at Algiers,
- drawing the border of the USSR bloc/Europe at the Urals and not in Siberia,
- finally, wishing to deal with Moscow *before* the liberation of Bucharest.

The entire politics of Europe will consist in creating its strength and in showing its power to the USSR in order to bring the latter to a greater realism. We love as much as anybody, if not more, peace and freedom. But we know equally that arms — their possession, not necessarily their use — are the first and indispensable basis of independence. The USSR has a greater need than Europe for a total peace, because our economy is not perpetually short-winded like its economy is: the future of the industrial and economic power of the continent is with us. The steel that one forges in the Ruhr could very well serve to protect Vladivostok.

But the *great precondition* of our entire politics of rapprochement with Moscow, the historical condition *sine qua non*, is the liberation of our provinces and capitals of the centre and the east of our great European fatherland. The entire political key to the relations of Europe and the USSR is found there. Any other perspective signifies only deception and subjugation for the peoples of our continent.

---

12   Chita is a city in Eastern Siberia.

13   Khabarovsk is a city in the Russian Far East, north of Vladivostok.

CHAPTER II

THE STYLE OF THE UNITARIAN EUROPEAN STATE

France should not at all be a collection of small nations which are governed separately, as democracies; it is not at all a collection of states; it is a unique whole composed of integrating parts, these parts must not at all have a complete existence separately, because they are not at all simply units but parts forming a single whole.

Emmanuel-Joseph Siéyès,
Discours devant la Constituante, 7/9/1789.

And as for our enemies, they are at the mercy of our work. They are only strong through our own faults. We walk through a storm; but, beyond, is the sun.

… Europe is emancipated; it has been that since Marathon. That day, the eastern stationary principle was defeated forever; freedom baptised our soil; Europe marched. It is still marching; and it is not through some worthless pieces of paper that one will stop its march.

Giuseppe Mazzini

The radical impression that to exist is to resist had become among them a veritable instinct; they felt, as it were, that life consists in planting one's fingers in the soil in order not to be dragged away by the currents. In an age such as ours, where everything is 'currents' and 'renunciations', it is good to make contact with men who 'do not allow themselves to be dragged away'.

Ortega y Gasset

Nations that want protectors will find masters.

Fisher Ames,
lecture in Boston

Europe Began at Salamis and at Himera

EUROPE BEGAN IN 480 B.C. at Salamis through the victory of the Greeks of Themistocles over the invaders from Asia.[1] The same year, through a sort of sacred coincidence, the same Greeks, under the command of Gelo, broke at Himera in Sicily the offensive of the Carthaginians.[2]

In this epoch Greece was Europe just as, a little later, Rome became Europe.

It is remarkable and symbolic that, at that time, just as today, we were assailed by numerous and powerful enemies, and simultaneously in the East and in the West.

Thus the Greeks, our historical ancestors, opened the European era through two unexpected and twin victories.

Taking turns, many nations have assumed the role of Europe. Spain in the High Middle Ages, which contained and then drove back the Moors; the Slavs, who repulsed the Tatars; Habsburg Austria, which stopped the Ottomans for three centuries — all of them have contributed in some way to save Europe. Then Portugal, Spain, the Netherlands, England, France, Italy bore the European presence in the universe. Of unitarian Europe there are three historical prefigurations,

---

[1] In the Battle of Salamis, the Greek city-states under General Themistocles defeated the Persian navy of Xerxes.

[2] Gelo was a Sicilian ruler, who, along with his ally Theron of Acragas, defeated the Carthaginian invaders under Hamilcar.

which are Greek Europe, Roman Europe and the Europe of the Holy German Empire of the Hohenstaufens.[3]

Europe has already existed for a long time unknown to those who made it, those who lived it.

For 25 Years the Solidarity of European destiny Has Been Sanctified by Blood Spilt in Common

To those whom an absence of character added to a poor understanding of history cause to doubt the future of Europe, we should oppose the historic sacrifices that, through 25 centuries of fighting, have formed Europe — often even unknown to those who fell.

The Russians are in Budapest, the Americans occupy Frankfurt. That does not prevent us for one moment from wishing their departure nor, for one moment, from being certain of it.

The Asiatics imprudently came to challenge us up to Athens. The Carthaginians ravaged the fields of Italy. The Huns laid waste to the land 160 km from Paris. We have suffered the Muslims at Bordeaux and the Turks before Vienna.

Many among them have left their corpses in our lands and their survivors have had to flee. Lucky still when we have not been to combat their proud nations up to their homes by destroying the Persian Empire, razing Carthage to the ground, conquering the Muslim world, ruining the Ottoman Empire. Europe, stronger, has always picked itself up, always triumphed. Twenty-five centuries of tests, twenty-five centuries of combat.

Europe, a powerful and fecund race, has metamorphosised itself through several of its nations, taking at one time the Greek mask, at another the Roman mask. At present, its metamorphoses are going to

---

3   The Hohenstaufens were a Swabian dynasty that ruled from 1138 to 1254. Three members of the dynasty became Holy Roman Emperors, Frederick I, Heinrich VI and Frederick II.

be accomplished and Europe is going to adopt its specific, definitive, unitarian appearance without having to use any mask. Our unitarian Europe will sweep away from its lands the big pink oafs of the US Army and the police militia of Moscow. We have had, in our history, to combat enemies more vigorous, and we have vanquished them.

Europe was forged in trials. It has tempered itself thereby, it has unified itself through blood spilt in common. Europe is woven on a gigantic framework of struggles without which today it would not exist. The heroic actors of these tragedies have not been able — when alive — to measure the extent of their sacrifices. Only the distance of history allows us to appreciate the gigantic prospect designed through 25 centuries.

Marathon — 490 B.C.: Victory of Militiades over the generals of Darius I.[4]

Salamis and Himera — 480 B.C.: Themistocles crushes Xerxes near Athens. The Asiatic peril has since that time been removed. The same year, symbolic coincidence, the Greeks of Sicily beat and push back the Carthaginians at Himera.

Plataea — 479 B.C.: The Greek military leaders, Pausanias and Aristides, crush the Persian general Mardonius.[5]

Granicus — 334 B.C.: Victory of Alexander of Macedon, in Asia Minor, over Darius III,[6] whose army was infinitely superior in number.

Arbil — 331 B.C.: Arbil, in Iraq, sees a big victory of Alexander, who, setting out from Egypt, after having traversed the Syrian desert,

---

[4] Militiades was a Greek general under the supreme commander Callimachus at the Battle of Marathon in 490 B.C.

[5] The Battle of Plataea, which followed the Battle of Salamis, saw another victory of the Greeks over the remnant army of Xerxes I under Mardonius.

[6] Alexander of Macedon invaded the Persian Empire in 334 B.C. and succeeded in taking Persepolis in 330 B.C.

crosses the Euphrates and the Tigris and comes to crush the Persians there.[7]

Carthage — 146 B.C.: Rome has, for Europe, taken the helm from Greece. After the long and painful Punic Wars, the year 146 finally sees Hasdrubal surrendering and Scipio Aemilianus ordering the destruction of Carthage.[8]

Catalaunian Plains — A.D. 451: After the centuries of order, the Pax Romana — one of the peaks of our history — we pass, in the 5th century, some difficult moments. No matter. We recover and, in the plains of Champagne, in the region of the Catalauni, some twenty kilometres from the present town of Troyes, in the Campus Mauriacus, Atilla, at the head of the Huns, is defeated and driven back.[9] The Huns were at that time 160 km from Paris. Aetius, leader of the Roman military, and allied with the Burgundians, commands a coalition formed of Visigoths of Spain with, at their head, Theodoric, and Salian Franks commanded by Merovich.

Poitiers — A.D. 732: Abderame, chief of the Saracens of Spain,[10] crosses the Pyrenees and occupies Bordeaux. He goes towards the north in the direction of Paris and is stopped only 300 kilometres from it, at Poitiers, by Charles Martel, a duke of the Franks, son of Pepin of Herstal.

Jerusalem — A.D. 1099: Godefroy de Bouillon, a principal personage of the 1st Crusade, born in Baisy in the Wallonian Brabant, Duke of Lower Lorraine, at the head of the knights of the lands between the

---

7 Alexander defeated Darius III decisively at the Battle of Gaugamela fought near Arbil in 331 B.C.

8 Hasdrubal was the son of Hamilcar and brother of Hannibal. Scipio Aemilianus was called Scipio Africanus Minor after his destruction of Carthage.

9 The Catalaunian Fields are located in present-day Châlons-en-Champagne, in North-Eastern France.

10 Abderame is the French form of Abdul Rahman Al Ghafiqi, an Arab who was made governor of Andalusia in 730.

Meuse and the Moselle, beats the Egyptian Army at Ascalon in Syria, and enters victoriously into Jerusalem in 1099.[11]

Granada — A.D. 1492: On 2 January, the Catholic kings make their solemn entrance into the Alhambra of Granada. It was the crowning achievement of the long *Reconquista*, starting some centuries before from a Visigoth centre imprudently forgotten by the Arab occupiers in the Asturian Mountains.[12] The battles of the *Reconquista* were so numerous that we can cite here only the historic crowning achievement.

Although solidly and for long implanted in the Iberian Peninsula, the Muslims were pushed out of it finally. The glory of that is due to some rough men of arms, descended from Navarre, Leon, Castile and Aragon.

Vienna — A.D. 1529: Vienna, in Austria, at the heart of Europe. The Turks are at its walls in 1529 after having, under the command of Suleiman II, occupied Belgrade in 1521, Rhodes in 1522, a large part of Hungary in 1526. Ferdinand of Austria, brother of Charles Quint, beats the Turks and pushes them away.

Lepanto — A.D. 1571: This time we are on the sea and it is again the Turks that we fight at Lepanto in the Gulf of Corinth in Greece. Don Juan of Austria commands there the fleet of the Holy League under the guidance of Spain, Venice and the Pope — Sebastiano Venier and Agostino Barbarigo, famous Venetian sailors, fought there as heroes. Miguel de Cervantes was seriously wounded there.

Saint Gotthard — A.D. 1664: This little town of Hungary in the comitat of Vas, on the Raab, sees numerous Turks — they were almost 100,000 — beaten by a European army of 25,000 men commanded by Montecuculli. A remarkable symbol was that Louis XIV had sent to

---

11 Godefroy de Bouillon was made ruler of the Kingdom of Jerusalem that was created after his victory in the First Crusade.
12 The Spanish Reconquista, which lasted around 800 years, is dated from the Battle of Covadonga (ca. 720 B.C.), when a group of Visigoth nobles led by Pelagius defeated the Umayyad Caliphate's army in the mountains of northern Iberia and established an independent Kingdom of Asturias.

the Austrians a reinforcement of 6,000 French volunteers under the orders of Jean de Coligny.

Vienna—A.D. 1683: On a little church that dominates a hill one can, even today, decipher a marble plaque which says: '*Mit dem auf dieser Bergeshöhe am 12.IX.1683 durch Pater Marco d'Aviano dargebrachten Hl. Messopfer begann der Entsatz Wiens und hiermit die Rettung abendländischer christlicher Kultur*' ('With the holy sacrifice made by Father Marco d'Aviano on top of this mountain on 12/9/1683 the relief of Vienna and thus the rescue of occidental Christian culture began'). For the second time, the Turks are before Vienna, in the heart of Europe. At that moment, Louis XIV reigns over France and people dance at Versailles. Vienna is defended by Duke Charles of Lorraine. He is powerfully aided by Jan Sobieski, at the head of the Polish Army, and the grand vizier Kara Mustapha loses the battle there, before losing his life.

Then there begins the brilliant period of expansion of Europe, in a somewhat interrupted fashion, up to the last European civil war of 1939–1945, tragic years, if ever there were any, for our continent. The Russians at Vienna, the Russians at Berlin. What does it matter! We have had the Huns and the Arabs a few steps from Paris, we have had the Turks before Vienna. Each time Europe tightened its fists, did battle and rose to its feet again. There is not a single people in Europe that did not spill its blood to allow the survival of Europe. Each one in its turn, sometimes some of them united and coalesced, have been, at a given moment, *Europe in arms*. The Poles who died to defend Vienna, the Italians in Greece during the battle of Lepanto and, before them, the Spanish who marked out with their skeletons the long route from Oviedo[13] to Granada, died to allow the birth of the European Nation.

The legendary race of Agamemnon and Ulysses is not dead. The attacks that have been made against us have always been avenged and our history has only been a series of Illiads.

---

13   Oviedo was made the capital of the Kingdom of Asturias during the reign of Alfonso II (791–842).

Races more proud and stronger than the Soviet Russians or the United States broke against the courage and the will of the men of Europe.

Against the Europe of Nations — Which Is Only a Sum of Rancours and Weaknesses

We do not wish a Europe of nations dear to the 'balkanisers' of the extreme right, a sort of Harlequin cloak over cowardly clothes.

This Europe of nations is nothing but the momentary and precarious sum of rancours and weaknesses. We all know that the sum of weaknesses equals zero or virtually zero. The petty narrow nationalisms cancel one another, as algebraic values of opposite signs cancel each other. The petty 'suppressed' nationalisms derive in general a semblance of vigour only from the hatred of a neighbour or the memory of it. This is nonsense, it is a formal contradiction to hope to derive a positive force from ossified and distrustful particularisms.

For us the fatherland is a FUTURE in common much more than a past in common. The customary fatherland: Belgium, the fatherland of memory: Germany of 1964, the fatherland of one's heritage: France, can suit only fatigued people possessed of conservative wishful thinking.

We wish a fatherland of expansion and not a fatherland of veneration. Such will be our European fatherland.

Consequently, we condemn the narrow and mean nationalisms that maintain the divisions between citizens of the European nation. These nationalisms should be sublimated and serve as a springboard for the greater and finer conception of the great European nation. The love of the fatherland should grow with the love for Europe.

Faced with the Russian and American nationalisms one should create a European nationalism.

We despise the paralytic patriotism of cemeteries, the vain patriotism of the wearers of decorations and trinkets. We do not count merely on the spirits of Joan of Arc — or of Bismarck — to save Europe. *We count solely on ourselves to do that.* But we are aware of the value of tradition enriched by a lucid will directed towards the future.

Reduced to the state of the survival of the past, the fatherland is nothing more than a trifle. The only true fatherland is a fatherland that is in the process of becoming.

Europe should be unitarian: federal Europe or a Europe of nations are conceptions whose inaccuracy and complication hardly hide the lack of sincerity or senility of those who defend them and disguise their ulterior motive and their schemes. However, Europe could pass through a very brief intermediary stage of federalism. Federal Europe would be the transition between the Europe of nations — which is the present pseudo-Europe — and the unitarian Europe which will be the Europe of Europeans, that is to say, the Europe of all the people of Europe.

Our Nationalism: a Community of Destiny

When men, peoples, have arrived at almost identical levels of maturity, when a culture is common to them, when the geography makes immediate neighbours of them and the same dangers and the same enemies threaten them, the conditions are given to create a nation.

For us, nationalism is the identity of destiny wished for in light of a great common plan.

We are opposed to the DIVIDERS constituted by the nationalists of fragmentation, the provincialists, the secessionists. The Breton, Wallon, Basque or Sicilian autonomists are at most, in the perspective of history, colourful and amusing folklorists. No real political thought animates them, they are childish romantics. These secessionists go against the human adventure. Their explanations barely hide inferiority complexes or, at best, a total lack of culture.

At present, in France, people who resist or oppose the unification of Europe *belong exactly to the same type of men* as those who refused the creative centralising work of the Capetians.[14]

We are likewise opposed to the CONSERVATIVES, to the adherents of the ossified nationalism, which exhausts its argument in memories. They hold on to the *nation of heritage*. *We do not refuse heritage: we wish to make it greater.* The French, German or Italian nationalists wish to stop the march of time. It is hardly less contemptible than the senseless intention of those who wish to distort its course by calling it, wrongly, 'historic sense'.

Other forms of nationalism not less harmful to our European design are contemptible: for example, those based on race. Europe is composed of several races — of which there are three big groups, that is, the Slav, the Germanic and the Latin-Mediterranean. This existence in the heart of Europe of a diversity of races causes us to formally and irrevocably condemn racism as a political argument. Racism within Europe should remain the affair of ethnologists.

Nationalism based on language is hardly worth more. Besides, homogeneity of race and language has always followed political unification. Blood and language alone have never engendered a great national state. It is, on the contrary, the national state which has levelled the original differences. The 'Frenchification' of the French provinces under the centralising power of the kings and the 'Castilinisation' of Spain of the 11th to 16th centuries provide eloquent examples of that. Our nationalism is therefore neither the conservation of the past nor a secession, nor racism.

Our nationalism is *a future in common* and those that it will unify will be welded one to the other by an identity of historical destiny.

---

14 The Capetian dynasty, beginning with the Frankish king Hugh Capet (ca. 941-96), was responsible for the formation of France as a state — which the Capetian dynasty ruled for more than eight centuries, until 1848.

Unitarian Europe will be a nation realised through a revolutionary elite.

Against All Discriminations All Ostracism: The Europe of All Europeans

Some people dream of a socialist Europe, others of a Catholic Europe, some of a Latin Europe or a Germanic Europe. In the meanwhile, all these dreamers accept servilely an American Europe.

We see, for example, the Flemish nationalists refusing, through resentment, all contact with the French culture, which is European, and not being able to perceive that they are being Americanised even to the most intimate part of their lives.

The Europe that we will make will be that of all Europeans. There will not be any question of excluding Slavic, Germanic or Latin people from it; there will not be any question of excluding Christians or Masons from it, of excluding people from it because they have eyes or hair of a certain colour, or because they belong to this or that faith.

Just as we do not tolerate the exclusion of Spain from Europe under the pretext of a real, imitated, degenerate or caricatural Fascism, no more shall we tomorrow tolerate the exclusion of the peoples of Eastern Europe, now under the Communist yoke.

For us a Spaniard is European before being a Francoist and a Pole is a European before being a Communist. Tomorrow, we shall welcome into Europe the prodigal brothers and the brothers abused by Communism in Eastern Europe, separating carefully and cautiously their fate from that of the agents and servile or bloody henchmen of the Muscovite occupier.

We will not hold anything against the youth of Eastern Europe on account of the fact they will have been conditioned by a long captivity suffered from birth.

Unitarian Europe will detach, state by state, all the satellites of Moscow every time that the opportunity for that presents itself. And just as, today, we demand the entrance of Francoist Spain into the European community, tomorrow we shall recuperate our provinces of the East.

Today we do not accept the pretext of 'Fascist' contamination to reject Spain, tomorrow we shall not accept the pretext of 'Communist' contamination to reject Poland, Hungary, Yugoslavia or any other European province temporarily occupied by the enemy.

Only unitarian Europe can suppress the contradictions between the divisions of the present political borders, on the one hand, and of the ethnic, linguistic and economic borders, on the other.

An objective and even cursory examination immediately reveals that the divisions of the present political Europe frequently do not correspond to the other 'borders', which may be distinguished in linguistic, ethnic and finally, most importantly, economic perspectives.

Thus an Alsatian is politically French and linguistically German. A Flemish worker of Courtrai will be economically French but linguistically Dutch (thousands of Flemish people find work only in the industrial basin of the north of France). The ports of Anvers and Rotterdam, politically Belgian and Dutch, are economically German.

In a country like France, races as different as the Normans and the Corsicans speak the same language. In a country like Belgium, two very different languages, Dutch and French, are spoken by a same race (ethnically the Flemish and Walloons are strictly of the same group).

The majority of the Northern French are of Germanic race, many East Germans are of Slavic origin (names with Slavic consonants abound in East Germany). In the latter case, who is the 'better German', the one who is ethnically German and speaks French or, on the contrary, the one who is linguistically German but whose ethnic origin is in fact Slavic? We see immediately in what an imbroglio we can fall. We see equally the absurdity of trying to base nations on race or on language.

If one tries to draw four maps of Europe on a transparent paper, political, ethnic, linguistic and economic maps, and one then superimposes them, one discovers that only the EXTERNAL borders of Europe coincide perfectly and that the INTERNAL borders, on the contrary, are mixed in an extraordinarily complicated manner.

One of the pretexts of the last war was the port of Danzig, a town linguistically German as well as economically Polish. Danzig had more need of Poland than Poland needed Danzig.

If we wish to make Europe, it is so that such situations do not engender further conflicts between European brothers. In the past it was the NON-COINCIDENCE of political borders with the ethnic, linguistic and economic borders which, on the one hand, created the hotbeds of dangerous discord constituted by minorities and, on the other, sustained by rapine appetites.

Some anachronists or some petty nationalists would like to make a Europe of nations. Okay. But of what nations? In fact there are PERMANENT CONTESTATIONS of the limits of these nations, between the petty nationalists themselves. In fact, the petty nationalists have already 2,000 years of wars in their past. So, to speak of a Europe of nations is to speak of *an impossible Europe.*

For those that belong to minorities, oppressed or not, there is only one solution that does not humiliate anybody, and this solution is Europe. As much as the external borders of unitarian Europe will be rigid and powerfully armed, the future administrative divisions within Europe will be supple and mobile.

The present nations are constrained, by historical determination, to create their unity or to reinforce it, to bully or to break the recalcitrant minorities.

France cannot recognise that Eastern Alsace is linguistically German. Italy cannot admit that South Tyrol is linguistically German. It is a question of the political and military interests of these nations. On the contrary, with the formula of a unitarian Europe, everything changes. *Europe then contains what France and Italy constrain.* In the unitarian Europe there will no longer be the Italian military general staff to demand (at the level of the military art, pertinently) the Brenner border;[15] in the unitarian Europe there will no longer be French Déroulèdes[16] to make us think that the Sarre[17] should return to France or to make us think that all the Alsatians are perfectly integrated 'Frenchmen'.

As we have suggested above, it appears then that a European individual or citizen is susceptible of several affiliations simultaneously.

The citizens of Europe will have only one political loyalty, that to the unitarian and indivisible Europe. There will be only one obedience, that to the European Army.

On the contrary, every liberty will be given to him to remain loyal to such or such cultural group, and every liberty will be assured to him to find his social fulfilment in such or such an economic region within Europe.

In the unitarian Europe, the administrative divisions will be made on the basis of efficiency alone, without the least care for 'nationalist' pride or vanity. Good management will be the only objective sought.

The few preceding lines show sufficiently that the unitarian Europe can be constructed only on the plans of a nation that has been engendered by a community of destiny. Europe will be this community of destiny. There exists, in this regard, in the history of Europe a model nation. It is, quite paradoxically, Great Britain — made up of Celts, Anglo-Saxons, and Scots. For a long time these peoples tore one another apart, collided with each other, and fought one another. For almost four centuries, they have formed, indisputably, a unitarian

---

15 The Brenner Pass in the Eastern Alps forms the border between Italy and Austria.

16 Paul Déroulède (1846–1914) was the founder of the *Ligue des Patriotes* to promote France's '*revanche*' (revenge) against Germany and especially the latter's control of Alsace and Lorraine.

17 The Sarre was a French department created in 1798 on the left bank of the Rhine. It was lost to Prussia after Napoleon's defeat in 1814.

NATION. That shows that one can very well make a great unitarian nation with former 'hereditary enemies'. The Empire which Great Britain cut out for itself in the 17th, 18th and 19th centuries was cut out with the blood of Celts, Anglo-Saxons and Scots, mixed without distinction or discrimination. I do not think that a Scotland of 1964 feels 'oppressed' or 'denationalised' by Great Britain.

The loyalty that Celts, Anglo-Saxons and Scots have shown for four centuries to the Crown will tomorrow be an example for the peoples of Europe when they will have to vow to give total loyalty to the UNITARIAN EUROPEAN STATE, without, for that reason, renouncing anything of their origins and cultures.

Federal Europe, No! Unitarian Europe, Yes! Why?

A brief glance at the past reveals in an obvious manner that all the great pages of history were written by states of unitarian structure and that the states of federal structure have hardly done anything but suffer events.

Until 1860–1870, Italy and Germany, not having benefited from a unitarian centralism, have been, and for centuries at that, arenas and stakes.

During this same epoch, the French, English, Spanish unities were already several centuries old. These three nations — France, England and Spain — interfered constantly in the politics of neighbours with more loose structures. Thus we have seen in history a French Italy and a Spanish Italy, whereas we have never seen an Italian France. We have seen a French Germany, but we have never seen a German France. Without European unity we see today an American Europe and a Russian Europe. Europe is in 1964 what Italy was in 1530: torn and shared between France and Spain.

Unitarian states possess a cohesion and a homogeneity which allow them aggressive politics. Unitarian France has for centuries maintained, to its own benefit, particularist anarchy in Germany. No retaliation is possible: the divided Germans were incapable of doing the same thing with regard to France. The Germanic Reich was a heavy monster on account of the fact of its federal state and, in spite of the remarkable efforts of the Hohenstaufens, was never able to realise the enterprises that its dimensions allowed it to hope for. In every federal formula the power is regularly contested, the continuity of the latter is not assured, the hierarchical connections are constantly questioned.

There are good historical models, such as France, England and Spain, and bad ones, such as Italy and Germany.

We have chosen for Europe the tested model, that of unitarianism. Let us not forget that, in the 15th century, Italy had everything to be the dominant nation in Europe: population, soldiers, wealth; it was not the dominant nation because it lacked one thing: UNITY.

Confederate Europe is the formula of classic alliances, and of ulterior motives as classic as dishonest.

Confederate Europe or, in other words, the Europe of nations is the formula in which each nation conserves its own army and its own diplomacy. This Europe is dangerous because the nations which compose it appeal to extra-European powers to support their politics.

Thus the England of 1964 introduces the American Trojan horse into Europe, and Gaullist France risks introducing to us the Communist Trojan horse tomorrow. This confederate Europe is criminal: it resembles Italy of 1525, whose princes called for help sometimes from France, sometimes from Spain, sometimes from the Germanic Reich. Italy lost each time. This Europe of nations is uncertain, one enters into and leaves it as in a permanent cinema.

We condemn it because it is the Europe open to foreign influences. Federal Europe constitutes already a great progress to the formula mentioned above.

In the federal solution, diplomacy and army become common, the economic borders fall. In the short term, it is a possible and transitory formula. We insist: in the short term, and for a very limited duration.

Because the federal formula consists, germinally, in the possibility of secessions or, at least, internal crises. Federal Europe is in fact the Europe of lawyers. By conserving, for each confederated state, different civil, commercial and penal legislations, one opens up an era of contestations and legal proceedings.

Modern life within Europe is going to lead to exchanges of populations and activities that are increasingly intense. So, to conserve several civil codes, several different commercial codes, is to rush towards judicial anarchy, even in the most down-to-earth questions: imagine for a moment the complexity of a divorce demanded in Madrid for a couple constituted of an Austrian man and a Polish woman married in Rome. Four legislations would intervene in this case, one would have to unite eight lawyers to resolve this contentious issue. It is unthinkable. It is inadmissible in a modern state.

It would not enter anybody's mind to contest the pressing need of a code of a SINGLE sort for all of Europe. Therefore one cannot any longer refute or refuse the pressing need of a single civil code, of a single commercial code, of a single penal code. *That is unitarian Europe, clarity and order.*

To our mind, a federal Europe (single army) could be the *preparatory* stage to a unitarian Europe: it would strictly be a stage on the way, it would certainly not be the terminus.

The confederate formula is calculation and ulterior motives; the federal formula is confusion; the unitarian formula is method, order and clarity.

Only the feudals who fear to lose a portion of their present power reject centralism.

In the United States, the shrewd legislator tends to systematically eliminate local laws and substitute them with 'federal laws', applicable to the 50 states which form the federation. These 'federal laws' are in fact the beginning of the unitarian American state. Everybody knows the weakness of the American system which allows a governor to mock or to tire the central power through judicial quibbles. The same phenomenon, but more marked, can be observed in Brazil, which is also federal and dramatically unstable.

All the great personages of history have been unitarianists, from Caesar to Bismarck to Philip the Fair,[18] followed by all the Capetians, Frederick II of Hohenstaufen, Richelieu, Mazzini or Stalin. We shall end by saying that confederate Europe is concubinage, federal Europe engagement and unitarian Europe marriage.

In a Unitarian Europe There Are No More Problems of Minorities

Everybody knows the quasi-insoluble problems of the minorities in Europe. They exist elsewhere than in the Balkans. Their complexity prevents all other solutions than solutions of force. In order to correct the injustices imposed on the German minorities, Hitler ended by acting unjustly with regard to other ethnies.

In the problem of 'memberships', there are several truths and none of them are negligible. Thus South Tyrol is geographically indisputably Italian, even though the people that live there are indisputably *linguistically* German. Certain minorities have integrated themselves admirably: the French Huguenots who emigrated to Prussia have, during the course of centuries, provided an elite of Prussian military leaders. Other minorities do not allow themselves to be assimilated. Searching in history, one ascertains that every people has some atrocity or injustice to claim of its neighbour. The Germans could hold against the French the destruction of the Palatinate,[19] the French against the English the massacre of Mers El Kebir,[20] the Italians against

---

18 Philippe le Bel (1268–1314) was instrumental in turning France into a centralized state with an uncontested monarchy.

19 The Rhenish Palatinate is a region in Southwestern Germany.

20 During the Battle of Mers-el-Kébir in 1940, during the Vichy government, the British attacked and damaged the French Navy on the Algerian coast.

the French the bloody occupation of Rome by General Oudinot.[21] As for finding a historical — chronological — truth, to what date should we go back? At what epoch should we stop? One realises very quickly the impossibility of resolving, to the satisfaction of everybody, all the problems of minorities, oppressed or not. The mono-ethnic state, a mono-linguistic state, has an interest, if not obligation, to employ force or coercion to assimilate the minorities. It is a question of its cohesion and its homogeneity.

France had the historic obligation to Frenchify the Italians of Nice, the Germans of Strasbourg and the Flemish of Dunkirk. A mono-ethnic state *must* do that if it wishes to survive.

The Germany of the Middle Ages, in its thrust towards the East, had to Germanise the conquered Slavs, unitarian France in its historic thrust had to Frenchify the Alsatians. These nations, France and Germany, could not tolerate within their bosom minorities susceptible of becoming one day Trojan horses in their state for the benefit of a neighbouring state.

Insofar as Italy could fear an offensive Austrian return, it *had to* crush and reduce the Germanic minorities of the Alto Adige[22]. Within a Europe where the possibility of Germano-French or Austro-Italian conflicts is now TOTALLY excluded, France and Italy no longer have anything to fear from the minorities they rule. For that is the real problem *at the start*: a nation fears the foreign minorities that it absorbs. That is why it should dismantle them before integrating them.

It happens quite differently in a polyethnic state (Latins + Germans + Slavs) like Europe, a nation of destiny which, containing everybody, obviously has no reason to harass anybody.

---

21 Charles Oudinot (1791–1863) was the French commander who in 1849 took Rome from the short-lived 'Roman Republic' of Mazzini and re-established Pope Pius IX as the temporal leader of Rome.
22 The Alto Adige is constituted of two autonomous provinces, Trentino and South Tyrol.

The problem of minorities becomes acute and violent when it is aggravated by the air-tightness of the borders of the small states. The moment that these borders fall, the minority is no longer cut off from its mother nation, we mean here the cultural nation, and all drama is instantly defused.

The European state was essentially of a polyethnic type, obviously does not have anything to fear of certain minorities. It has therefore no reason to harass them.

We Should Prepare an Ideological War

Our combat, which is historically identical to the combat of Europe, will be doubly active: it will be a political offensive at first, and it will also be an ideological offensive, which, according to our pragmatic conception of European National Communitarianism, will replace the myth of Communism, the fraudulent panacea.

This conception will be opposed to the morbid defeatism of those who, despairing of our garrulous and impotent pseudo-democracies but not finding any dynamic ideal of replacement, wait, in timid opposition to any change, for the enslavement to the Red termite-mound.

To those who have been disappointed or disgusted by the parliamentary pseudo-democracy, to those who, through despair or spite, could slide towards Communism, we bring a living and aggressive ideology, European National Communitarianism. There are multiple types of wars, from military war to ideological war, to psychological war, revolutionary war, cold war and the war of nerves. We should seriously retain the hypothesis that atomic war will not take place on account of the balance of terror. It is not for that reason that Moscow will give up advancing its pawns to improve its positions. *Direct military competition being rendered impossible by the certainty of a bilateral massacre, other kinds of competition will be attempted or tried.*

Industrial competition, social competition. In these two cases, even present-day Europe is, and will remain, in a situation of strength.

But if it comes to ideological war, this Europe has nothing to oppose to Communism.

What is ideological war and in what, for example, does it differ essentially from psychological war? *Psychological war* is essentially negative, it seeks to weaken the enemy morale through information, lies, propaganda, fabrication …

In contrast, *ideological war* is essentially positive, it does not have any other goal than to present to the adversary a constructive and appealing solution ACCEPTABLE to the latter.

Tomorrow the technology of audio-visual telecommunication is going to permit, thanks to satellites, the literal bombarding of the whole world with selected information issuing from one point on the earth.

In ten years, Moscow will inundate us with its television, and its own propaganda. The Communists will then present their solution as being susceptible of producing *'the happiness of humanity'* … *'Of which YOU are part'*, they will say to their adversaries, whom they will wish to shake in their determination to resist.

The pseudo-democratic Europe of chatterboxes has nothing to oppose to this Communist mystique — and the fact that it is false does not, alas, take anything away from its efficacy.

Thus the 'moral ornaments' of the thought of our enemy are present among us, but the thought of the democratic West has never been present on the other side of the Iron Curtain.

In such conditions, the ideological war is lost in advance. That is why we have to be able as soon as possible to bear an efficacious message to the men on the other side of the Iron Curtain. And this message can only be that of Communitarianism. If the Communism of the middle of the 19th century claims to be in accord with the 'sense of history', we shall say that Communitarianism is now in accord with the SENSE OF HUMAN EVOLUTION.

Communism is dogmatic. Thereby it condemns itself to being rejected by facts, by historical reality. Thus its *rigidity* leads it to agricultural failure, to industrial mess and, what is more, to sustaining petty nationalism among its victims or 'associates'. Communism can maintain itself only through coercion. It is a *fraud* that will collapse once it is deprived of its police apparatus.

In the ideological war that WE will oppose to Communism, we will propose to the oppressed populations a plan of society applicable to them as it is to us: the Communitarian society.

The pseudo-democracy which at present weakens Europe is incapable of desacralising Communism. But we will do it, for we shall oppose to an outdated ideology a new, dynamic, aggressive ideology.

We will win the ideological war with the message of Communitarianism.

Against Anti-White Racism: All Ethnic Groups Have a Right to a Certain Privacy

To deny the difference between races is as ridiculous as to deny the fundamental difference between men of the same race. These inequalities are observable facts, experimental ethnological scientific facts. There are two attitudes as ridiculous as they are indefensible: that of racists who project into politics ethnological knowledge and that of those, like the 'progressives', who embarrassingly deny these same ethnological truths.

We declare that the races are different, which means that there are good and less good ones at the level of intellectual creativity. We cannot help it if the blacks have been incapable of inventing the wheel, if they have not developed a script and if, in 1900, they did not know anything about the geometry conceived 25 centuries ago by our Greek ancestors. Nevertheless, we shall not have the harshness to enlarge these inequalities.

The sorcerer's apprentice politicians who today wish to practise a forced integration of the races will lead us to bloody social disturbances—disturbances from which, besides, it may be mentioned in passing, the whites will emerge victors from the fact of their number and their intrinsic qualities.

In the years to come, the war of the races ignited precisely by the so-called anti-racists is going to transplant the CLASS STRUGGLE with a racial one and give it a cruel significance. The only wise solution consists in the formula of cohabitation and of good neighbourliness—of the states politically controlled by the blacks (the ex-Belgian Congo, for example), where the whites will be welcomed as guests but without political rights and, on the other hand, of states politically controlled by whites (Transvaal for example), where the blacks are accepted as guests but without political rights.

Any other solution, that of integration, for example, will lead to a social reclassification, in which the blacks will form a sort of sub-proletariat. *A country like Brazil, which is absolutely not 'racist', manifests the racial differences* de facto *by the differences in social level. And this is more humiliating for the people of colour. They cannot have any more illusions: they are in their place.*

There exist within the ethnic groups private interests that it would be dangerous to break. The Jewish community, for example, has in our country numerous Jewish schools—subsidised by the state, like the others. Nobody would have the absurd idea of forcing the Jewish community to accept into their schools little Flemish children. If one did that, one would immediately cry out about a crime against humanity. But when the white community refuses to mix with heterogeneous black elements, as in the United States, the conscience of humanity, duly directed and orchestrated, feels offended.

When a father of a family refuses the hand of his daughter to a suitor (of the same race as his family) because the latter is a good-for-nothing, uncultivated or unstable, everybody—rightly—finds that normal and fair. But if the same white father conducts himself in this way with regard to a black BECAUSE THIS BLACK IS ALSO a good-for-nothing, uncultivated and unstable, people will cry out about murderous racism.

This situation cannot leave us indifferent. *Anti-racism has, in the last ten years, become a machine destined to give a guilt-complex to the Europeans. We have been colonisers and not colonialists as people try to make us believe.*

We have taught the blacks everything, including the technologies that they turn against us today. Anti-racism, which happens to be politically an instrument in the hands of the sworn enemies of Europe, is in fact an anti-white racism that does not dare speak its name.

When they assassinate whites in Katanga,[23] the press sends out a short notice of 10 lines. When a black singer is beaten by a white on a road in Mississippi, the television gratifies us with a 15-minute broadcast. A black student has never been raped in Paris or in Brussels; however, not a month passes in the black countries recently freed from our tutelage without there being a violation of white women.

In the hysteria of racial masochism, certain whites, contemptible specimens of their groups, begin to conduct themselves like intellectual homosexuals. In the Belgian universities, the bad black students are not failed because the academic authorities apply pressure to see that inferiority complexes do not arise among the blacks. A mediocre or stupid black student has a right to a diploma that is refused to a similar stupid white.

Our correctional tribunals punish whites who fight against blacks in the dance clubs with six months in prison — it is not a question here of Fascists but of party animals, and for the same fights between whites and in the same conditions the penal sentence is eight days in prison with reprieve. They try to make blacks sacred cows. That is supremely annoying. We condemn the projection of racism into politics

---

23 Katanga is a province in the Democratic Republic of the Congo (Zaire), which broke away in 1960 under Moise Tshombe from the Republic of Congo-Léopoldville that was established when the Belgian Congo became independent of Belgium. Tshombe surrendered in 1962 to UN forces.

and we say that a superiority born of a difference does not justify an exploitation or a genocide that we forbid ourselves from practising for moral reasons and not for reasons of absence of power in our leaders — we demand that the others do the same.

We whites do not have to produce guilt complexes to cure the blacks of their present inferiority complexes.

Fascism and Anti-Fascism: Anachronisms

Fascism and National Socialism are historical phenomena and no longer present political facts. Therefore all Fascist or anti-Fascist polemics are puerile, anachronistic and useless, even harmful for the future of Europe.

History alone will be able to judge, and with the large vision indispensable to scientific objectivity, Fascism and National Socialism as socio-political phenomena. To wish to judge these two phenomena today is quite premature, just as it would have been to wish to judge Bonaparte in 1829. Between 1815 and 1830 as injurious and inaccurate things — if not more — were written against Bonaparte as against Hitler between 1945 and 1960. The atrocities attributed to National Socialism are shared by its enemies. The useless butchery of Hiroshima and the Anglo-American phosphorus bombings of April and May 1945 on German cities have for the moment been evaded by the victors. Atrocities have been the fact of all men at all times, one cannot reasonably impute to an ideology, and as a monopoly, atrocities invented and practised by all and for millennia. Or one would have to condemn Catholicism for its anti-Semitism and its stakes of the past centuries and demolish the Soviet Union to punish it for accommodating an ideology that has killed or caused to kill many more men than all the Fascisms together. Which would be, to say the least, wrong.

Political life has been encumbered by bearers of icons who cannot decide to leave the stage. The heroic qualities demonstrated in 1943 do not prove anything regarding the maturity and the creativity of the political sense in 1964. One can have been a hero of the Resistance or a hero of the Eastern Front in 1943 and be a political dunce in 1964. It is remarkable to note that, at all times, the people who are nostalgic have not preserved of the past any of its qualities, they have only conserved its RITES.

Resistance and Fascism, National Socialism and anti-Fascism belong already to the postcard phase. But the bearers of these nostalgias do not wish to, or cannot, see it. If you go and see what remains in Waterloo of Napoleon's sword, you will see many postcard houses, fried dishes, cafés, dance clubs. There the postcard phenomenon is blinding. For the recent past, that of Fascism and anti-Fascism, if the phenomenon is less apparent, it is not for that any less real. Some confuse patriotism with old-age homes and civicism, along with its conformism, others confuse National Socialism with boots and swastikas.

From the recent past we should draw two lessons, namely: first, that the political combatants of the 39/45 era do not have the right to force the present youth to resume their heritage of hatred, and my statement is directed to the two camps—secondly, those who are incapable of an intellectual reconversion and an ideological adaptation must abstain from encumbering the paths of the contemporary political scene. If they wish to tie themselves at all costs to the past, let them at least abstain from encumbering the present.

To the extent to which we condemn those who tie themselves to the attitudes and hatreds of the past, we open wide our doors to all those of the two camps who, leaving in the locker room their old ideological rags, come to us to fight in for Europe. *As much as we strike the old ideologies with ostracism, so much do we refuse to apply the least ostracism to the old militants of these ideologies insofar as they reconvert themselves sincerely to a new ideology in the service of a new fight.*

The myth of neo-Nazism remains one of the great needs of Communist propaganda to divide the West, which it wishes to crush.

Moscow needs neo-Nazism. Some 'orchestra conductors' with a cold and calculating mind manipulate in this activity a handful of naïve stooges who become real unconscious provocateurs. These manipulated stooges are precisely these nostalgic people with mediocre culture and very limited intelligence, such as the Colin Jordans[24] and the Rockwells,[25] ridiculous caricatures of what the National Socialists were. But these ridiculous caricatures serve to revive the old conditioning of hatred, which divides anti-Communism.

By perpetuating this division and hatred among old (NON-Communist) anti-Fascists and old Fascists, Moscow removes all vigour from the anti-Communist fight. The anti-Communist fight for the liberation of Europe demands the right number of Fascists as well as of ex-Resistance fighters. I insist on the prefix 'ex'.

---

24 Colin Jordan (1923–2009) was a British neo-Nazi leader of the British National Party (1960) and of the World Union of National Socialists (1962), which included Lincoln Rockwell as his deputy.

25 Lincoln Rockwell (1918–67) was an American neo-Nazi who founded the American Nazi Party in 1959.

CHAPTER III

THE FRIENDS AND ENEMIES OF UNITARIAN EUROPE

If therefore one wishes to understand this point well, one should consider if those who seek new things can do something by themselves or if they depend on others; that is to say, if they count on prayers or on force to lead their enterprise to success. In the first case, they always finish badly and do not succeed in finishing anything; but, when they depend on themselves and can use force, then it is only rarely that they fail. FROM THIS ARISES THE FACT THAT ALL THE WELL-ARMED PROPHETS WERE VICTORS.

> Niccolò Machiavelli

Do not trust Europe, men of America. You are young, it is younger than you …

> Georges Bernanos

We do not think that there is a possible agreement, of equals, among peoples who agree to risk war and of peoples who refuse to risk it.

> Henri de Montherlant

Freedom is Power.

> Thomas Hobbes

It is a shame that the soul becomes weak while the body does not.

> Marcus Aurelius,
> Book VI

The Refugees From the East, First European Citizens

AT PRESENT the refugees from the provinces of Eastern Europe are received with more or less 'charity' in the provinces of Western Europe. The good ladies of the Red Cross offer them blankets and certain ham actors, whether in a soutane or not, exploit in the media the miseries of our brothers in the East. As for work, ignoble employers profit from the uncertain status of the refugee to employ him at a reduced salary.

Should we speak also of the American secret services, which recruit, from Munich to Istanbul and from Hamburg to Thessaloniki, our brothers of the East, freshly escaped from the Soviet nightmare in order to make them 'agents' of the Pentagon?

The scandalous imprudence of these American secret services has already cost the lives of hundreds of them launched imprudently into operations that are most often useless. If each of us must hold one's life at the disposal of the cause of the liberation and reunification of Europe, none of us must be sacrificed to extra-European, and especially American, interests.

We demand for our brothers who are refugees from the East, immediate European citizenship, giving them all of the civil and political rights in all of Western Europe.

The refugees from the East are AT HOME here in the West. We will not allow that they be classified as 'tolerated foreigners'. Whereas, in countries like France, Belgium and Italy, the native Communists and the imported Communists have total latitude in devoting themselves openly to their work of subversion for the profit of a foreign and ENEMY power, in fact the USSR, it is scandalous that Europeans should here be victims of harassment, of humiliating and discriminating measures, or even of extortion on the part of the police in the West. More serious is the fact that very often Communists infiltrated our police in the West, in England, France, Belgium and nearly everywhere in Western Europe, and provided the Soviet police services with information that allows the Communists in Moscow to exercise reprisals against the families of our comrades who have remained in the East.

Within the scope of historical rights for our refugee comrades with immediate European nationality, there is occasion *to steer them from now on into political formations designed to prepare the reconquest of our provinces of the East.*

Among the young escaped from the East we will find the elite elements who will tomorrow be at the head of the combat for the liberation of their provinces, either in political action or in the action of groups of partisans.

We reject the defeatism which consists in wishing to 'assimilate' the refugees from the East, in removing from them all hope of returning one day to their country. We will return to Bucharest, without cannons or at the cannon, through diplomacy or through our tanks, but *we will return to it.*

As soon as Western Europe is cleansed of pro-American collaborators, we will recall to Europe the hundreds of thousands of young Baltic, Hungarian, Polish, Czechoslovak, Romanian and Bulgarian comrades to educate and instruct them in view of the assault against the Communist (concentration) camp. Our brothers of the East will participate in the reconquest of their provinces; we do not wish that they be lost in emigration to South America and North America, or to Australia. Being first citizens of Europe, they will also be the first soldiers of Europe.

Europe Should Withdraw From the UN Circus, Which We Reject From This Moment on

Europe should withdraw from the UN. This organism combines, at an international level, the vices of the pseudo-democratic and Communist regimes in a scandalous demagogic flagrancy. Europe can and should regulate its internal affairs by itself and guarantee its external interests by itself. It does not have to submit either to the tutelage or to the good offices of the UN, that is, in fact, to the hustling of the Soviet and American blocs, which, for twenty years, have been in an alliance to despoil it in favour of the stupid UN arithmetic. In this assembly, which pushes to the point of absurdity the principle of universal suffrage—the vote of Sierra Leone is equal to that of France, the vote of Zanzibar is equal to that of England, Liberia has a vote, Germany does not. Thus the majority of the votes are in the hands of the Afro-Asiatics in a state of economic beggarliness and therefore easily manipulated by Moscow or bought by Washington.

After 1918, the League of Nations was created by naïve people, who promised for it a moral prestige, and by crooked diplomats, who drew profits from it. The League of Nations was at first, in the hands of Paris and London, an anti-Russian and anti-German instrument; a little later an anti-Italian instrument. The League of Nations was for 15 years a moral façade—of cardboard—for the diplomatic calculations of the Quai d'Orsay.[1] The failure of the League of Nations was total during the Ethiopia affair and on the occasion of the Civil War in Spain; at this moment everybody, even the most naïve, had ripped off its mask. The League of Nations died in a general indifference.

The awakening of Europe will ring the death knell of this exotic farce. The assassinations of Belgians in Katanga will not remain unpunished any more than the atrocities committed in Angola by the

---

[1] The French Ministry of Foreign Affairs is located in the Quai d'Orsay in Paris.

terrorists of Holden Roberto[2] and we shall, if necessary, find those responsible for them.

From this moment on we reject the UN and we reject its intrusion into our problems and into our European national interests.

The 'scattered Europeans' who will have collaborated excessively with this organism will be judged and treated as agents of an enemy power.

We shall never grant judicial status to the white mercenaries of the UN who have assassinated our European brothers in Africa in 1961 and 1962; it will be the same for our political clowns who are the 'intellectual' accomplices of this anti-European machination.

Fighting Against Active Defeatism

Tired bodies with cowardly minds wallow in morbid defeatism. Some maintain that Europe cannot '*go beyond*' the American tutelage. Others think that already everything is lost. Weak, they would wish that others be that too; blind, they would wish others to be that too; cowardly, they would wish that others become that too. Now, for Europe, nothing is lost if it recovers its determination. In a much more desperate situation, the Greeks did not throw in the towel after the occupation of Athens by the Persians; they finally won at Salamis; the Romans did not capitulate when Hannibal seemed 'irreversibly' victorious.

Defeatism should be denounced, fought, restrained penally in the most severe fashion. Passive defeatism serves the cause of Communism; it should therefore be punished. Europe is demographically strong with its 400 million men, strong in its industry, prodigiously rich in technologists. Europe constitutes a potential force that is superior to the American force and the Soviet force.

---

2   Holden Roberto (1923–2007) was the leader of the *Frente Nacional de Libertação de Angola* (National Front for the Liberation of Angola) from 1962 to 1999.

Europe lacks only political unity to become, from a potential great power that it is at present, a world power, the first world power.

Intellectual perversion should lead to the dock, and then to prison, all those who revel in it, those who wallow in it and those who live off it.

Breaking Active Treason

When half of our European fatherland has for twenty years suffered a bloody occupation by the Red Army, which the latter constantly threatens us with, the suicidal stupidity of our leaders tolerates, in Western Europe, Communist parties, undisguised agents of treason.

Moscow, through the Communist parties, introduces into the European defence an authentic politico-military Trojan horse.

The Communist fifth column within Western Europe — at a time when, for the moment, we do not have any similar agency in the Soviet world — falsifies all diplomatic negotiations with Moscow.

As long as the Kremlin can foster the hope of unleashing internal revolutions among us, there is no reason that it should take the negotiations really seriously at the level of the governments. The probable and indispensable dialogue with the USSR should be preceded by the destruction of the Communist parties in the West. In our countries Communism should be treated as a manifestation of mental disturbance or active treason. To the die-hards of foreign Communism we will apply either the care required for lunatics or the measures that traitors call for. The last irredeemable residues of Communism in Western Europe should take the path to the lunatic asylum or to prison.

It is partially inexact to claim that Communism serves the Soviet state. In reality it is the Soviet state that serves Communism. The internationalist religion is egregiously in the service of a classic pan-Russian nationalism. In fact, it is especially the Russian state that lends some prestige to Communism and then makes use of it to undertake a work of '*idealistic espionage*' or to undermine its enemies.

We should above all not allow ourselves to be softened by the fact that the Communist agents might be disinterested idealists abused by a religion. They are agents of an enemy power and should be treated as such.

Those Who Wish to Destroy Us Aim at the Nation Through Society

To accelerate the biological decadence of the Red Indians, the Americans took enormous pleasure in procuring alcohol for them. Genocide through alcohol is a little less rapid than by the Winchester but it has the advantage of keeping morality on its side, since nobody is 'obliged' to buy alcohol.

Should we recall the Opium War between England and China in 1840? The present occupation of Hong Kong by the English is the last benefit derived by them from this little edifying affair. England in 1840 waged war against China because the latter wished to prohibit the consumption of opium by its natives. The sale of opium fabulously enriched the very British East India Company…

Our contemporary enemies, Communism on one hand, Yankee mercantile Capitalism on the other, systematically look for everything that could shake the structures of our SOCIETY. We say here SOCIETY, and not STATE or nation. A society possesses a series of moral regulations and traditions, which allow it to find stability in a prosperous period and to resist the historical shocks coming from outside in a bad period.

A nation that possesses a strong society can easily allow itself a weak state. On the contrary, a nation that has only a weak society or no society at all is obliged to have recourse to an inquisitorial state, to a repressive state, to a police state.

To the extent that the moral regulations are powerful, the repressive laws will be less numerous and rarely used. And vice versa.

It is the same with subversion. A nation whose society is strong possesses the tranquil assurance of its superiority or its personality. It remains impermeable to the temptations of subversion. Our adversaries know this. For this reason they will try everything that is possible to prepare our collapse by undermining, by sapping, the values of our society. Having disintegrated the political structures of the state, there will remain nothing before them that can keep the nation standing and allow it to resist the crisis. *For, when a nation possesses a strong society, it can easily survive the momentary destruction of its state structures, its political structures.* Ancient Republican Rome was, through the rigour of its customs, structured in such a way that, after military disasters or terrible political crises, it seemed hardly shaken.

Our adversaries will thus try to destroy our moral values, our traditions that cement the nation.

How will they do this?

By means that are at first glance very anodyne.

The authority of the head of the family being constantly contested will lead easily to the contestation of no matter what authority. The cult of ease in private life will easily lead to military defeatism. In this psychological war that Communism waged against us at the time of the conflict of Algeria — it ESPECIALLY did not place any emphasis on the ideological war between the West and Moscow but, with infinitely more ruse, it undermined, shook the 'contingent' by whispering in its ear: '*What are you doing boring yourself in this dump when there are girls in St. Tropez …?*' Don't smile: this was a reality recently experienced by all. From ease to defeatism there is only one step, one step on one and the same path. Cinema, more than any other method, pushes towards the destruction of our society. It offers us false heroes, heroes of comfort, heroes of cowardice. The progressive cinema of the Italo-French school proposes to our masses the cult of the bidet. Popular pornography — that is to say, cheap — at the price of a ticket to the cinema — exercises terrible ravages on the youth, destroying the notions of family by destroying the respect that is due to it. The reign of television only perfects this technique of moral corruption.

Now, the family is — I speak here as a sociologist and not as a moralist — the basic cell of a stable society. To ruin its family is to open the gates to all individual and collective neuroses.

The solidity of families, the authority exercised by the head of the family, is reflected faithfully in the society that they form.

The commercial media are equally associated with this destruction. Through cinema, through commercial advertising, the young man who starts life thinks that he will be a free person, a hard man, a hero, if he smokes that famous cigarette, the cigarette of virile men — if he drinks that famous apéritif, the apéritif of sportsmen and hard men — if he gives himself up to that debauchery that the cinema suggests to him as the supreme manifestation of virility.

Look where the youth seek their model heroes: Brigitte Bardot and Johnny Hallyday, contemptible products, if ever there were, of human fauna serve as models to an entire youth. With the Brigitte Bardot copies one cannot make mothers of balanced families; with Johnny Hallyday copies one cannot make either workers or warriors.

Our local politicians must also coarsen the masses in order to remove from them any critical sense and thus prepare them for elections.

The solicitation of popular votes has lost all relation to the original representative system and has completely degenerated into a Barnumesque media operation: they voted for Kennedy because he was a handsome boy and not on account of his capacities as a statesman. It is normal in these conditions that one must 'drug' the people before any scrutiny occurs. Similarly, the big distributors of whiskey or of cigarettes must condition the purchasing masses and for that equally remove any critical sense from them.

The coarsening of the voter, the coarsening of the consumer and finally, and especially, the vilification of the citizen, all that contributes to the destruction of a society.

Without morality, without traditions, without customs, this society or spinelessness is presented with seductive features, and will not be able to resist the shaking of its political structures.

The morality of a nation is determined by the solidity of its society. In this view, the fight for the construction of a united and strong Europe cannot avoid denouncing today, and hunting down tomorrow, all those who wish to destroy the traditional values from which we derive our moral strength.

We Do Not Wish to Become a Practice Target Area: From the Bomb on Peking to the Bomb on Paris

One of the reasons for the Peking-Moscow divorce rests in the Russian refusal to communicate with their Chinese 'brothers' about atomic military secrets.

There is no doubt, besides, that tomorrow, what will accelerate the USA-Europe split will be the Yankee refusal to give to the Europeans the control of the use of atomic weapons based in Europe.

Europe and China run an immense danger: that of serving as a practice target area *without possibility of retaliation*.

China and France are aware of this, whence their opposition to the Moscow Treaty of 1963.[3]

It is not at all excluded that the temptation may come from the Soviet and American general staffs, in case of a conflict, to spray Europe and China with *'small tactical bombs'* even while avoiding, at the same time, in order not to poison matters, bombarding the

---

3   The Partial Test Ban Treaty of 1963 was signed in Moscow by the USSR, the United States and the United Kingdom. It prohibited all nuclear test detonations except those conducted underground.

American and Russian territories. This hypothesis must be seriously maintained.

We have very little taste for the role of victims and we are not at all enthusiastic about the formula which would couple Peking and Frankfurt, Shanghai and Paris, Canton and Rome.

If a coupling must take place, it must strike the first users of the atomic weapons in their countries and not among their satellites, which are considered their friends.

The argument of small bombs and big bombs does not hold. A Chinese submarine with a 'small bomb' can destroy San Francisco and we can even now destroy Odessa or Kiev with a French or English 'small bomb'. One can kill as easily with a .22 calibre as with a .45 calibre. Therefore one can defend oneself very WELL with a small calibre gun. Even if this atomic delay may be very difficult to compensate rapidly when European unity will be realised.

We have more scientists than the USSR and the USA combined and our industry is as powerful. I present the argument of the 'small bomb' to emphasise its indisputable efficacy even now, and while waiting for our 'big' bomb.

Knowing the stupidity and, especially, the cowardice of the Americans, Moscow could be tempted to attack us even with the atomic bomb, counting on the fear of the Yankees of seeing the massacre extend to their country. The danger of a 'massacre' for which we will pay the cost following an implicit treaty between Moscow and Washington is very plausible.

The external field of 'limited' battle was already chosen in Korea, Vietnam and Laos. There is no reason that it may not be conceived on a little larger level.

That is why there is no security for Europe without autonomous atomic weapons. The military and political authorities of the present European states which accept the American military atomic monopoly betray the peoples whom they have a mission to defend.

Europe with its 400 million inhabitants has another role to play in the history of the world than that of a colonial infantry of the Pentagon or as a practice target area.

For a European Army with Nuclear Armaments. NATO Is an Instrument of the Vassalisation of Europe by the USA

Nearly 300 million Western Europeans are no longer in the state to defend themselves alone. This humiliating situation cannot last. If one adds up the military expenses of each European state and the numbers of their national armies, Europe does not appear disarmed any longer. Its military weakness results solely from the fact that one finds in it a dozen armies and not a single strong army.

Today Europe is a stake between Washington and Moscow, tomorrow it can become an arena where a devastating war will take place. We will substitute NATO, which has made Western Europe a military glacis destined to receive Soviet bombs, with a defence organisation purely European.

In the present state of affairs, that is to say, while waiting for Europe to be capable of assuming its defence by itself, and protecting its neutrality, NATO must be, very provisionally, maintained with a care to untie ourselves from the USA as rapidly as possible. NATO is an imposture which makes Europe serve as a 'colonial infantry' for the USA. We do not wish to be the Senegalese of the Pentagon. The European Army cannot be conceived without its own atomic weapons. Atomic power is at present the only effective guarantee of European neutrality between the two USA and USSR blocs, united when it is a question of dispossessing Europe but antagonists in other regards.

The French atomic bomb will tomorrow be the European atomic bomb. In this view, the French initiative, which is childish in its initial size, is in fact rich with possibilities in an imminent future.

A superficial reasoning causes people to say that '*the balance of terror*' will prevent in any event the utilisation of atomic weapons and that, therefore, it is better to turn one's efforts to the modern revolutionary army and leave to the Americans the COSTS of the constitution of a nuclear army. That is the argument that I heard one of the big leaders of the OAS[4] say and one should refute it with vigour. In fact, one should refrain from monomanias. It is fitting to foresee and at the same time to prepare for both the atomic and the revolutionary wars.

A modern state which wishes to be politically independent must possess an economic independence but also a military independence and a military autonomy. It is possible that one does NOT use atomic weapons, but one should nevertheless possess them to be able to dissuade the adversary through deterrence.

A military conception which complacently talks of an '*American nuclear umbrella*' above Europe is intimately connected to an American political tutelage.

Let us suppose for a moment that the Americans become politically our sincere friends. Even in this hypothesis one must foresee the forced evacuation of the Americans from Europe — not on account of us — but on account of the deterioration of the political situation in the two Americas. The Communist leprosy of Cuba is inevitably going to extend to South America; the black problem is insoluble in the United States. The fall of the dollar following the economic crisis, of which the initial stages are already evident, the probable racial war at the heart of the USA itself, the active extension of Castroism, are

---

4   The *Organisation de l'armée secrete* (Organisation of the Secret Army) was a paramilitary organisation formed in 1961 by French nationalists to hinder the independence of Algeria through the January 1961 referendum on self-determination declared by de Gaulle.

going to reduce the USA in a few years from the first rank to that of a secondary power.

In this hypothesis — that of the forced evacuation of the US Army from Europe — will Europe remain fully exposed, without nuclear armaments, before Moscow? Those who do not foresee this situation are politically short-sighted: criminal. *One should have even now a European atomic military plan that may be substituted immediately in the case of the 'premature' departure of the Yankees from Europe.*

In fact, WE, Europeans, are quite determined to drive out the Americans who occupy Western Europe. But it might be that historically we do not even have the time to do that and that the Americans may leave by themselves in a 'premature' way before we even actively do anything about that.

There is no state without an army. For us the unitarian European state will commence its historic existence the day when the popular Army of Free Europe will be set up with nuclear weapons.

CHAPTER IV

LEGAL EUROPE AGAINST COMBATANT EUROPE

Bad luck to one who wishes to make a revolution without being slandered.

Honoré de Mirabeau

The great souls are not those who have fewer passions and more virtues than the common souls, but those alone who have greater plans.

François de la Rochefoucauld

Revolution is the work of a resolute minority, inaccessible to discouragement, of a minority whose first moves the masses do not understand because, victims of a period of decadence, they have lost that precious thing that is internal light.

José Antonio Primo de Rivera

But if we look closer at that of which national patriotisms are constituted, is it not that which European patriotism lacks? Formidable question, but that all those who wish to make a powerful Europe cannot continue to avoid.

Marcel Grégoire

It is never acting that dishonours, it is being acted on.

Walter Rathenau

Courage is a thing that is organised, that lives and dies, that one should look after like guns.

André Malraux

ଈ

The great dates of fighting Europe:
East Germany: Berlin 12 June 1953
Czechoslovakia: Pilsen 1953
Poland: Poznan 28 June 1956
Hungary: Budapest 20 October 1956
Czechoslovakia: Prague 1 May 1964

We Are the Legitimate Europe and Reject the 'Legal' Europe

WE REJECT that which is only a theoretical Europe, this 'legal' Europe, that of Strasbourg, for its crimes of incapacity and impotence, first of all, and then for the crime of treason.

In fact, the treason of this 'legal' Europe materialised first in the cowardly acceptance of the definitive abandon of Eastern Europe, and then in the total subjection of the West to Washington.

This legal Europe is only a construction on paper, and it has no more consistency than the Humanity with a capital H, or Humankind with a capital H, invoked by the UN. Western Europe, the rump of the politics of the White House, exists only as a parody destined to deceive the peoples who serve, as we have said, as a colonial infantry for the Yankee politics!

'Legal' Europe does not exist because it is not independent; it is only a sort of American super-Panama.

If the American Army should leave Europe, at that moment the construction of Strasbourg will collapse just as a satellite disappears when its mother planet is extinguished.

Similarly, in the East, only the Russian Army guarantees the 'Pax Sovietica'.

There is no nation where there is no independence. There is no independence where there is an occupier.

To this 'legal' Europe that we reject we oppose the legitimate Europe of peoples, *the Europe of combatants*, OUR EUROPE.

We are EUROPE as a NATION.

The legitimate Europe exists, it is present everywhere, combatant everywhere. It is that of the insurgents of East Berlin of 17 June 1953, it is that of the heroes of Budapest of October 1956. It is also that of the combatants of Algeria who, by fighting to maintain this land, defended Europe consciously or unconsciously.

In the balance of history, the life of a sole heroic insurgent will be worth a hundred times more than the life of a chatterbox of Strasbourg. The legitimate Europe is represented by the men who, not only in words, but also in daily deeds, do everything in their power to drive out the two OCCUPIERS, the Americans from the West and the Russians from the East. These determined men fight in difficult conditions, and the prisons often close upon them in the West as well as in the East.

A certain press subject to the occupiers tries vainly to vilify the European combatants by representing them as desperados, by trying to condemn them before an opinion already systematically conditioned. But from month to month, the youth, this unexpected youth that was twenty years old in the sixties, brings a scathing refutation of the controlling pessimism of the occupiers, by joining the ranks of combatant Europe. The latter already demonstrates its efficacity to such a degree that the accomplices of the occupiers have been obliged to establish a 'Police Europe' to try to arrest our rising tide.

United, trained, and then united around the principal idea of the liberation of Europe, and of its reunification, the men of combatant Europe will send 'Rump Europe' and 'Police Europe' to hell.

It is too late to stop us. One could knock off some leaders 'just as one could kill some propagators' — a political assassination here in the West would then be attributed to some enthusiastic Communist whom the psychiatric specialists of the political police have ready at hand — but it is too late, the seed of the liberation of Europe has been sown in the furrows.

And the idea, like the seed, can lie for a while in frozen land beaten by winds and drenched by rain; when spring returns, the seed rises. THE IDEA HAS BEEN SOWN.

Against the Europe of Good Wishes, of Clubs and Youth Associations — Against Academism

Europe should be lived and not uttered. It should be a reality of flesh and blood and not a construction of rhetoricians.

Too many socialites, boy scouts and 'intellectuals' distract from the attention and effort which should be consecrated first of all to making Europe a Nation.

As long as the concept of Europe as a Nation has not penetrated the working masses, as long as it has not inspired all of the youth, there will not be Europe. Europe is a thousand times more than the Europe of economists and administrators — no matter how competent and well-intentioned they may be. One should create a mystique of Europe, a patrimony of Europe. Those who scatter the efforts in 'cultural' European circles, those who discuss it excessively at banquets or while exchanging souvenir medals, waste energy. The Europe of chapels or the Europe of salons are caricatures. Europe needs steel before needing 'fraternity' members. Europe needs enthusiasm before needing jurists. Europe needs combatants and leaders and not profiteers and public figures. We are those who seek every reason to MAKE Europe and not those who raise all sorts of difficulties in order to slow it down, restrain it or stop it. It is our way of life, we seek always, with regard to any situation, every reason to MAKE something. The Neo-Byzantines, as decadents, also find pretexts NOT TO DO something. A century ago 'charity' was a pretext for balls and celebration. Today, in bourgeois circles, Europe performs a function analogous to the 'charity' of the past. One enrols in a European 'club' just as one enrols in a golf club or in a gourmet club. All of that is only puerile and sterile academism, all of that is only a window display, exhibitionism of social vanity. As for the intellectuals, they act within academic circles, blacken pages and go through the motions when they are not entering lavish fluff called 'foundations' of this or that — 'European' foundations, of course …

Europe does not need 'goodwill'. Europe needs steel wills, combatant wills. The will of the militant is a steel will, a combatant will. 'Goodwill' is a virtue for an old church-going woman or for a timid bourgeois.

This *academic Europe*, this 'Europe of socialites', does not advance our liberation one step: so we despise it and denounce it.

The most sincere — or the most naïve — of this cohort of scholars and anemics can, at most, claim to represent the *Europe of herbal teas*.

The innumerable movements are fully controlled by the systems in place, they themselves subject to the American politics. Their function is that of an outlet destined to distract, especially among the youth, forces which otherwise would be engaged in a real combat.

Since the 'Prague Coup' of February 1948, the Pseudo-Democracy Has Proven Its Inability to Defend Europe

The degenerate parliamentary democracy, otherwise called the democracy of chatterboxes, is incapable of defending us against Communism; without calling for the interested aid of American capitalism.

The 'struggle' of our pseudo-democrats against Communism has only been a long series of combats for delay, a long series of renunciations, of abandonments. Our pseudo-democracies only seek to avoid coups, and are very happy when they can foresee them. Their divisions allow Communism to find allies among the very people who claim to oppose it.

The finest illustration of the stupidity of the politics of balance and of the inconsequence of the pseudo-democrats is that of the 'Prague coup' in February 1948,[1] followed by the UN treaty signed on 4 April 1949; the democrat Beneš, in spite of his ruse, was, in it, rapidly surpassed by the Communists with whom he thought he could 'coexist'.

Or, from naivety to fear.

Politicians who call themselves Europeans oscillate regularly between gullibility with regard to the Communist world and a demand for American protection.

Our so-called '*statesmen*' (sic) have been acting for eighteen years like loose women of politics and diplomacy.

Incapable of thinking and, *a fortiori*, of willing an *intrinsically* European politics, they jump from one bed to another; on Monday they dream of 'peaceful coexistence' with the Communists, on Tuesday, like in Prague in 1948, they are cheated, deceived, humiliated by them, on Wednesday they run to Washington to whine and ask for aid. Then the next week new Mondays attract them. The best example of this is provided by the 'European' Spaak[2] who, after having proclaimed that he was afraid of the Soviet danger, runs today to Warsaw to support there the Rapacki plan of European neutralisation.[3] But not once has the idea occurred to these cowardly politicians of a politics *specifically* European, without illusions regarding Moscow, without complacence regarding Washington.

---

1   The Prague Coup marked the beginning of the total control of Czechoslovakia by the Czech Communist Party, supported by the Soviet Union. Klement Gottwald, the General Secretary of the Czech Communist Party, who was Prime Minister at that time, became the President of the Czech Socialist Republic in June 1948.

2   Paul-Henri Spaak (1899–1972) was a Belgian politician, who is considered one of the founders of the European Economic Community in 1957.

3   The Rapacki Plan, named after the Polish Foreign Minister, Adam Rapacki, presented a proposal to the UN General Assembly in 1957 for a nuclear-free zone in Central Europe. It was opposed by the NATO organisation in Europe and never implemented.

We have dozens of Beneš' in reserve in 'democratic' Europe. Not only are these people incapable of defending Europe but, furthermore, they are not worthy of doing so.

Resisting the Communist imperialism under the leadership of people who regularly cause intellectual disease is a suicidal snare. And when the disease leaves them, following an electrical shock of the voltage of Prague, they dash off to hide behind the skirt of beautiful America.

These 'European' politicians have neither the calibre nor the scope to be the leaders that the destiny of our great fatherland calls for.

To wish to defend Europe with these people and their method, to oppose 'democracy' to the Russian Communist totalitarianism, is the same as building castles in the air.

This immense mediocracy of the Western politicians has let all the opportunities to defend Europe aggressively pass by. It has let the Czechs fall in 1948, the Germans in 1953, the Polish in June 1956, the Hungarians in October 1956. Not a single gun was sent to our insurgent brothers.

Four times the opportunity of causing, at little expense, the entire unstable edifice of the Soviet occupation of Eastern Europe to collapse has not been exploited. Lack of imagination, stupidity, cowardice or complicity with Moscow? One should, in my opinion, impute the four charges to them.

In fact, the people who signed at Yalta — and the English were there — in February 1945 had already explicitly admitted the Russians being set into orbit over Eastern Europe.

Today it is the same people who speak of organising '*the defence of Europe*'. They are first of all incapable of it — and they do not have a right to do it either.

From the Spirit of Resistance to the Spirit of Revolution — From the Defensive Conception to the Offensive Conception

For fifteen years people have been speaking, from time to time — between two eruptions of an ideological epidemic — of 'resisting' Communism and 'defending' against the imperialist intrigues of the Kremlin on our lands, with a conviction more rhetorical than determined.

We do not wish to resist and do not wish to defend. We wish to bring to the European man a spirit of revolution with the power that it might contain; Communism we wish to attack *in its colonies*. In Eastern Europe and among its abused clientele, the working class of the East.

The Moscow edifice is far from being as solid as it seems to the frightened bourgeois of the West. If, in spite of the bloody Russian police occupation, the Czech, Polish, German and Hungarian WORKERS revolted (the spirit of revolution), it was because the yoke hurt very much, but also because the yoke was very badly adjusted.

In the West, the American psychological clumsinesses has powerfully contributed to the development of the European national sentiment but let us not forget that, in the East, the gross blunders of the Russian imperialism, especially its pillage, have awoken powerful reactions, among which is in the first rank Titoism, a phenomenon that is not to be underestimated. Within the framework of an ideological offensive against Russian Communism, the European national sentiment can constitute a formidable arm, an extraordinary revolutionary lever.

It is normal that many Europeans of the East hesitate to change occupiers: the idea that their uprising against the Russians will definitely benefit only the Americans and their socio-economic system does not enthuse them nor even incite them. The situation becomes quite different if the appeal to revolt against the Russian occupation is cast by a communitarian Western Europe. Then it is an appeal to brothers. To the extent that we guarantee real social conquests to the populations of Eastern Europe, our European nationalism becomes a natural force that can internally destroy the Russian protectorate.

It is the spirit of revolution and the offensive spirit. It is war brought to the adversary as the principles of revolutionary war teach.

This will turn us away from the recantations and bargaining to which the NATO 'allies' subject themselves in order to 'resist' Communism.

Eastern Europe must constitute a capital element of our entire military political strategy. But the only possible instrument of this strategy is the message of a communitarian Europe. The little edifying spectacle of a corrupt Western plutocracy, servilely obeying Wall Street, can only discourage all ideas of revolt among the prisoners of the East.

Communitarian and unitarian Europe will have at its disposal tomorrow an extraordinary offensive arsenal for the PSYCHOLOGICAL WAR against Moscow, whereas this offensive arsenal is prohibited, on account of its plutocratic structures, to the present day 'Western world', which is damned in advance to defeat.

Where the plutocracy can at best hope to 'defend itself', we can speak of an offensive and of revolution.

CHAPTER V

THE PLACE AND THE ROLE OF MAN IN THE EUROPEAN COMMUNITARIAN SOCIETY

In truth, man does not have rights but he has needs. Right is a philosophical principle, need a scientific concept.

ALEXIS CARREL

To be of the Left or the Right is to choose one of the innumerable ways that are offered to man of being an imbecile; both, in fact, are forms of moral hemiplegia.

JOSÉ ORTEGA Y GASSET,
La rebelión de las masas

Democracy is the right of lice to eat lions.

MARCELIN BERTELOT

It is madness to choose the leaders of the Republic with beans when nobody would like to employ a pilot designated by the bean.

SOCRATES

But historical reality does not know any ideals, it knows only facts. There are no truths, there are only realities. There is no reason, no justice, no conciliation, no end; there are only facts. Let the one who does not understand write books on politics but stop making it.

OSWALD SPENGLER

Neither Communism nor Plutocracy

COMMUNITARIAN EUROPE will organise its social structures in a conception more removed from Communism than from plutocracy. To wish to subject man to systems, to wish to make him conform to ideological phantoms, is to run the risk of a politics of permanent coercion, it is Communism with all its retinue of vexations and cruelties. On the contrary, to allow a man to give himself up, without reservation, to his appetites is to rapidly end up in the reign of egoism which leads fatally to plutocracy. The Communitarian organisation of European society will take into account the realities of man. We know that the deprivation of liberty — and the economico-social constraint is one such — can make of a man who was productive, creative and enthusiastic a sterile, nihilistic and passive individual.

This is what the systems that try to make man an ant, to make man a collective individual, end up as.

The man held within collectivism loses all his qualities, his vitality, his spirit of initiative, his creative spirit; he is then — *in a social captivity* — like the splendid wild cat in a zoo and, like the latter, a terrible apathy takes hold of him. Compare a buffalo or a tiger that is free and one in captivity in a botanical garden; all the qualities which blossom in conditions of freedom wither in captivity.

We know also that an excess of social liberty leads rapidly to social licentiousness, and it is then plutocracy hypocritically camouflaged behind a parliamentary democracy, of which it pulls all the strings. The financial capitalists have everything to fear from a popular and authoritarian regime, while, on the other hand, — and they recognise it themselves — '*with members of parliament there is always a way of arranging things*'. When one has in mind at present the politico-financial scandals that periodically flourish in the regimes called democratic, one can measure all the cynical significance of this statement.

The concern of the European Communitarian society will therefore consist in allowing enough economico-social freedom to man so that he might conserve the taste of initiative, risk, creation and effort and in imposing a minimum of discipline in order to prevent the birth of exploitative inclinations on the part of very few men towards a lot of men and for the sole benefit of the former.

Communitarian Europe will thus be established in the struggle at once against the Communist materialism and against the Yankee materialism. The first is that of the poor, the second of the rich; they do not differ essentially, there is between them only a difference of degree.

We are nevertheless not among those who claim to fight against materialism with a metaphysics. The latter has nothing to do with the reality of the politics of mankind. Materialism is a reality, but it is not an end, it cannot be a goal.

The material realities constitute a means of capital importance in the realisation of the human adventure, but never its end. Now, the American 'civilisation' is already there; the 'Communist civilisation' is definitely getting there. Both of them are already in an impasse.

If one removes from man a goal that surpasses him one removes from him through the same action his will to ascend, to surpass himself.

European society will not have fewer automobiles or fridges than the materialist Yankee or Communist societies, but it will have in addition an ethical aim, a Promethean will, for which Russians and Americans manifest no appetite, no attraction.

We shall surpass the 'realised materialism' of the Yankees and Communists and to the satiety of the body we shall add the demands and ambitions of the Promethean spirit.

We place emphasis on the fact that our anti-Communism is not reactionary, that is to say, passive or backward-looking. We do not defend the present impotent and mercantile pseudo-democratic regimes corrupted by an anachronistic and selfish degenerate liberalism and by the stateless hypercapitalism. Our anti-Communism, our anti-materialism (materialism as a goal in itself) is revolutionary, that is to say, active. Europe does not have to repeat the political pediatric diseases that dominate the USA and the USSR at the moment. These two nations have not yet reached historical puberty and the problems that move them must not compromise our maturity, our equilibrium. We do not have to receive from them historical or social lessons. Washington does not have to teach us democracy: we have tried it, or suffered it, for twenty-five centuries and we know that we should beware of it and that it must be rejected. Moscow does not have to teach us socialism: for twenty-five centuries we have tried all the formulae and we have, through these rich experiences, extracted precious lessons. Europe is an adult nation, which has had some historical scarlet fever, whooping cough and measles during centuries, with its Cathars, Anabaptists, its Jacobins and Spartacists.

Young folk like the Americans wish to teach us democracy, young folk like the Russians wish to teach us socialism and the most recent, the young folk of the petty and ridiculous Afro-Asiatic nations, wish to teach us nationalism.

Europe has had all these illnesses and does not have to undergo them again.

The big oaf Americans cannot impress us with their very recent Lincolns and Jeffersons. If we wish to compare to them our great ancestors, just those in Greece and Rome, we can display the Dracos,[1]

---

[1] Draco was a 7th century B.C. Athenian legislator, who was the first to formulate a legal code for Athens. The harshness of his laws, however, have led to the use

the Solons,[2] the Peisistratos',[3] the Themistocles',[4] the Thucydides',[5] the Gracchi.[6] The bearded advocate of the American Civil War[7] has nothing to teach us.

Should we speak of the philosophical or political Popovs?[8] The comparison would be much more humiliating for them ...

Europe is maturity, experience; Europe, in its concert of nations, is the big brother, more instructed, stronger, more in touch with things.

It is not a question of speaking of Europe as a third power but of Europe as the first. The priority belongs to us *de facto*. Europe does not need to import ideologies or infantile systems coming from Moscow or Washington. By drawing from its rich and long historical experience, Europe will find the elements to propose new structures of society: the Communitarian structures.

On the contrary, later it will be Europe that 'exports' its social structures and disciplines.

It will not only be bigger and more advanced militarily, industrially, intellectually, *it will be that also socially.*

---

of his name in the term 'draconian'.

2   Solon (ca. 638-558 B.C.) was an Athenian statesman and legislator, who repealed most of Solon's laws and instituted several constitutional and economic reforms.

3   Peisistratos (6th c. B.C.) was an autocratic ruler of Athens, who succeeded in restoring order after the departure of Solon. Although a 'tyrannos', Peisistratos was quite popular during his reign.

4   Themistocles (ca. 524-459 B.C.) was an Athenian statesman and general, who fought at the Battle of Marathon (490 B.C.) and was instrumental in achieving the decisive Greek victory over the Persians in the Battle of Salamis (480 B.C.).

5   Thucydides (ca. 460-400 B.C.) was an Athenian general and historian, famous for his *History of the Peloponnesian War* recounting the war between Athens and Sparta from 431 B.C. to 404 B.C.

6   The Gracchus brothers, Tiberius and Gaius (late 2nd c. B.C.), were plebeian Roman tribunes, who attempted to pass land reforms favouring the poor. Both the brothers were assassinated by their opponents.

7   Abraham Lincoln (1809-65) practiced as a lawyer from 1836 to around 1852.

8   Alexander Popov (1859-1905) was the Russian inventor of the radio.

The fireplace of culture lit in ancient Greece and developed in Europe prefigures *the Promethean destiny of man.*

The United States, ensnared in their infantile material enjoyments of self-gratification, and the Communist world, obsessed by its inferiority complex of a materialism of the poor, do not have the qualities required to lead humanity. Only Europe, the bearer of THE culture and TRUE *guiding nation*, is capable of indicating to humanity the paths of its Promethean destiny.

Collectivist Society, Selfish Society or Society of Solidarity?

We consider a collectivist society to be a society at the core of which there does not exist any hierarchy any longer, any differentiation. Everything belongs to everybody, and everybody is theoretically rewarded *'according to his needs'*. That is a myth, which is hard to blow up, for it exists only as a *'utopian tomorrow'*. Absolute Communism is impossible, impossible on account of the nature of men.

At present we live in a selfish society, where everybody fends for himself. In this selfish society the total of particular interests is not the general interest, as one tries to make us believe. The one cancels out the other and vice versa. It is the anarchy of our bourgeois society, where the struggles between groups are conducted through the bias of the state, which abandons in this way its role of arbiter to play that of a policeman supporting this or that coterie. In this society we sometimes see the industrial selfishnesses inviting the state to bully the agrarian interests.

One example taken from hundreds.

The energies are being cancelled instead of being accumulated. From anarchy arises an unquestionable sterility.

That which we shall call the society of solidarity will avoid at the same time the pitfalls of harmful naiveties contained in the conception of a collectivist society and the sterilising effects of a society torn by selfishnesses.

The society that we shall call that of solidarity starts from the real man, animated by appetites, instincts, and not from an ideal man that has never existed, will never exist and would hypothetically be animated by an overflowing brotherly love.

Through a discipline of the state it is possible to add the selfishnesses up and to make of it something efficacious; a society of solidarity. This society of solidarity, starting from different individuals, unequal individuals, must take care to see that the best can freely give their full measure in the service of the community.

The society of solidarity will be egalitarian as regards the chances at the initial stage — and will be that with caution — but it will, on the other hand, be made hierarchic as regards the manifestations of capacities and efforts.

'*To each according to his needs*' is a satisfying viewpoint at a philosophical level but inconsistent on the political landscape. To the extent that the initial conditions are falsified (sons of privileged fathers, for example, who enter in too great a proportion into universities) by caste privileges, the natural selection is distorted, which engenders a congestion of society.

But in a society where the initial chances are rigorously guaranteed, the formula 'To each according to his needs' remains the most just formula and the most efficient. We shall add to it, however: '*And according to his efforts*', for merit derives as much from effort as from inner aptitudes.

Financial Capitalism Not to Be Confused With Free Enterprise

The birth of unitarian and Communitarian political Europe will thus go in tandem with a radical transformation of the present social structures. Europe cannot be and will not be the simple enlarged projection of the vices of our present regimes. We are *a priori* for free enterprise against state economic management. We are that especially for reasons of efficiency. We shall tolerate only a civic capitalism, a disciplined and, if necessary, controlled capitalism, a capitalism in service of the European nation.

We are for the joint ownership of production, for the benefit of ALL who work in it; but we remain opposed to the notion of the joint ownership of the means of production. Again for reasons of efficiency, clarity, method, justice.

State ownership of the means of production is a costly trick for the producers themselves — and we classify the workers among the producers. An intelligent, modern, scientific socialism must ALSO apply the natural criteria of competition and of its corollary, selection. It is the very condition of its durability, its survival. It is highly immoral and, worse, more dangerous for the future of a nation to push solidarity to include good-for-nothing or useless people. It is highly immoral to have the financial transformations of factory X, caused by the firing of 10,000 badly guided or badly utilised workers, supported by 10,000 disciplined workers of factory Y. *Initiative, responsibility, competition and selection are notions to be introduced into the economy of a scientific socialism.*

The ownership of all the means of production in the hands of the state leads to the substitution of the reign of anonymous capitalist companies with the reign of irresponsible economico-humanitarian societies; one passes from selfishness and pure profit to incompetence and chaos. Between 1945 and 1960, in Italy, France and England, the nationalisations not only diminished the capacity of production of the affected sectors but provoked a social regression attested to by the endemic discontent of the workers who were occupied in it. For us the state is — on the economic level — an organiser, a controller, a judge — but never a manager — never a monopolist and thereby a stultifying owner.

We establish a clear discrimination between free enterprise and capitalism. For us free enterprise employs the surest, the most tested and the most efficient means to attain and maintain a high level of productivity. We are for free enterprise as a means but not for capitalism as an end. It is in this that we differ from the adherents of liberal plutocracy and stateless financiers. We are not demagogues and we have the merit of having compared objectively the results of the capitalist production, on the one hand, and the collectivist production, on the other hand. The assessment is positive, in a striking fashion, in favour of capitalism.

The means used by capitalism are thus better. Which does not at all mean that its ends are honest or moral.

Now, these means that are used reside precisely in free enterprise. Of capitalism we shall retain in free enterprise the management, for one who talks of free enterprise talks also of responsible enterprises, and we shall reject pure profit as an end and especially the excess of financial power of certain oligarchies, which are involved in this way, in an unacceptable way, in the political management of the nation.

The present plutocratic regime, camouflaged coyly as a parliamentary democracy, in fact considers capitalism as an end — a very profitable one, besides. We see in free enterprise a means. A means which, through competition, emulation, initiative and responsibility, guarantees SELECTION, which in its turn engenders PRODUCTIVITY.

No Individual Political Freedom Without Personal Economic Independence

We are not among those who confuse freedom and licence nor, especially, freedom and whining. A power should be able to remove itself from grumbling and raving and not confuse the latter with the 'popular will'. As if the masses had wills or, furthermore, competences, led as they are at present by false shepherds and by demagogues.

We think that a power should be assured stability, longevity and, finally, continuity. A power cannot be connected to outbreaks of the public opinion fever that is constantly solicited by demagogues.

Public opinion. on the one hand, and power, on the other hand, must be at once intimately connected in the realm of reciprocal information but also clearly separated in the realm of public MANAGEMENT. That said, we will all the more be authorised to denounce the progressive stifling of freedom in our pseudo-democracies.

An individual whose accommodation is granted by the state, whose employment is offered by the state, does not have any liberty any more. His landlord and his employer are one and the same person. Further, when one slides towards a generalised statism, it is not even possible any longer to change the landlord or to change the employer, which was still possible yesterday under the reign of integral capitalism.

Freedom is directly and intimately linked to economic independence. The collectivist society stifles the individual, it silences him and threatens him with social death.

That is what happens in certain 'socialist' states, where freedom of opinion is guaranteed in forms but belied by facts.

The man who baulks or revolts is no longer imprisoned but he loses his employment (to the state), he loses his accommodation (of the state), he cannot send his son to the university (of the state). This is not only true in the USSR but already very often in the Western pseudo-democracies, where social blackmail cancels the use of political freedom.

In an insidious, hypocritical, but systematic and implacable manner, an immense cloak of obligatory conformism is thus thrown over free men — in our pseudo-democracies.

Bad luck to the one who attempts to baulk: economic death and social death await him. One of my friends said pertinently that freedoms are guaranteed to those who promise not to make use of them. That which may seem to be only a witticism is in fact a tragic reality that is already present.

Political freedom is connected to economic independence, that is indeed why our collectivists wish to enrol the last 'independents' as civil servants: doctors, technicians, teachers.

That is also why we are the most determined partisans of free enterprise that conditions and guarantees political freedom. *The security needs should not in any case stifle the demands of freedom.*

We want a strong state made up of free and vigorous men and not a weak collectivist state built on mediocrity and conformism.

State Control and Corporatism Can Stifle and Then Ruin a Nation

An encroaching and interfering state control and a jealous and narrow corporatism can weaken a society and then destroy a nation. Parliamentary democracy tries to prolong its agony with the construction of a dense network of regulations that claim to be some social, and others professional. In fact, through these practices, it weakens the nation by discouraging the last men capable of initiative when it does not penalise them. The 'Christian social' ideal of contemporary Western politicians is not new; it is made up of envy, of jealousy with regard to the strong, and it wishes to substitute a society that is certainly often unjust with a mediocre society. The phenomenon is not original; the same parasitical organism has many times attacked a state and the most edifying example remains that of the Roman Empire of the 4th century, an authentic 'Christian socialist empire'. Let us ask the historians to describe this paradise to us.

The state had become an immense galley ship, where each received his post and where no one could leave. The Roman legislature tended to prohibit the quitting of a position. The disorder of the state economy had provoked numerous famines towards the end of the 3rd century in the Empire.

The people then straightaway caught hold of the bakers. Result: the number of bakers diminished rapidly. The profession was dangerous without being profitable (cost of taxed bread); so people avoided it. Maxentius[9] prohibited through a law the bakers from leaving their profession or the place where they practised it.

Decadence would make of the free corporations of the early Empire the forced corporations of the late Empire: professional constraints would arise. Vital industries would be nationalised, turned into the public sector, and in order to prevent workers from abandoning production, they would be attached by law to their jobs. The late Empire practised all the recipes that one wishes to impose on us today in our moribund so-called democracy: creation of the state, corporative constraints, fixing of prices (Diocletian, 'Edict on Maximum Prices'). Between 317 and 426 an impressive series of laws bound the civil servants and their descendants to their posts.

In 332, Constantine reinforced the bonds attaching settlers to their lands. Towards the end, in 396, Arcadius[10] prohibited members of the municipal councils from fleeing to the country. In 400, Honorius[11] orders that the members of corporations be searched for and brought

---

9   Maxentius (ca. 278-312) was Roman Emperor from 306-312. He was engaged in a civil war that ended in his defeat by Constantine in the Battle of the Milvian Bridge in 312.
10 Arcadius (377-408) was Eastern Roman Emperor from 395.
11 Honorius (384-423), brother of Arcadius, was Western Roman Emperor from 393.

back to their profession. Later, in 458, emperor Majorian wanted to put back in their original positions all those who had fled them.

This overview of the past should make us better understand the inanity of the plans of politicians camouflaged as pseudo-statesmen, who, claiming to improve matters, ruin them definitely. For nearly half a century now, people have been concerned in most parts of Western Europe with introducing regulations to determine the access to certain professions. This is frequently justified — to the extent that it is limited to the demands of competence alone. But we can never be sufficiently warned against the abuse of all the legal provisions that suppress or even limit the natural conditions of competition, initiative and responsibility, which alone can guarantee creative results and abundant fruits.

To produce human happiness through a ramification of regulations is a naïve dream periodically caressed by a number of mediocre reformers, who are ignorant of man's power of passive resistance. Captivity causes certain species of animals to waste away and sometimes even refuse to reproduce. Systematic constraint causes man to quickly stop being creative and constructive — good and bad work being rewarded materially and morally in the same fashion, he stops making the effort, that EFFORT without which no progress is possible.

Competition is sometimes a harsh law but it is always a creative law because through it punishment *follows close on* incapacity and reward *follows close on* effort. Its justice is rapid and efficient. As harmful as it would be to maintain men in rigid cadres and social classes, so harmful would it be to wish to insert and then tie them into a narrow corporatism.

The imperfections, indeed the disorders, of liberal economics are nothing in comparison to the economic sterilisation provoked, on the one hand, by 'socialist' (note the inverted commas) reformers and, on the other hand, by the partisans of rigid professional regulations. The state should take care to maintain economic freedom within limits, but it should take care of the maintenance of this freedom as well.

The political quacks 'of the left', who think of bringing into line certain social egoisms—to replace them with others—through laws restricting economic freedom, are mistaken—just as the other political quacks 'of the right', who think they have found a miraculous elixir in a systematic corporatism. The ramification of restrictive laws is the formal index of the decadence of any given society; the abundance of these is, like the abundance of pharmaceutical prescriptions for an individual, the sign of a sickness.

The State Should Take Care to Maintain Competition, That Is, Competitiveness

It is inaccurate and unjust to impute to free enterprise or to the principle of liberalism, the mistake of the liberal capitalist economy. In fact, liberalism has frequently tricked itself and, preaching free enterprise to the public, has secretly solicited the protectionism of the state or it has organised the suppression of competition through certain alliances. For example, in Belgium, the coal industry bosses, using the threat of dismissal of personnel, had obtained from the state the isolation of the Belgian market solely for their benefit, whereas, thanks to the state subsidies, they wasted billions which should have served the modernisation of equipment.

Before the Common Market, the automobile industry in Italy and in France enjoyed an economically unhealthy and technologically sterile protectionism.

The creative vitality of a nation, at the industrial and economic level, is connected to the rigorous maintenance of competition, that is to say, to the maintenance of competitiveness.

Two sorts of people tend to suppress competition: big capitalism, on the one hand, and the parasitical hopefuls of collectivism, on the other hand.

The Communitarian national state should therefore take care jealously that, on the one hand, the big enterprises cannot suffocate the small enterprises or the growing enterprises and that, on the other hand, the bureaucrats cannot turn the economy into a civil service, that is to say, 'Malthusianise' it.

The cyclical crises of capitalism are due much more to the struggle between capitalist groups than to the principle of free enterprise and competition.

Big or small capitalism has almost always yielded to the temptation of ease, which consisted in getting protected by protectionist regulations (customs and others). The same capitalism has also regularly established alliances destined to maintain prices or to prevent the creation or development of new competitors.

In an earlier chapter, we explained that scientific socialism should also take care to maintain the natural laws of competition/selection in its own interest. We shall add that free enterprise needs, in order to guarantee its vitality, a framework of free competition.

And we know that, by an apparent paradox, it is often the state that should take care to maintain freedom of competition in the sectors called 'free enterprise'.

We declare therefore that the state should guarantee the good functioning of competition by breaking up monopolies.

Of the Different Forms of Property: Property and Possession

In the liberal capitalist view, property is something essentially destined to be bought, sold, trafficked, mortgaged, speculated or bequeathed.

In the Marxist view, the ownership of everything is theoretically with the collectivity. In practice, if the apple tree belongs to everybody, the picking of apples is carefully made hierarchical and the 'advantages' of common ownership are completely sidestepped by the inequality of distribution.

In the more modern conception of Communitarianism, ownership can be total, as in the liberal economy, can, in rare cases, be of the state, as in the Marxist economy, but, further, can be equally restrictive and limited. This third form of ownership is that which gives the enjoyment of a property (land, for example) without giving the power of resale, transfer or speculation. This is what we call possession as opposed to ownership.

It is, on the other hand, *shared* ownership, a superior formula to that of anonymous ownership.

Communitarianism wishes a maximum possible of private ownership within the limits of a) non-exploitation of the labour of the masses, b) a non-interference in politics through hypertrophy of concentration of economic power, c) a non-collaboration with interests foreign to Europe and to its benefit.

We prefer to see the worker as owner of his house rather than tenant of the state; we prefer to see the workers participate in the ownership of the enterprise rather than see the state there.

In order to ensure for the state a maximum of moral authority, one should take care that it develops a minimum of direct interference. Marxism wishes to move society from private capitalism to state capitalism, in which case the masses hardly change their harness but only the colour of their harness.

On the contrary, we wish to transfer ownership from the hands of speculation to those of production.

For us, workers and producers (as a class) are inseparable and have united interests against financial speculators, or against state capitalism and its retinue of parasites (the little friends of the Party), or even against foreign finance.

For the Specific Organisation of the Economy and For a Dimensional Regulation of the Enterprise

The error committed by capitalist liberalism consists in leaving in the hands of private, if not often foreign, interests the management of certain sectors that present a strategico-military interest or means of exercising blackmail on the internal politics of the nation.

These sectors are the primary sectors of energy and of certain raw materials.

The error cultivated by the Marxists consists in wishing to impose structures identical from top to bottom of the economic apparatus, from the hydro-electric exchange to the corner dairy shop, from the steelworks to the cobbler, from the coal mine to the street vendor.

We think, contrary to the capitalist liberals and the Marxists, that it is necessary to vary the matrix of economic organisation of enterprises regarding:

a) the type of the enterprise

b) the size of the enterprise

In certain cases, the property will be of the state and the management of the state; in other cases, the property will be of the state and the management private; in yet other cases, the property will be private and the management will be private.

Here are three examples of this:

1. State property and state management: in the case of hydro-electric energy;
2. State property and private management: state leasing of an oil-producing territory to an industrial group;
3. Private property and private management: almost all of industry

For each sector, the specific organisation will determine the form to be chosen in terms of:

a) the superior interests of the European nation;

b) the productive efficiency

Practice and experience reveal that, in certain sectors, state management is more creative — for the nation — than capitalist management. Conversely, there are very many sectors where free enterprise proves to be much more efficient than the state.

Against Social Anthills and Barracks, for a Socialism Detached from the Bureaucracy

We reject the anthill socialism proposed by police socialism. We reject the civilisation of application forms. In this sad world, from which risk, initiative and responsibility are banished — the individual is crushed, choked to the level of a termite or an ant. It is useless to suppress the defects born of the egoism of the liberal society if it is to be replaced with the cumbersome and costly parasitism of the new 'socialist' bureaucracy.

Social neo-parasitism, the only truly concrete expression of parliamentary socialism, has no other goal than to make the '*priests of progress*' live handsomely and to instal as a new ruling class a sort of feudalism of clerks.

We will notice besides that, in the present efforts of degenerate socialism (state socialism), only the nominal ownership of the means of production has been changed.

That is where the entire swindle of parliamentary socialism or state socialism lies: if the means of production pass from the hands of the financiers, bankers and foreign exchange dealers into the hands of senators, trade union fakirs and friends of the Party, the fruits of production are always shared as before: a large portion for the parasitical cabal, whether it be financial or political, and a small portion for the producers (workers, technical cadres and enterprise leaders).

The new ruling class, in this case, is not less greedy than the old. Alas, alas! It is often much more incompetent.

To replace the parasitical sectors of finance with the parasitical sectors of a titular pseudo-socialism is not an ideal for us.

A true socialism, a scientific socialism, must subject itself to the natural criteria of competition, responsibility, competence and initiative. The socialism of application forms is destined to stifle a nation just as the creeper stifles the oak. That is a hypocrisy to be denounced and a danger to be combated.

Against the Parasitism of Titular Socialism, Against the Dogmatism of Communism, for the Efficiency of Communitarian Socialism

On the economic level, the socialism of the state, that of the parliamentary socialist parties, can only live, like the creeper clinging to the oak, as a parasite on the capitalist economy.

On the political level, state socialism lives only from the blackmail exercised on a greedy and cowardly bourgeoisie. This bourgeoisie pays for 'having peace'. The socialist politicians, abusive intermediaries, comfortably and handsomely encrust themselves between the bourgeoisie, which they from time to time frighten by reviving an old conditioning — that of the fear of the 'street' — and the masses, carefully kept stupid, who, they believe, will snatch the rights *'from the wicked capitalist'* through a 'sustained battle'.

In fact, the last thing the advocates of socialism wish for is the disappearance of capitalism, the only justification for their job, that of expensive go-betweens.

Soviet Communism possesses the entirety of political power. It is no longer an intermediary but a direct manager. This management is catastrophic, and the shambles have been crumbling for more than 40 years. The fact is that Communism thinks in terms that are already a hundred years old: the catechism written by Karl Marx is scrupulously respected by the dogmatic leaders of Moscow and by the Protestants of the Party. It would not enter anybody's mind to apply medicine according to the only scientific rules known in 1870. That is, however, what Communism wishes to do by clinging to an economico-social idea that is a century old, not only in its basis but in its most narrow form. Communitarian socialism knows social progress only as a goal. It knows that social progress depends on scientific and technological progress. In order to realise its objectives, it does not intend to arouse or inflame the hatred between classes; it knows that all the men of the same society are united in the flourishing and expansion of the latter. It wants a strong sole power, alone capable of checking the appetites of some people and the demagogy of others.

Communitarian socialism obeys not only economic laws but also psychological and human laws. It does not commit the error of wishing to cause the happiness of humankind through 'perfect laws' applied to naturally imperfect men; *it starts from man* and it does not proceed from perfect theoretical principles.

For The Deproletarisation of the Worker, the Recruitment and the Rise of Elites

The principal preoccupation of all our progressive politicians and of the majority of the syndicate fakirs consists in establishing themselves as a clergy, which is considered to be indispensable to the masses who remain perpetually minors.

The European National Communitarian Revolution will remove the worker from his sustained stultification as a proletarian to make of him a conscious worker and an organised citizen, aware of his rights but also of his responsibilities. The worker should learn to take care of his interests and his development by himself. At present, he is a citizen who is politically a MINOR, who cannot undertake anything without going through the channel of the 'socialist priests'.

We wish for the *direct interest* of the worker in his social and political condition in order to put an end to the present hypocritical *proxy socialism* — profitable to the political cabal.

We shall demonstrate to the worker that his promotion will especially go along the path of a highly advanced technical qualification.

The professional education of the youth and the study holidays for this purpose constitute one of the bases of our social politics. *Another of its bases will be to guarantee at every moment of the professional career the possibility of resuming or continuing studies leading to a superior qualification. Thus the recruitment and ascent of the news elites, essential conditions for the vigour of a society, will be ensured.*

Finally, we shall reveal to the workers that the state is also them and especially them, that often the fight against the state or the pillage of the state is, in fact, for them only a sort of self-destruction.

The classes called inferior constitute a reserve of inexhaustible recruitment in the midst of which one can draw a human resource destined to compensate the natural depletion of the elites in power. The elites cannot perpetuate themselves hereditarily: they can do that only through co-optation. That is why one should take care to see that all the external conditions are realised to allow exceptional values to be highlighted and brought to light.

In our bourgeois societies, the stereotyping into social classes is done almost as a sort of academic grade obtained at the age of eighteen or twenty-five. The social selection conducted as a mere sheepskin leads to the creation of an abundant caste of greedy clerks and good-for-nothings, who claimed yesterday to be the 'guardians of the Christian ideal' and today the guarantors of the 'true socialism'. Yesterday and today they are the same people, it is this same clergy speaking of an abundance of spiritual or humanitarian values but in fact especially taking care to divide society into social classes in order to maintain its privileges. The structures of the Communitarian national state will offer every chance to the individuals of value to distinguish themselves, to emerge and to distance themselves from the group not once, on the occasion of their schooling, but in the course of their entire lives. *The search for exceptional aptitudes cannot be limited to education alone.*

The de-stultification and de-proletarianisation of the masses constitute the first measures favourable to the search for elites in combating the eternal discouragement that prevails in the so-called inferior classes and keeps them in a sort of social fatalism, or herd-like resignation. It is necessary that, at any moment of their lives, the individuals of value from this mass might rise.

Subtracting the Salary from Commerce

In the disorder of the capitalist economy, founded on the sole law of supply and demand, one arrives at the somewhat appalling situation where the sale price determines the cost price, whereas in good logic one should be faced with the contrary situation.

Capitalism, in its sometimes anarchic competition, arrives at investing abroad (before 1940, Europe did it in China, India, Africa and, after 1945, the USA does it in Japan and in Europe) in a preferential manner and with the sole goal of paying lowing salaries. This is why the capitalism of pure profit is frequently without any civic sense, and is frequently anti-national.

This little capitalist game is possible only due to the borders which separate the economies and isolate them in different stages.

These practices are contrary to the national interests, on the one hand, and allow extraordinary extortions vis-à-vis the labour force, on the other.

This system is at this point vicious and immoral so that we have seen some American workers' syndicates trying to financially sustain strikes in Europe in order to fight against the American financiers who invested there with the aim of exploiting a cheaper labour force.

Besides, the same American financial interests exercised at the same time extortion and corruption, with regard to the European trade union leaders, with the threat of a lock-out or of a *'transfer of the industry',* in order to force the salaries down here.

It is useless to insist on the fate of the salaried labour force in this international imbroglio of rackets, extortions and corruption.

The big international trusts should be combated for two peremptory reasons: first, for the practice that consists in expatriating industries of strategic interest, second, for the practice which consists in lowering our local salaries by pointing to lower salaries in underdeveloped countries, in this way curtailing all social expansion. One finds in this anti-European practice one of the real reasons for the 'aid' to the underdeveloped countries which has nothing humanitarian about it but proceeds from the sole concern of capitalist profit.

The European salary should be subtracted from the 'international commerce in labour force'. It will be that in a closed economy, but closed within a large enclosure. This large enclosure is a Europe of 420 million men and tomorrow it will be a Euroafrica of 700 million men.

As harmful as the autarkic economy is in small circuits so defendable is it in large circuits.

We shall therefore fight against the commercialisation of work and we shall subtract it from the law of international speculation.

Within Europe, the circulation of the labour force having to be guaranteed, the alignment of the social laws being ensured in all the regions, and finally a protective belt being opposed to the practices of dumping of international finance, the salaries will be able to find an intrinsic value, a human value, independent of speculation and extortion.

For the Self-Management of Social Organisations by the Workers and Producers

We shall render the trade unions independent of the parties, we shall render the health insurance funds independent of the state.

The state should be the instrument of pure political power, of a power that dominates every other; it cannot, at the risk of being weakened, disperse it in enterprises that demand a great deal of supervision for a zero direct profit. The state does not have to dilute its energy and its authority in tasks that do not belong to it and that can be better guaranteed by the cooperative sector. To be a judge and a party is to be inevitably exposed to cede very to moral fraudulence. The state cannot be an insurer, doctor, pharmacist and at the same time a social arbiter. Now the mission of an arbiter, at all levels and in particular at the social, is the essential role of the state.

The trade union organisations, the social organisations, will be denationalised, removed from the state and the parties, and returned to the hands of the workers and producers to whom they belong collectively. Thus the state will be substituted by the cooperative private sector.

Today, the politicians of the parliamentary state obstruct with their creations all the trade unions, mutual, cooperative and parasitical. Tomorrow we shall entrust the ownership of all these organisations to those who, through their contributions, cause them to exist and for whom alone they should exist.

Further, in order to prevent abuses and embezzlements, the principle of the publication of the balance sheets of the management will be applied to all the cooperative sectors.

It is necessary that the most modest of the co-operators may obtain, with full right and without the least delay of procedure, delivery of the details of the management of a community (trade union or health insurance fund) to which the law obliges him to belong.

Today there indeed exists a control of management: it is that exercised — at least theoretically — by the elected representatives designated for this purpose. It should be stated that first the elections are duly 'prepared' and then, every time that the control is exercised solely by power of attorney, the bearers of the latter allow themselves to be easily and rapidly circumvented. *Appointed to discover abuses or frauds, they find it most of the time easier to participate in it themselves.*

There is reason to initiate the workers and producers into the management of their social organisations. First of all, that would give them a sense of the enterprise, then the nanny state will be demystified. In this way they will be faced with the realities. The present social fussing which consists in making one believe that the state can pay for everything will be instantly unmasked.

The fight against waste, against distributive demagogy, will be — due to the cooperative private management — exercised by the interests themselves: trade unionists and mutualists.[12]

Today the worker shrugs his shoulders when one points out fraud or waste to him. He lives in the belief that the state works with a plate full of notes and that, in any case, the latter's money is not his. About which he is evidently and absurdly mistaken.

The worker and the producer should realise that each wasted franc is lost in fact by every person. At the moment that we will have inculcated in the masses the notion that they participate intimately in the wastage of the services of the state — and we should stress that they participate in it passively as a duped party — they will modify their attitude completely and will pass from indifference to vigilance.

It is necessary to make the worker, the labourer, a responsible citizen. He should be given responsibilities and the ideal realm to initiate him, to make him participate in the responsibilities, is that of social insurances and the trade union. Then the constructive spirit will take

---

12   Mutualism is a movement that promotes mutual organisations, mutual insurance and mutual funds.

the place of the spirit of denigration, vigilance that of indifference, economy that of parasitism.

For an Increased, Responsible and European Syndicalism

As we explain in another chapter, syndicalism should end in a form of direct power and have at its disposal its own organ of political representation: the European trade union senate.

At present, the politicians use syndicalism for their own ends, most of the time without any relation to the material interests of the trade union members. In Belgium, during the royal affair, the trade union leaders had recourse, with an exclusively political aim, without any social implication, to the weapon of social struggle: the strike. In the Europe that we shall make syndicalism will no longer be political but professional, it will no longer be national but European. It should not have to suffer the obligation of an intermediary politician but will have its own political representation.

More developed than today and endowed with infinitely large powers, it will become more responsible than today and the publicising of the accounts will ensure the control of the management by the union members themselves. The present political trade unionists do not have any legal responsibility not having a civil or thus financial personality, which allows them to yield to an unrestrained demagogy. This responsibility should not be applied merely to the workers' trade unions but equally to the employers' unions.

It goes without saying that syndicalism will contain internal contradictions if it remains in the form called 'petty national', a form that is already, in fact, really provincial with regard to Europe. Each trade union will thus be on a European scale, and it will no longer be a question of starting a strike in the steel mills of Liège while those of the Ruhr do extra hours — or vice versa. Such are the present contradictions of a narrow syndicalism on account of its 'petty nationalism'.

Capitalism, endowed with better cadres than the present political syndicalism, has understood all the possibilities of a Europeanism applied systematically and rapidly. And Capitalism has also made ITS Europe twenty years at least before that of the workers, for the latter are represented by mediocre stipend-chasers of no calibre or perspicacity.

Access to Raw Materials — One of the Keys to Independence

After 1945, American high finance has sought to systematically dispossess European capitalism of all its international positions: Indonesia, the Middle East, Indochina, Algeria, Katanga.

The victory of 1945 of '*Democracy over Fascism*' is the sentimental explanation proposed to regularly deceived masses. The real historical fact was the organised destruction of the European hegemony over the world in order to replace it with the Yankee hegemony.

This was, in fact, under the logomachic cover of the war of ideologies and of 'eternal principles', a war, at first hypocritical and then cynical, waged against European capitalism by American capitalism.

This war, begun in 'friendship' from '40 to '45, continues at this moment too, the hypocritical mask less. The USA does not hide its appetites any more.

We have no fondness, *a priori*, for European capitalism, but it is true that we are its heirs in fact and rightfully so. An heir cannot legitimately be uninterested in his heritage.

Before 1939, Europe supplied to itself in Asia and in Africa sources of raw materials which belonged to it or that it directly controlled. Today, we are obliged to buy from the Americans the raw materials whose sources once belonged to us. Thus our suppliers are only our exploiters. The Americans resell today to us raw materials extracted from the mines and rigs that we, Europeans, dug or constructed yesterday.

However, it must be admitted that the eviction of Europe from its empire was facilitated by the form of colonisation itself, quite superficial, practised by our capitalist societies. If we had proceeded to a colonisation in depth, of settlement and not of exploitation, American imperialism, which, besides, repeats the same error at this moment, would not have dispossessed us so easily.

Not only the financiers of Wall Street took possession of our sources of raw materials but, what is worse, the routes of communication between Europe and these sources were cut by the American military forces. The powerful American squadrons in the Mediterranean which pass from Gibraltar to Istanbul form a screen between us and Africa, between us and Asia Minor. That is a situation that a unitarian Europe cannot tolerate and the evacuation of the Mediterranean by the US Navy will assume an importance equal to the evacuation of Bucharest by the Red Army.

Europe too will have its Monroe Doctrine,[13] and in this sense will consider the Mediterranean as a European 'lake'. We have not forgotten the hostile attitude of Washington at the time of the Budapest affair. *At the very moment that Moscow took possession of Hungary for the second time, the Americans strangled the European economy by cutting from it the petrol of the Middle East.* In the hypothetical case where we would have had here in Europe, in 1956, something other than weak governments, and that we would have wished to bring aid to the insurgent Hungarian people, an American action, by depriving us of petrol, would have blocked our armies and stifled our industries.

The lesson will never be forgotten: we guarantee that. We will empty the Mediterranean of the American presence. The access to the sources of raw materials assumes a capital importance, a colossal importance.

This problem has three aspects, of which each is vital for Europe.

---

13 The Monroe Doctrine promulgated by President James Monroe in 1823 opposed any further colonisation efforts in the Americas by European powers.

First of all, the economic control of the sources of raw materials leads to the fact that the speculation '*directed or oriented*' by Wall Street can create a hidden blockade of our industries. The cost price of our industrial production consists in good part of the sale price of the raw materials that nourish it. Thus the one who controls the sale prices of petrol or of copper controls indirectly the cost prices of our manufacturing production. An indirect control, but irresistible. The American tutelage is more than evident, it is in plain sight.

The second aspect, equally as humiliating and mortal for us, is the military result, the strategic consequence of the American control of our sources of supply. Uranium and petrol are inseparable from the strategic needs of a nation.

A nation without an army does not exist or, if it does, as a fiction, and those who place their hopes in the protection of another nation find masters in searching for protectors. There is no Europe without a European Army and no European Army without strategic minerals and without fuels.

Mr. Kennedy, who will in 1963 be the hand of the butchers in Budapest of 1956, could have been tempted, one day, to prevent us from liberating our provinces of the east by stifling our armed forces through a naval blockade in the Mediterranean. The Americans will thus leave this sea which is our lake. Willingly or unwillingly. Which obviously does not signify the necessity of a military war against the USA.

The configuration of this sea leads to the fact that it can be easily transformed into a magnificent mass.

The third aspect of the problem of the access to the sources is the social aspect. And here again the consequences of our humiliating economic tutelage can be considerable.

No real socialism, which would displease the Americans, can in fact be applied when the latter control a part, and not the least, of our economic circuit.

The demagogues who dream of establishing 'socialism' in Europe would be quite incapable of doing so. All the constructs that are called 'socialist' are in fact constructed on mined territory. The political puppets who play at verbal socialism, at the Hague, in Brussels, in Vienna, in fact move in a void.

Let us imagine hypothetically — quite freely, for our left-wing politicians have had no problem refusing the ambassadors, proconsuls in fact, of the States — that our indigenous demagogues nationalise industry in Europe. What would we see then? *Socialist economic systems in the humiliating condition of depending on capitalist sources of raw materials. This expresses the entire verbal character of the least reform that is truly socialist in Europe as long as a foreign power, the USA, controls our sources of raw materials.*

One can therefore declare that, without the protection of a powerful European nationalism, it is not possible to speak reasonably of a real social emancipation in Europe.

The Europe of 1964 is organised according to the fine and classical scheme of colonial economy for the benefit of the United States. In order to break this colonialism of the dollar, Europe needs its unity and a strong political power.

Without the guarantee of a strong European political power, no economic independence is possible; without economic independence, no social progress is possible.

Without a powerful European nationalism, no possible real socialism, no possible Communitarianism. Our political strength is here the precondition and guarantee of our economic and social prosperity.

Against International Miserabilism and a Begging Economy

For 20 years American capitalism has systematically eliminated its direct competitors, the European capitalists, from all the zones called 'colonial' and rich in raw materials.

The Americans have stretched their deviousness to the point of imposing on our rump governments, docile satellites of Washington, the obligation of entertaining the Afro-Asiatic politicians under the cover of *'aid to the underdeveloped'*.

Thus, it is American finance that exploits the natural resources and gathers cobalt, copper and petrol while we can content ourselves — the height of misfortune and irony — with entertaining black political puppets. Washington and Wall Street know what they are doing. By possessing our old colonial positions, they possess the taps of the sources of raw materials and can thus control our industries by acting on their sale price — first — and — secondly — retarding our industrial expansion in Europe by exhausting our finances through the haemorrhage that the obligatory aid to the underdeveloped countries constitutes for it.

That is not all. Certain European capitalists — and it will not surprise us when one knows the lack of civicism of these milieus (*'Our only fatherland is money'*) — find it convenient that the public finances of the states of Europe serve to gratify the black, yellow and brown politicians as tips. These 'European' capitalists have a great interest in our ex-colonies and they know that it would be difficult for them to maintain their enterprises without abundant means of corruption. Instead of paying by themselves the price of the corruption and removing to their advantage the indispensable tips that oil the wheels of the 'political life' of *'young liberated nations'* [sic], they have the impertinence to make us pay them. In the past one made the indigenous people sweat to ensure lavish benefits. Today the metropolitan taxpayer has picked up the bill.

Thus the billions in taxes, which could be more intelligently devoted to the development of our industries in Europe itself and to the improvement of the fate of our workers in Europe, serve to indirectly augment the profits of American finance and its servile 'collaborators', the unscrupulous capitalists of Europe. One tries frequently to soften sensitive as well as naïve hearts by showing them extraordinary photos of undernourished children, with swelling stomachs, rickety beyond belief.

It is a question here of a sinister volley of propaganda, and if the photos came from Hollywood, you would hardly notice the difference. Of course, there are children that die of hunger in the underdeveloped countries. But whose fault is it? When we 'aid' these people, for the benefit of whom and what are these funds being diverted?

The least informed know that the billions collected for the 'underdeveloped' serve partly to maintain political cliques of colour, on the one hand, and to buy arms, on the other hand.

Thus the billions subtracted from the producers of Europe are devoted to the purchase of Cadillacs or Mercedes' for the coloured politicians the purchase of superfluous arms for their states.

Mr. Nehru wants to make us feel sorry for his poor and he details to us complacently his famines, somewhat as the beggars of the Middle Ages exhibited their wounds on the bridges of Florence or Paris, but at the same time he pays for military planes, frigates, submarines for himself …

Thus the negroes of Léopoldville[14] hold a frantic party with the money of the Belgian taxpayer; the Algerians buy American or Czechoslovak arms with the money of the French taxpayer.

The jackpot is so abundant that the black politicians manage, in spite of the expensive luxury in which they live, to build up a nest egg, and to save money. Hundreds of millions are poured each year into their private accounts in neutral countries. The Swiss, Swedish, Mexican banks shelter prodigious current accounts of African politicians. That is the real aspect of aid to the underdeveloped. The corruption, however famous, of the South American politicians and colonels has been surpassed a hundred times by that of African politicians.

---

14 Léopoldville is the old name of Kinshasa, the capital of the Democratic Republic of the Congo, a state which began in 1885 as a personal property of King Leopold II of Belgium, called the Congo Free State and which was then annexed by the Belgian state in 1908 as the Belgian Congo.

Africa has, at this moment, need of an abundant technological middle class, it needs welders, mechanics, electricians, agriculturists, livestock farmers. It would not be contrary to our interests in the long term to aid Africa to create for itself this class without which it will never start up and we shall not, if need be, refuse it. But what do we see at his moment? When they are not too tired of the life of perpetual nightclubbing that they lead, in Europe, of dancing and whoring, the so-called 'student' blacks show themselves sometimes in the classrooms of the universities. Not in the technological and scientific faculties, not in the faculties that are difficult and useful to a nation, but invariably in literary faculties and especially those of law, where verbalism reigns.

Thus these 'young black nations' [sic], which will not possess even in ten years a good locksmith or a good clockmaker, will have a line of hundreds and hundreds of advocates who, for lack of employment, — and this phenomenon is already observable among us — will enlarge the ranks of politicians. Why not economise on these black politicians and the studies that we pay for them? The white political animal is abundant to such a point that we could easily yield to the underdeveloped countries a numerous contingent without risking weakening our public life in any aspect whatsoever.

We therefore resolutely take a stand against the swindle that consists in retarding the progression of salaries of our workers of Europe to fatten the black political feudalisms and to enrich American finance.

We have firmly decided to eliminate the white political parasites; with greater justification we will not agree to maintain the political parasites of 'underdeveloped' countries to the detriment of our European industrial producers, engineers and workers.

Lead the underdeveloped countries out of chaos? Yes. But on precise conditions and with rigorous guarantees.

International capitalism derives at present lavish benefits from these 'underdeveloped' countries, where the political power is weak and easily corruptible. It is not for us to help it in this.

This 'charity' — besides often extorted through international political blackmail — does not go to the 'poor' but to the vicious, to coloured corrupt people and white sharks.

No More Social Classes, But Classes of Men

The division of society into horizontal sections corresponds to the classification into 'social classes'.

Respect, prestige and power are, in this case, attributed according to the sole criteria of wealth, well or ill-gained, when it has not been gained from one of the family predecessors.

People say then that someone belongs to an elevated social class when his bank account is important. It is the characteristic of decadent societies to be based solely on money. The late Roman Empire has given us an example of this. We live today in the late empire of the workers.

Power belongs, in fact, to these elevated social classes, either openly or through the intermediary of the political bureaucracy.

It goes without saying that the criterion of fortune constitutes almost an inverse selection in the human species. The one explains the other, and the political decadence of our regime consists in part in the fact that it is in the hands of a pseudo-elite. It would be grotesque to maintain that the value of an individual is connected to his social condition alone, that is to say, to his wealth.

To place civic virtue or even human virtue itself in a single social category would be to not dissociate the intrinsic value of an individual from his bank value. One school of thought tries to make us believe that the only human virtues are those to be found in the leisured social classes, another school tries, not less incorrectly, to make us believe in the original and inflexible virtue of the poor social class. This is ridiculous, and it is dishonest.

In fact, there are rich people whom wealth has not corrupted and there are poor people whom misery has not freed of corruption or baseness. And vice-versa. The present politics, the pseudo-democratic or plutocratic politics, making the value of money the standard of society, it is normal that, as a consequence, the conflicts that shake it are conflicts of more or less rich against more or less poor people, the latter cursing the former, while praying ardently, in their internal faith, that they might take the place of the others and perpetuate, but this time to their benefit, the practices condemned with indignation, for the requirements of polemics.

The struggle of the social classes is in fact the struggle of envy. Which does not make the assailants greater nor excuse the attacked. If there should be competition and if selection should follow from it and is desirable, it should start from classes of men.

The horizontal division of society we hope to substitute not with a division but a classification, and a vertical classification. Classes of men, that's it. They are distinguished by the degree of courage, creative power and nobility. And here the superior class of men traverses all the social classes, just as the inferior class of men runs through all the social classes from end to end.

We do not believe in the equality of men, Nature weakens at every moment this view of the mind: men are different, men are unequal.

In a society of elevated ethics, the differentiation should operate according to the characteristic values of the individual — physical courage, moral courage, intellectual aptitudes, and a demanding and strenuous morality — and not according to his social values, bank account or salary. Society should be made hierarchical if it wishes to be ordered. Again it should be specified by what hierarchy.

Also, we shall declare that tomorrow there will exist as today upper classes and lower classes, but that the upper class will not be a socially elevated class but an elevated class of men, a superior class of men. An elevated class, a class of responsibility, a class of service. And to 'service' we give the noble sense, the original sense.

Aristocracy, in the etymological sense, is found from the bottom to the top of the social scale; it is this aristocracy which should be found, which should be reunited. This recruitment of the aristocracy cannot be hereditary at the risk of rapid degeneration, but should proceed from a perpetual renewal.

Bound in false classifications, men of value are thrown one against the other through the sterile game of the politicians. Besides, they, the better and the worse, are confused when characterised by their financial condition alone. We consider the struggle of the social classes as sterile, harmful to the nation and thus highly condemnable.

This social war does not allow the true elites to be drawn out, it retards, if it does not prevent their discovery.

And the quality and the power of a nation are direct functions of the nature of its elites. The war of classes engenders pseudo-elites eager for material enjoyment as well as weak in the face of adversity and even in the face of hardship itself.

We see here one of the major reasons of our present political decadence in the world. We should proceed as quickly as possible to a new classification and substitute the domination of the upper social class with the domination of the superior class of men.

The State of Producers Against That of Politicians and Financiers

In the European National Communitarian state there will be no question of '*right to work*' but of obligation to work.

The Manichean division into 'good workers' and 'frightful capitalists' is too crude, and the messianic mission of the working class is part of the décor of the Marxist theatre and not of historical reality.

There is no class that is essentially virtuous and predestined to a justicialist[15] mission.

In all the present social classes there are healthy elements and crazy elements.

It is an idealised image to depict, on the one hand, good workers duped and exploited and, on the other, industrial cynics amassing, without any difficulty, immense and immoral profits.

The middle class and the bourgeoisie offer us extremely interesting specimens, full of initiative, hard workers, creators, from the artisan to the industry chief. These are the directors of factories who '*come to the office*' on Saturday morning and who, during the week, finish two or three hours after the end-of-day siren.

This species of man we classify among the producers, the creators of work and wealth. The heart of the industry, they constitute a social cadre of high quality, from which it would be suicidal — socially speaking — to separate ourselves. The other part of the same bourgeoisie offers the little edifying spectacle of lazybones who go around from milliner's shops to tea rooms and from dates to jewellery shops. Their companions haunt the racecourses in the afternoon and the bar from six in the evening.

Speculators, revellers, parasites, all those constitute the shady part of the bourgeoisie. All that will be swept away in Communitarian Europe, and laws on obligatory work will be applied, precisely in this asocial case without hesitation. The idle and indifferent children of this rotten bourgeoisie will change their sports car for a shovel and the nightclubs of Cannes for the work camp, which will make them men again.

In this way we divide the bourgeoisie into positive elements and negative elements and we avoid the sterile and unjust generalisation which consists in approving or condemning EN MASSE one of the present social classes.

---

15   Social justice. The term 'justicialist' is typically associated with the Justicialist Party created in Argentina by Juan Perón in 1947.

As for the working class we will, just as much, avoid yielding to the temptation of generalising. This class: neither more nor less virtuous than the others.

This class produces equally elements that are little productive socially, such as the congenital unemployed person, the penpushers and the entire little political bureaucracy. The working class also has its 'malign people' and it contains — potentially — within itself 'exploiters' at least as greedy as certain of those that we know today.

The fight against parasitism will constitute an important task among those Communitarianism will assign to itself.

The Communitarian nation is interested in those who produce, and slowly, when the term is better understood, we shall speak only of producers — without having to add 'workers' — for a producer is essentially a worker but a worker who is not limited to those that wear helmets or to those that have callous hands. We shall substitute the notion of the proletariat, a puerile and inefficient messianic view, with the hegemony of producers in the economico-political life of the European state; verbal politicians as well as dishonest ones, fake financiers, gluttonous trade union bureaucrats, all that is parasitism, all that should be eliminated to ensure the health of Europe.

The present pseudo-democracy barely hides behind a façade of cardboard, a real plutocracy greedy for profits as well as cowardly before historical responsibilities. We live and we suffer the uncontested reign of the financiers associated with politicians.

Communitarian Europe will make tight again the connections which must unite the professional producers with the producers of the bottom. For, if there is a particularly interesting vertical class, it is that of the PRODUCERS. Tomorrow the rudder will be in its hands.

Europe: the Minimum Size for Economic Planning

We are decided partisans of free enterprise and of a free economy to the extent where freedom is not disorder, to the extent that freedom is not licence.

On the other hand, and moreover, strategic imperatives must have priority over the attachment to the principles of free competition. Let us take a concrete case as an example: there is a poor mineral resource in Europe, a rich one in New Caledonia;[16] this mineral resource is principally used for military needs. It goes without saying that the exploitation here, in Europe, of the poor mineral resource — exploitation more costly than that of a rich mineral resource — will be encouraged and protected. The military necessities do not authorise us to be dependent on sources of supply that are distant and therefore vulnerable in their communications with the European big city. In the specific case evoked above, Communitarian Europe will be interventionist and protectionist, without denying for that reason its attachment to the principles of competition, rivalry and free enterprise.

We may declare, at the outset, that Europe, within its borders and within its market of 400 million men, will live in a free economy. Conversely, and vis-à-vis what will be external to Europe, we shall give preference to free exchange WHEN IT IS POSSIBLE, but we shall not hesitate to practise the most severe autarky in the contrary case. The free economy of the relations external to Europe will be applied after our strategic needs will have been guaranteed and after the basic minimum for our population will have been ensured. The last point deserves a short elaboration.

The vicissitudes of history have caused that a Venetian Europe, then a Portuguese Europe, then the Dutch and especially the English

---

16   New Caledonia is an overseas French territory in the Southwest Pacific Ocean.

Europe have given us the habit of maritime relations and we have turned away from our real vocation, which is continental.

We have in this way neglected Eastern Europe for the benefit of oceanic adventurers and have built maritime empires, which have later shown themselves to be extremely fragile.

The real vocation of Europe is, geopolitically, continental. It is time to understand this. We have dispersed and worn ourselves out in creating colonies that have one by one turned against us. If we had diverted into Eastern Europe—over the head of the Habsburgs, exhausted against the Turks from the 16th to the 18th centuries—the human potential that we have devoted to what has become the USA and Latin America, we would now have European territories, profoundly European, up to Istanbul at the very least and probably beyond it.

Out of sight, out of mind. The North America that we have made slips through our fingers. The explanation of this phenomenon rests in the 4,000 kilometres of ocean.

But let us return to economics.

We cannot permit that western Europe buy its asparagus—in boxes—from California when Eastern Europe can provide us with it—fresh. Romania and Bulgaria are extraordinary vegetable gardens, remarkable producers of cereals. And what do we see? Our apples, peaches, many of the fruits and vegetables that we consume, are imported from the USA.

Similarly for grain, cattle and poultry.

This situation cannot be imputed to the Iron Curtain alone and to the Soviet occupation alone; in fact it existed before 1939. Thus it happened that Greece bought its grain from Canada and refused Bulgarian grain, that of its neighbour.

Two explanations for this situation: the maritime orientation of the expansionist politics of Western Europe and—already—American finance.

In the 1920s and 1930s, the jousts of the Yankee financiers, sometimes on the wheat of Manitoba, at other times on that of Argentina, have maintained the pauperisation of agricultural Eastern Europe.

Tomorrow, in the unitarian and Communitarian Europe, it will no longer be a question of buying Californian asparagus as long as all the European asparagus has not been absorbed by our consumers. It will no longer be permitted to retard the expansion of Eastern Europe for the benefit of the USA. We shall eat first the Romanian chickens before importing American chickens.

An isolated Western Europe is deficient in agriculture, an isolated Eastern Europe is deficient in industry. The complementarity of the two Europes is remarkable. That is indeed why the recuperation of our Eastern provinces is, in our view, essential and that this concern take priority over all others.

We shall buy chickens from the Romanians and tomatoes from the Bulgarians in order that they might buy French cars and German trucks.

The two halves of reunited Europe can live in a quasi-autarky but, separated, remain dependent, one on the USA for its agricultural food supplies, the other on the USSR for its equipment.

Relative economic autarky permits a nation to be politically independent: a half Europe cannot claim to be that, only a whole Europe can attain that; however, there are some primitive politicians, demagogues, who sometimes in Belgium, sometimes in Tyrol, would like to make things '*as small as possible*'. Western Europe is already economically subjected to the USA: what would an independent Wallonia or an autonomous Flanders then be? It is quite simply grotesque.

The smaller a nation is, the more chances it has of becoming a satellite. And the monomanias of regional autonomy — inspired either by romanticism or by inferiority complexes or by demagogy –, by refusing to be part of a large Communitarian nation, of which they are constituents, will find themselves one by one reduced to the state of colonies. One of the keys to the political independence of nations is economic independence. Short of the size of unitarian Europe from Brest to Bucharest, there cannot be any question of economic independence, and *a fortiori*, of political independence. And since we wish the second, we shall build the first.

CHAPTER VI

THE UNIVERSAL MISSION OF EUROPEANISM, OUR NATURAL RIGHT TO HEGEMONY

Intelligence chooses, for taking its flight, the miniscule promontory that Asia thrusts into the Atlantic Ocean, in the north of the Mediterranean …

Alexis Carrel

There are still millions of men in the world who think of Europe as their last chance.

Georges Bernanos

All these men deep and of a broad mind that this century has seen have tended towards this end: the secret work of their thought. All have in common the same aspiration, that is, the soul of a united Europe which, under the prodigious diversity of formulas, makes an effort towards something else, towards a thing of the future and more elevated.

Friedrich Nietzsche

It would be of little importance if Europe were to cease to command, if there were someone capable of replacing it.

But we do not see even the shadow of a substitute. New York and Moscow are nothing new in relation to Europe. They are both only two fragments of European command that, by dissociating themselves from the rest, have lost all their meaning …

José Ortega y Gasset

'Nobility obliges' is said of Europe vis-à-vis a world that takes it at its word, but whose plebs do not oblige it to anything.

Alexis Curvers

Culture and Civilisation, Creation and Utilisation

CULTURE AND CIVILISATION are concepts that are essentially different though closely connected.

Culture creates and permits civilisation, civilisation is impossible without culture. Culture is the tree, civilisation the fruits.

Few people have shown themselves capable of planting these trees; on the other hand, many people have regularly profited from the fruits.

There is thus a European culture — accompanied of course by a European civilisation — facing an American civilisation WITHOUT an American culture.

The American civilisation draws its substance from the European culture. The converse is not true, for there does NOT exist any American culture.

Civilisation is, in some way, to culture what technology is to science.

In the course of history, the appearances of culture have been extremely rare: it is, in the geopolitical order, an 'accident', a mutation.

It is the Greek miracle, a colossal phenomenon, perhaps the greatest in history up to our days. Up to the present it has been followed only by the European culture begun in the 13th century, in full maturity in the 17th.

The mathematicians, the astronomers of the 17th century reach at that time summits similar to those that the fathers of ancient Greek geometry reached.

This sort of miracle demands, at the start, at least two conditions: a biologically superior race and a favourable terrain—soil and climate—not too harsh so as to coarsen the species (the country being too cold or too hot) but sufficiently hard to oblige it to daily struggle for survival. The second miracle has been that which was born in the 13th century between Edinburgh and Padua, between Nuremberg and Canterbury. It was there that European culture was born, which gave birth to the civilisation adopted internationally today. If tomorrow European culture were to disappear, the international civilisation would no longer progress.

It is from this knowledge that we derive our pride and justify our supremacy.

We cannot admit the insolence of peoples who, having received the use of our civilisation, imagine that they have become our equals in the misunderstanding they have of the obligatory origin of a civilisation from its genesis: first, a culture. *The black who buys a car cannot in his primitiveness differentiate POSSESSION from CREATION*. And let us make clear that the creation of the car which can be related again to a superior phenomenon of CIVILISATION itself depends on pure science, geometry, chemistry, physics, phenomena of CULTURE.

The black politician, who travels in a plane, possesses a transistor radio, is fitted out by a good haberdasher in London, imagines, in his infantilism, in absolute good faith besides, that he has become our equal. Such childishness runs through the homily used to deceive our stultified masses, and then one hears, '*They are people like us, they eat with a fork and brush their teeth*'. A monkey dressed as a conductor does not make a Claude Debussy.

The difference between creative power and utilising capacity is particularly evident in black Africa. There is no doubt that if we, the whites of Europe, should totally abandon Africa to its fate, it would return in a few generations to the absolutely primitive state in which we had found it. The same phenomenon has been observed among the Indians in Paraguay after the forced abandonment by the Jesuits of the reductions.[1]

Let us imagine, hypothetically, black Africa totally isolated for a hundred years, without any contact with the external world. If one returned there a hundred years later, one would no longer find any trace of any engine, obligatory education, the roads would have once again become trails. What could be observed five years after the initial departure of the French, English and the Belgians is terribly revealing in this regard.

It is not my intention to hope to see certain species — the black race in particular — deprived of the benefits and advantages of civilisation. But it is important to highlight a certain hierarchy of values and avoid the confusion created by a theoretical, abstract and unrealistic egalitarianism.

In the train of history we depict the energy that impels the locomotive and the blacks represent the wagons. It is certain that the wagons owe respect, if not recognition, to the engine. Now what do we see today? The wagons try to teach morality to the engine. This is the world upside down. We shall set it straight.

The modern biologists teach us not to draw excessive glory from our intellectual qualities; they say that it is a chromosome disposition that determines this quality. The merit of being more intelligent than another is derived more from a biological lottery than from a mark of interest of the gods with regard to us, or from personal merit. Certain people are creative and generous, in others nature has shown itself particularly arid.

---

1   Reductions were the Jesuit settlements in Argentina and Paraguay for native peoples who were converted to Christianity. The reductions enjoyed a certain degree of autonomy from the Spanish colonial empire until the expulsion of the Jesuits in 1767.

Within the framework of a race, the same considerations are true for individuals.

It is not our fault if the blacks had not yet discovered the wheel when Stanley crossed Africa, we cannot do anything about it if they owe to us the writing that we have had for four thousand years.

But it is nevertheless good to recall this from time to time, in order to put everybody in his place.

In any case, the *nouveaux riches* of civilisation — its utilisers — should not interfere in the work and the progress of those who are the creators. The work of creation is not yet finished, it will never be in the view of the Promethean man. This ASCENT should not at any cost be disturbed or hindered by the fantasies of a human egalitarianism constantly contradicted by the observation of facts.

Today as yesterday, tomorrow as today, Europe must be able to continue to develop its POWER IN CULTURE. We do not contest the Americans' practice of a high civilisation nor the blacks' enjoyment of a relative civilisation.

But there is a difference in the measure of value between culture and civilisation.

We do not intend to contest this hierarchy.

However unpleasant it might be to decadent rhetoricians, the mind sometimes defends itself with the sword and, if it forgets this, it disappears.

Athena was armed,[2] let us remember.

---

[2] Athena Pallas is the Athenian goddess of wisdom and war and was often represented in armour since she was considered the companion of heroes.

Priority of the Individual Over the Ant and the Greatness of the Exceptional Man

The individual is the only authentic and creative force of community. By virtue of this, he determines the collectivity. Man is reality and community is a convention.

What constituted the Greek genius, what permitted the prodigious expansion of European man is the possibility of development of the individual within a society. Europe is *par excellence* the land of choice of the EXCEPTIONAL MAN.

Two forms of solidarity can weld men together and give birth to organised societies: first of all, the bond of resemblance, the tribal bond, the mystical bond, the magical bond of primitive groups, and that is in a way a *mechanical, in other words, gregarious solidarity*; on the other hand, the bonds of common dependence, the pact of selfishnesses, the social contract, the alliance of diversified aptitudes, is the consciously accepted organic solidarity.

In the first form, that of mechanical solidarity, there hardly exists any exceptional man; only the collective man is admitted into it. This man is nothing outside his tribe, his clan. This type of man is found equally in the societies of primitives, in the modern collectivist societies (USSR-China) and, finally, in the materialist societies (USA).

A frightful conformism stultifies, wastes the American man and 'mediocritises' him exactly as the dogmatism of the Marxist religion coarsens and crushes the Soviet man. American man is reduced to the role of a consumer and voter, the former in particular. He is a luxury robot created as if unleashed for industry; the latter has much interest in standardising him in order to facilitate the task of distribution of consumer products. American man, prepared for this for three centuries by the stifling Puritan religious conformism, has not had any difficulty in submitting himself to the norms of industry.

Soviet man is another robot, much less luxurious. He struggles and must, further, glorify his struggle. In his mediocrity, in his life, he does not even have the compensation of satiety experienced by the American robot. A detail that is particularly vexing for him — he must not only glorify but it happens also that the programme might be changed without his being warned and he may in this way find himself in prison, no matter for Stalinism or anti-Stalinism, without fully understanding what it is about. He is, in a way, a broken man whose programming his operator has failed to restart.

The democratism that at present ploughs on in Europe, this collectivist dullness (Christian or not) tends to attain the same objectives. Man is less and less differentiated, both in his salary and in his thought (he becomes a SUBJECT): the social subject is the indigenous robot of our countries.

We rebel against the coarsening of man, his reduction to the level of a robot. This form of society composed of collective mass men signals decadence.

These mediocritised societies present a terrible danger for the future of the species: by their structures they prevent the appearance of a substitute elite, a reserve elite. If at each harvest one destroys the corncobs that are bigger, in some decades one will obtain a decadent species of wheat, for the bigger corncobs are cut and destroyed and those that hang close to the ground are spared.

These 'collectivist' human societies, equalised and admirably passive and docile in the hands of those who direct them, have manifested themselves many times. At the first shock issuing from the OUTSIDE, the edifice has crumbled in a general indifference.

These societies that discard everything unexpected, every risk and every initiative, do not possess any more men of decision and command, they do not have any substitute elite. It is enough then for an external agent to cause that which takes the place of its head to fall in order to take possession of the entire apparatus.

This phenomenon has been observed among the Persians of the Empire, defeated and then held in check by a handful of Macedonians. The former were docile SUBJECTS, the latter free men, warriors proud and hardened by danger.

From tranquillity and security only mediocrity and passivity can arise. At the very moment that the Persian emperor was eliminated and the Empire belonged to the Macedonians, we see thus the dominated and dominators in a ratio of 10,000 to 1, an extraordinary figure.

The phenomenon was repeated in Mexico with Cortes[3] and in Peru with Pizarro.[4] A handful of vigorous adventurers from Europe took possession of gigantic empires and their populations by decapitating the Aztec and Inca political edifices. The latter did not have any substitute elite. The people, accustomed to obey and never take the initiative, showed themselves incapable of making new Indian leaders emerge from their ranks to confront a laughable handful of adventurers. Pizarro, attempting his strike between Milan and Florence, had been crushed by a simple communal militia of turbulent but free men accustomed to risk and to initiative. But Pizarro had conquered an empire of robots. It was the same in ancient Rome.

At the beginning of its history Italy was invaded many times by the Celts and other peoples, particularly by Hannibal, who ravaged the entire peninsula and inflicted bloody defeats on the legions. But the Rome of that epoch was still full of vitality, it was constituted of free men, armed men. In every big Roman family one could find a general in reserve.

Six centuries later, after having suffered the moral decrepitude of the Christian social empire, Rome, rich and fat, yielded to

---

3 Hernan Cortes (1485–1547) was the Spanish conquistador who, during the reign of Charles V, conquered the Aztec Empire of Moctezuma II and brought the Mexican territories under Spanish colonial rule.

4 Francisco Pizarro (ca. 1471–1541), a distant relative of Cortes, was another conquistador responsible for the defeat of the South American Inca Empire of Atahualpa and its subjugation to Spanish rule.

barbarians ten times less numerous and ten times less strong than the Carthaginians had been. Why?

It is because the Rome of the Republic was constituted of free men bound by a national contract, of independent men united by a discipline and the Rome of Christian social decadence was now populated only by subjects, by ROBOTS:

The consuls governed turbulent but vigorous men; the emperors of the decadence reigned over subjects. The former handled strong men, the latter guarded sheep.

Our ideal society is that of a collection of men bound by a discipline in order to avoid the causes of decadence briefly evoked above.

Unity here is opposed to uniformity. The former is a fact of independent men who have consented to subject themselves to an iron discipline on a number of specific and limited points. They form a unitarian state that is concerned with few things but is concerned with them vigorously.

They are bound by an organic solidarity.

The second, uniformity, is the fact of standardised men who have lost their differentiation. They are then bound by resemblance in servitude and mediocrity. This is the mechanical solidarity.

The robotised man has only a single common life, official life being mixed with private life and the two being confused.

Everything is common, not only the service rendered to the nation — the service of arms, armed service, for example –, but also private life, personal life. The social anthill does not allow him a single moment of autonomy, it violates his personal life and provides him with distractions. Then the species degenerates.

Conversely, the exceptional man possesses two lives: a public life devoted to social obligations and a private life, the free sector of thought, initiative, risk and difference.

Public life is that of civil laws, of military demands, of social discipline, of the normalisation of public services. Here unitarian Europe cannot suffer the least indiscipline.

Private life is reflected in thought, the choice of personal life, the organisation of work, the arts, the genius of a region, the charm of a province. Here the state does not have the right to any interference.

The anthill is the invading state, covering a weak and mediocre society. The unitarian state — by contrast — is a discipline crowning a strong society. We oppose here (invasive) statism to society. We shall develop this topic further below. Europe should remain an expanding nation, a nation animated by the spirit of enterprise, by the taste of risk, by the sense of initiative. In this view, one should preserve the European man from the degeneration engendered by the conditions of life of the anthill, whether it be social or luxurious. Europe, an empire of 400 million subjects? NO.

Europe: an empire of 400 million free men, of disciplined citizens? YES.

Europe Bears the Destiny of Man

The history of life on our planet teaches us that nature, animated by a systematic pragmatism, has tried, or allowed to be tried, all the formulas possible only to finally reject those which were not viable and to finally adopt the best. Thousands of vegetable species, thousands of animal species have been 'tried' and from all these experiments only a few hundred have survived from thousands of attempts, and some dozens from hundreds. And, besides, I am being generous.

From life in the most elementary forms to life in the most complex forms — man — nature has always used the criterion of competition among species, followed inexorably by the law of selection, a cruel but creative law.

These tendencies have been applicable not only to men taken individually but also to men taken as a group, as collectivities, as races, nations.

One type of man has, over numerous centuries, emerged from the magma of peoples and races, European man.

His superiority does not allow any contradiction, the elements of proof are peremptory, striking, universal. What would Japan be today without Western sciences? A small traditional nation in the hands of the Cook travel agencies or American Express, no more.

Despite all his vain anti-European jabbering, Mr. Nehru must indeed teach European geometry in the Indian schools; the industrial expansion of China borrows ALL its disciplines from Europe, and the majority of the best professors, in the American universities, are still today 'imported' from Europe.

One plays Bach, Beethoven or Brahms in Santiago, Tokyo and Philadelphia. One does not play Chilean, Japanese or American composers in Vienna or Milan, and for a reason: one is still waiting for some immortal works of genius from them. Of course, at the same time, the negro music invades Europe, but one could not speak of culture with regard to this assemblage of sounds that express the most primary instincts.

Orientalism, as a cultural value, which could abuse unsuspecting people, is a myth easy to refute. The East has never been creative, except in the domains of metaphysics or mysticism, activities that are particularly little constructive. If one excepts the rare historical accidents, Alexander or the men come from the steppes through the North, India has been a region remarkably isolated from the big international confrontations. What emerged from this? A sort of life with a torpid rhythm. Geographically, demographically, historically, a great nation should have emerged from this peninsula blessed by climate and protected by the Himalayas. However, nothing of the sort emerged from it.

Let us look now at China, whose history is remarkable. We notice it under the Mings, later under the Manchu emperors, as already having lost its speed, ALREADY IN AN IMPASSE. This China of the 17th century and 18th had produced remarkable painters and poets and, already 2000 years earlier, a well-known philosopher, Lao Tzu, and a military moralist, Confucius; but it had to call to its aid Portuguese and Flemish Jesuits to construct its artillery and to calculate its calendar.

Four thousand years of civilisation to end in an impasse. Tomorrow, when an international civilisation will take greater shape than today, China will have brought its ceramics, its cuisine, its painting and its poetry. Nothing more.

We Europeans, we will have brought all the rest, that is to say EVERYTHING: mathematics, sociology, technologies, industries, morality and lifestyle.

Everywhere where other nations progress (China and Japan), everywhere where other nations try quite awkwardly or even grotesquely to progress (India and Africa), they have recourse to European technologies alone, recourse to European disciplines alone.

The other peoples cannot diminish their gap, make up their delay, except to the extent that they give up their culture and adopt our much more creative one.

Two nations, however, seem to wish — or, more precisely, hope — to snatch supremacy from Europe in culture and its works, civilisation. These are, on the one hand, the Soviets and, on the other, the Americans.

This ambition is the crowning of an infatuation born of a precarious military occupation (the occupation of Europe for 18 years, but what is 18 years in history?). That is for us at most a matter of annoyance and a page that we intend to efface.

But where the matter becomes more serious is that these two impostors of culture could, to a certain degree and within a certain time, influence the orientation of the history of man.

It is here that a possible tragedy is outlined.

The USSR and the USA are two children of Europe; on the level of civilisation totally, on the level of culture very partially.

But it is a question of two sterile branches. To the extent, and in the epochs when they were cut off from the SOURCES, the ROOTS,

Russians and Americans have rapidly run out of steam, rapidly come to the end of their tether.

This exclusivity of CREATIVE POWER that Europe has possessed for centuries is due to the conjunction of a type of man living on a type of terrain. Negroes placed in Burgundy would disappear and our race installed for a thousand years in the Ubangi would degenerate. That is a geo-ethnological phenomenon comparable — excuse the comparison — to that of the wine of Burgundy. I choose this example with the intention of vulgarisation.

The white inhabitants of the United States belong to the same genotype as those of Brussels, Basel or Vienna.

By contrast, the North American and the European are classified into two very different phenotypes.

Apart from heredity (our race) and milieu (Europe), Russians and Americans have been deprived, have even been deliberately deprived, of our historical experience and, thinking to go faster, have chosen to create a type of collective man, this lamentable MASS MAN.

And we find ourselves here at the centre of gravity of the tragedy that could strike the history of man: that humanity might choose the path of collective man, of stereotypical man, of mass man, or in simpler words, of American man or Russian man.

This accident is probable in the case that political Europe would not be present, would no longer be present, to guarantee and protect the type of man who for centuries has permitted the soaring of the species.

The conformism that wastes American man, which crushes Russian man, allows the nations that create this type to advance more rapidly, in the SHORT TERM — and at the same time condemns them irrevocably — in the LONG TERM. For the average man as the hero of a society, let us say, the mediocre man, is a perfect robot that can sometimes be a soldier, sometimes a consumer, sometimes a Stakhanovite,[5] sometimes a voter. But the benefit stops there.

In a system where everything that excels, where everything that is 'different', is rejected or crushed, there is no possible place for the mutations of man in the ascending direction of life. With standardised men, the human adventure is in sight of its end.

Men are the reality and society is a convention or a contract that WE know.

But for the Americans and the Russians, the 'society' dominates the individuals and those who deviate too much from the standardised world are rejected, banned, neutralised and ostracised from it.

Europe is a society of diversified men bound by a social contract, everyone conserving his own individuality, his particular spirit. This is an immense accumulation of individualities of personalities reinforced by an interaction that multiplies its potential.

Unless there is an accident we are going visibly towards a type of international civilisation engendered by a particular culture, the European culture.

It is — therefore — of prime importance — not only for the future of Europe but for the future of humanity — that the type of civilisation adopted or imposed correspond to the most evolved, the most creative formula: ours.

Our civilisation constituted of individualised men has been prodigiously rich, the fruits are there before our eyes, and everybody vies for them.

But the United States and the USSR today tend to develop a type of mass man. At the end of the American experience, at the end of the

---

5 The Stakhanovite movement was based on the exemplary effort of a miner, Alexei Stakhanov, who, in 1935, exceeded his work quota fourteenfold. The Stakhanovite movement was supported by the Communist Party and sought to encourage competition among workers during the second Five Year Plan of 1935.

Russian experience, there could be a tragedy infinitely greater than that of the disappearance of historical Europe.

On the success or the disappearance of Europe as a political state (organised city, defended city) depends the rise or the disappearance of man as a Promethean adventure and even as a species, the famous 'thinking reed' of Europe. Europe holds in its hands the choice of the history of man.

Either the mass man (USSR-USA versions) leads us towards dead ends, towards impasses and human evolution ends in fact in the anthill or the termite hill — whether they are comfortable or even luxurious does not take away anything from the horrible character of these ends — or the individual man continues the ascent of the species, and through combats, convulsions, selections, mutations, announces Promethean man.

Europe does not bear only its own destiny. It bears also the destiny of men living outside its borders, it bears the destiny of humanity.

Europe — a National Arena or a Pilot Nation?

Soviets and Americans would be strongly mistaken in imagining that they could easily and eternally perpetuate in Europe a situation analogous to that of Korea or to that of former Indochina.

The laws that can be applied to small nations cannot be applied as easily to a big nation. Just the half of Europe, the Western part, with its 300 million inhabitants, constitutes a group more important even than that of the occupying force: the USA.

In February 1945, at Yalta, when the USA and the USSR shared the world, Europe seemed definitely worn out, and China destined to never emerge from its Middle Ages of the 'warlords'.[6]

---

6   In the fourteenth century, when China was ruled by the Mongol Yuan dynasty, several provincial aristocrats ruled independently of the emperor as warlords.

Eighteen years later, Europe is in full economic expansion and America comes to beg monetary aid from it.

Eighteen years later, Red China already begins a new imperialist politics. In 1945, the international game consisted of two protagonists; today it consists of four.

It consists of four, but people try or pretend not to know this.

The tremors that are going to shake the world in the decades to come will have as their origin the fact that our planet is subjected to an 'order of two' with in fact four powers in line. The spirit of Yalta cannot satisfy either Europe or China.

Japanese imperialism was exhausted in China; the Russian imperialism also had to give up all expansion in this direction.

Now, China was, even a short while ago, a totally broken, disorganised, weakened nation and the one who had spoken thirty years ago of a possible Chinese imperialist policy would have aroused a torrent of jeers or sniggers. It will be the same for Europe tomorrow, and those who were not focussed on the phenomenon will not have seen it arising. We cannot tolerate much longer that Europe be a field of manoeuvres or a barracks for the American Army, nor that the Mediterranean be a lake for the American fleet. We cannot tolerate much longer the same situation — but that due to the Russians — in our Eastern provinces. The flourishing Europe of 1964 is no longer the exhausted Europe of 1945 and the conditions suffered by the latter are no longer tolerated by the former. Europe no longer wishes to play the role of an arena where two foreign imperialisms confront each other. An arena can be equally a field of military, diplomatic battle as a field of economic battle. Everybody, even the most obtuse, will agree that the vocation of being a battlefield hardly tempts us.

One should add that we have as much an aversion to seeing our fatherland constituted as a field of colonialist exploitation for the American capitalist economy as for the 'exciting' socialist 'experiments' of Moscow.

Finally, Europe can no longer tolerate seeing primitive and naïve ideologies like 'the American way of life' or brutal and dogmatic systems like Communism imposed on it.

We do not wish either a military arena Europe, nor an economic arena Europe nor an ideological arena Europe.

A nation whose roots go back 25 centuries of history and which has more than 400 million highly civilised inhabitants does not have to receive lessons from young presumptuous barbarians nor to tolerate much longer serving them as a makeshift stage for acrobats.

The first task for Europe is to constitute its political unity and the task immediately following is of RESUMING its natural role of elder nation, of pilot nation. For Europe is the older nation, the nation that has attained its maturity and which in its long and rich experience of the past can draw precious and principal lessons on the art of living and the art of governing.

Europe has a long time ago had its childhood illnesses As a nation, it has had its Anabaptists, its wars of religion and its civil wars. 1945 is a great date for our history, for it marked the end of our civil wars.

One cannot say as much of the recent nations like the USA or the USSR, which, lacking a thousand-year experience, could still be tempted to proceed to social or historical experiments, of which we, Europeans, know so well the vanity and pointlessness.

If tomorrow, in the concert of four or five great nations, which will constitute the new international balance, one must find one therein which could serve as a guide or pilot, that is indeed Europe, and none other. Older, more populated, more powerful, more civilised, Europe, through its experience drawn from its long past, will be able to present itself as an example and prevent other young nations from making again the experiments that we have already tried in the past.

The Europe of the last decades of the 20th century will then play, at the international political level, vis-à-vis other nations, a role analogous to that played by France vis-à-vis Europe — in the course of the century of Louis XIV — at the level of the arts and philosophy.

Absence of Europe: Rupture of the International Balance

The hate-filled men who had devised the Morgenthau Plan in 1945, a plan destined to pastoralise Germany,[7] were not themselves able to realise it for fear of a catastrophe through a rupture of the balance of nations. Thus even those who had conceived it had to, probably regretfully, abandon it.

Roosevelt, in his megalomaniacal hatred, had also dreamed of destroying the European power in a definitive manner. A dream already quite faded today and of which there will remain only a wisp tomorrow.

In Eastern Europe, Moscow began by proceeding with some years of an economy of systematic pillage — then, learning that it was more profitable for it, switched back on, for better or for worse, the economy of the East. Thus, from 1950, hardly five years after the capitulation of the Third Reich, its two conquerors had to rebuild both Germany and Europe.

At the economic level, this was already the *de facto* recognition of the European reality. Tomorrow, the attraction of the colossal economic power of Eastern Europe alone will provoke a political awareness in Eastern Europe. Moscow will not be able to ignore it for a long time for fear of being faced with internal tremors in its 'socialist world'. Thus, step by step, Europe reassumes its place — not through the intimate desire of its present occupiers but through the power of facts, the reality of its existence alone. The absence of Europe provokes a rupture of the international balance. The USA and the USSR are

---

7   The Morgenthau Plan, proposed in 1944 by the United States Secretary of the Treasury, Henry Morgenthau, Jr., was designed to deprive Germany of its armaments and heavy industries. Most of its points were formally accepted by Britain and the United States at the Second Quebec Conference in September 1944. However, it was not fully implemented after the war and substituted in April 1948 by the generous Marshall Plan.

absolutely not capable of replacing the presence of Europe in several parts of the globe, and in particular in Africa, for lack of possessing sufficient civilisatory capacities and practices. Everywhere where Europe has been forced — after the fact of arms alone in 1945 — to withdraw, anarchy was born and neither order nor prosperity ever returned again. In all the regions abandoned by Europe, there is occasion to make two principal observations. The first is that all these nations (Tunisia, Morocco, Algeria, Congo, etc.) are in a remarkable and indisputable social and economic regression.

The second is that, in all cases, without exception, where the USA has wished to supplant us and substitute us with itself, it has failed lamentably, if not ridiculously. One cannot improvise with impunity and suddenly a 'civilisatory nation'.

From Batavia to Léopoldville, through New Delhi, EVERYWHERE the USA has failed in its attempt to substitute us with itself. Not to mention the farces of the Soviet missions in black Africa: they smack of vaudeville, and the Russians themselves, piqued and discouraged, have most of the time removed their lynchpin from this black imbroglio. In order to regain its balance, the world should appeal to Europe — if we ourselves have not before that regained our place without asking for anybody's advice or paying attention to it.

Europe incarnates a power and a mass such as neither the USSR nor the USA will be able to absorb. The rupture of the international balance derives from the fact that this economic and civilisatory reality does not have a means of expression of its own political power: a political personality, a formal political entity.

Neither Moscow nor Washington will ever be able to master Europe; they cannot cultivate this illusion for much longer. It was perhaps possible in 1945.

From 1955, the most obtuse minds could see that we were regaining form and that there could not be any question of integrating Europe with the USA under the false flag of a 'West' or an 'Atlantic world' and much less with the East under the cover of a 'socialist world'.

The first of the two states, the USA or the USSR, which will admit this reality totally and which will draw the logical conclusions therefrom, that is to say, its DISENGAGEMENT from Europe, will be able to hope for an alliance with a Europe that has become once again an ENTITY. It is a matter of indifference if this be Moscow or Washington. Nations are directed by interests, by facts, not by ideologies. It would be more beneficial — all things considered — either for Moscow or for Washington to be able to count on the alliance with ALL of Europe than to be able to draw benefits from a precarious tutelage applied to HALF a Europe.

The ally of Europe will be chronologically the first of its two occupiers who will disengage and who, in exchange, will seek its 'positive neutrality'.

China, an economically asthenic nation, has freed itself of all tutelage; there is therefore no doubt that Europe in full economic expansion will (*a fortiori*) free itself of its occupiers more or less soon.

Europe will thus return to the concert of great nations, four or five, of the world.

The problem for Moscow as for Washington is to make a 'good exit'. Would they wish to cling on? They will end up like the French in the Tonkin Delta, decimated and destroyed one by one.

For there is no place to deceive oneself, ten or thirty years from now. 'THEY' should leave. If they do it in time, they could still leave with arms and baggage; if they are obstinate, it is with boycotts, with strikes, with terrorism, with armed insurrection (this is not war) that we will drive them out. It is better — much more for them than for us — that they understand this in time.

It would have been ridiculous in 1815 to want to efface from the map a country like France and to conceive a new European balance without it; it would be equally as ridiculous and dangerous to want to create a new international balance without Europe.

Warning of this is given to the blind adherents of this diplomatic recklessness.

Up to 1945, peace or war, in the whole world, depended on the solidity or the rupture of the European balance alone. After 1945, the USSR and the USA became indisputably international interlocutors; in 1964, China was added; tomorrow, Europe will return. It will be necessary to substitute the old European balance with a new international balance, and move to the superior historical denominator. The world of tomorrow will be dominated first of all by four giants: Europe (400 million), the USA (200 million), the USSR (220 million), China (700 million). Others will perhaps follow, such as Latin America and India, but this is not at all probable in the short term.

The rule for Europe will be to preferably seek a continental peace, thus conditions of non-aggression with the USSR; it will in this resume the Bismarckian policy of relations between Berlin and Petrograd.[8]

But this peace will be possible only when the last Russian soldier, the last Russian policeman will have evacuated Sofia and Bucharest. Not before. And if this solution is not possible, there is an alternative — and this should not seem ridiculous. The Pope indeed attempted an alliance with the Mongol against the Turk, François I one with the Turks against Austria, Richelieu, a Catholic prelate, one with the Protestant princes against the Habsburg Catholics.

Europe can neutralise the USSR through a Chinese game.

Let everybody realise in time the ineluctable character of the RETURN of Europe in the interest of the international balance, in order to spare many people's tears. One does not deprive 400 million men of their personality without danger.

---

8   St. Petersburg was on the outbreak of the First World War in 1914 named Petrograd. In 1924 it was named Leningrad and in 1991 renamed St. Petersburg.

Europe a Third Force or the First Force?

Fine minds think they are audacious in seeing Europe as a 'third force'. In fact, the brutal and sudden rise of China already puts us in the fourth place.

But let us specify—in the fourth place in order of appearance on the international stage. But the order of appearance is not the order of importance.

Everybody knows that, in a show, the star waits to be called and appears at the end of the programme.

To speak of Europe as a third force can cause a confusion to arise in the minds and lead them to mix up the order of appearance with the order of importance.

Europe will be the third or fourth international force in order of appearance. It is of little importance to us, but one thing is certain: Europe will be the first force in order of power.

This supremacy of Europe still escapes too many people who have inferiority complexes totally misplaced with regard to the realities.

The supremacy of Europe is registered both in quantity and quality; it is registered in the figures.

Demographically, Europe lines up more than 400 million men, the USSR 220 and the USA 200 (of which 20 million blacks of little competitive quality should be subtracted).

The same advantages are found at the industrial level and if, demographically, we crush each of the other candidates for world hegemony, we leave far behind us the USSR—much more underdeveloped in comparison with us; it has up to now had to give up every serious consumer industry for the benefit of its equipment industry. What to say then of China, which does not exist economically in spite of its 700 million inhabitants?

Military power flows in a direct line from industrial power. Thus the European military power will rise even tomorrow from the personality core of Europe. It is neither engineers nor factories that we lack, but solely the political leaders to plan military production.

When one comes to the comparison of intellectual resources, of creative human resources, the primacy of Europe then becomes striking. Let us not forget that the USA and the USSR are only branches of the European civilisation and that we are its trunk.

Thus it is necessary to explain the sentiment of timidity of certain Europeans through an ignorance of the figures and of the realities or, if not, through a genuine inferiority complex. Europe is not the 'third force', it is the first. In the concert of great nations, hegemony will revert to us in fact and by right; in fact because we are the most powerful, and by right because all our competitors, modern China included, have adopted OUR civilisation, this European civilisation, of which we are and will remain the only ones possessing the ROOTS: that is to say, European culture. In the international civilisation, we possess the fundamental parts. That gives us the right to supremacy. We no longer wish to hear of Europe as a 'third force'; this equivocal term should be banned from now on. We say — and we will prove it — Europe, the first force.

CHAPTER VII

HOW UNITARIAN EUROPE WILL BE FORMED

A state is first an idea, a historical conception.

> Jacques Doriot, Congress of the PPF,[9] 1942

And one cannot pass from the small society to the big through the same process. One needs here a coagulating factor, which, in the great majority of cases, is not the instinct of association but the instinct of domination. It is to the instinct of domination that the big system owes its existence.

The nation did not at first bring out its leaders for the simple reason that it did not exist before them, either in fact or in instinct.

> Bertrand de Jouvenel

Where there is a will there is a way.

> William of Orange

Only those will win who are ready not to win anything for themselves, for the future belongs to those who risk everything for an ideal. Wisdom is to live heroically.

> Alexis Carrel

A factual hierarchy must be founded on the need that a revolution has of revolutionaries. The most necessary ones are the first.

> Sergey Nechayev

The relative homogeneity of the race and language, which they enjoy, is the result of the prerequisite political unification. Consequently, neither blood nor language constitute the national state; on the contrary, it is the national state that levels the original differences of the red corpuscles and of the articulated sounds. And it was always so. Rarely, not to say never, will the state have coincided with a prerequisite identity of blood and language.

> José Ortega y Gasset

---

9   The *Parti Populaire Français* was founded by Doriot in 1936 as a French equivalent of National Socialism.

Pilot Nation or Pilot Party? Hegemon State or Springboard State?

A NUMEROUS BUT OLD school advances the formula of a process of unification of Europe starting from a preponderant nation.

Another school, ours, much more modern, maintains the technique of unification of Europe starting from a European party. Let us specify clearly, of an integrated party and especially not of a vague amalgam of 'nationalist specks of dust' (petty nationalists) reunited by the very loose bonds of a so-called 'coordination' or a fragile 'federation'. The party that unitarian Europe will herald should be — evidently — itself unitarian and centralised.

The Europe realised by and around a preponderant nation has been a formula tried several times and aborted several times. France tried it with Bonaparte, Germany with Hitler, de Gaulle flirts with it still and, which is better, his 'pretenders', that is to say, the last survivors of the CNR[1]-OAS, do the same.

The process of a strong nation, of a chosen nation, 'predestined' in a way, federating in its orbit the other nations of Europe, is condemned and to be condemned. In fact, every reactivation of any nationalism, yesterday the German, today the French, is of a nature to resuscitate immediately, and as a direct reaction, other small and old nationalisms. Europe came out of this infernal circle in 1945. Let us

---

1   The *Conseil National de la Résistance* was a secret organisation created in May 1962 for the defence of French Algeria.

not return to it. It is necessary to know what distrust the old nationalisms arouse — besides justified by the history of the recent centuries — in the neighbouring countries to never wish anything but their gradual but radical disappearance. We shall say that, for ten units of positive nationalist ENERGY in a determined nation, the reaction of negative ENERGY in all the neighbouring nations is five times that of the initial positive power. The result is therefore definitely tragically negative. The hypertrophy of any given nationalism unleashes dangerous allergies in all the neighbours.

It is nevertheless clear, up to the present, that Europe presents zones favourable to a revolutionary action and others that are unsuitable. The successors of Salazar, the successors of Franco, the successors of de Gaulle, may announce the worst and the best. But in any case, they will have profound and very wide repercussions. By contrast, one does not see that the European national revolution would be able to have at its disposal favourable conditions, either institutional or emotive, in Sweden or in the Netherlands.

The progression of the European revolutionary reality will therefore be very rapid in certain states, very slow in others. We have for that reason before us a hierarchy of terrains that are more or less favourable.

If a nation presents a terrain favourable to an accelerated awareness and the establishment of an apparatus, that gives it in no case any privilege — a privilege which would have emerged directly from the petty nationalist conception. Let us suppose that, in extremely favourable conditions, 'ONE' 'French' European party succeeds in attaining power in ONE specific country. Here, hypothetically, France. A real catastrophe would arise from this success. In fact, the French European party, buoyed in its success, would not resist the temptation of national nepotism in the European Revolution. With this, one would have only displaced the problem of conflicts between nations to that of conflicts between European parties.

VII. HOW UNITARIAN EUROPE WILL BE FORMED

The theoretical construction of a local European party helping the others after its personal success is an extremely dangerous heresy.

The orthodox conception at the revolutionary level is that THE (I say here THE as opposed to the term ONE used above) European nationalist party establishes its logistical bases in the first country of the old regime that will present conditions of weakness or trouble.

Which is the same as saying that, in case of the rise to power of THE European nationalist party in France, it should be realised first of all with powerful non-French assistance (what General Salan[2] was incapable of understanding and what Colonel Argoud[3] began to timidly perceive a little before his arrest), and then the party will have to be consolidated with the support of numerous non-French elements. These numerous contributions of non-French people would constitute a total guarantee that the new regime will not try to return to narrow nationalism, even if it be at the level of the party.

Thus the nation favourable for the installation of bases would not in any case be:

1. tempted to play the classic game of the preponderant nation,

2. tempted to hypertrophy ONE European party within a coalition of European parties.

Every construction of a Europe of coordinated nationalisms contains a mortal seed of impotence or of failure in the long term. This heretical conception should be opposed by the integrated European nationalism. The international of the nationalists is not only a chimera but a contradiction, a formal antinomy.

---

2 Raoul Salan (1899–1984) was a general of the French Army, who was one of the founders of the *Organisation Armée Secrete*, which sought to preserve French Algeria.

3 Antoine Argoud (1914–2004) was an ardent partisan of French Algeria and, after serving in the French Army in Algeria during the Algerian War, joined the executive committee of the *Organisation Armée Secrete* in 1961.

One would see then a sick state taken by storm by an integrated European revolutionary organism and then this revolutionary apparatus USING the conquered state as an operational base.

This concept will make numerous persons grind their teeth who have not yet been able to overcome, sublimate their present local nationalism.

But this is the condition itself of final success. In fact, in such conditions, this springboard state (a springboard state is especially not a hegemon state, commonly called a guide state) will have so many antennae in Europe that it will cause the structures of the old regime to split rapidly in all the neighbouring states. Hypothetically we shall say that if, from Paris the revolutionary action in Germany is orchestrated by a European apparatus containing numerous militants and cadres of German origin, it will obtain deep echoes of sympathy because this apparatus will thus have provided formal elements to arouse confidence. If, on the contrary, it is in the hands of French people, even the German Communists will easily reactivate the old German national feeling to cause the operation to fail.

The international Communist revolution failed already for a very simple reason and, in two cases, very precise. The reason is that in Moscow — since 1935 — people have been infinitely more Russian than Communist (in reality today Communism serves Russia; the contrary — and that was the situation in 1923 under Trotsky and Borodin[4] — has not been true for a long time). The 'International' of the song[5] is long dead.

---

4   Mikhail Borodin (né Gruzenberg) (1884–1951) was a Comintern agent, who operated in Mexico between 1919 and 1922 and in China between 1923 and 1927.

5   The 'Internationale' was adopted as the anthem of socialism at the Second International in Paris in 1889. Translated into Russian, the song was used after the Bolshevik Revolution of October 1917 by the Communist Party of the Soviet Union and continues to be used today by the Communist Party of the Russian Federation.

This Russian nationalism caused the integration of Eastern Europe to fail through Russia and caused the welding together of China and the USSR to be lacking.

The nationalist comportment of the Russian policy has aroused the classic and well-known reaction of other nationalists at the threshold itself of the Communist world. Poor Karl Marx, he must be turning in his grave.

This is the error that we should avoid with the greatest care even and especially within the European national party. Within the party all the vestiges of ancient nationalisms will have to be rapidly eliminated by an accelerated integration. The success of the European integration will depend on the preliminary development of integration within the ranks of the party. These conceptions are revolutionary and collide with the customs of many, we know, but they are the conditions *sine qua non* of success. We have discarded the formula of a preponderant state and later that of a 'European' party. But we have to speak of the pilot party, which we will do in the next paragraph.

On the Nation as a Creation, on the Nation as a Cult

The nations have never been pre-existent as unities within people's souls. However, all the 'nationalisms' reason as if that had been so. They do not know the history of the formation of nations. If we use the term nationalist in its classic significance, we shall say that the nationalists have followed the nation, and that they never, and emphatically never, preceded it: they have never been its fighters. By fighters I mean those who fought to make it. Of course they will fight to defend it. Why? Through lack of imagination, through lack of stature, through opposition to change, and conservatism.

Nations are — at the start — the fact of the will of a man or of some men, the entirety realised by the force of a fortunate war (England) or by an artifice of dynastic matrimonial connections (Austria).

A nation must be made, as it were, against everybody for it disturbs the customs and threatens the oligarchies. France was made against the French; in the same measure Europe will be made against many Europeans. It was not necessary to make people believe that the people would welcome Philip II of France[6] as a liberator or as a unifier in Normandy, Anjou, Aquitaine and Poitou. Only Philip II perhaps — and I say perhaps — nourished the grand plan of France in memory of the Carolingian adventure. At best, he — with his advisers — was the only one who understood the scope of this plan.

The same men who squawk, fulminate, grumble, chip away at unitarian Europe — under the stupid pretext that 'this has never existed' — did the same in 1210 against the rise of the Capetians. At that time, and they were the Maurassians[7] and the Barrèsians[8] of the 13th century, they were in revolt, in the name of some contemporary local petty nationalism, against the 'senseless' pride of the Capetians. There was not a pre-existing France wished for by God. There was France because some men wished for it and made it. I intend to emphasise that the French of the 13th century were against France just as many Europeans are (in fact) against Europe in the 20th century. The arguments are the same: 'It has never existed' or 'What do I have in common with a Dane?' In 1210, how many barons of Poitou did not say 'What do I have in common with a Champenois?'[9] Those who use

---

6 Philippe Auguste, or Philip II of France (1165–1223) was the first Capetian king to call himself 'King of France' rather than 'King of the Franks'. Philippe Auguste sought to destroy the power of the Angevin kings of England in France and waged war against Henry II of England (1133–89), who was Count of Anjou and Duke of Normandy and Aquitaine.

7 Charles Maurras (1868–1952) was a political thinker, who was the principal figure of the *Action Française* movement, which was anti-parliamentarian, monarchist and 'integral nationalist'.

8 Maurice Barrès (1862–1923) was a nationalist politician, who was a friend of both Charles Maurras and Paul Déroulède (see above).

9 A native of the province of Champagne, in Northeastern France.

such weak arguments awkwardly betray their incapacity to judge from the 'heights of history'.

To teach history I imagine a short calculation in the form of a quick cartoon, showing, in colours, the birth of a point that grows rapidly or of a stain that shrinks. One would then see being born or dying, expanding or disappearing, Aquitaine, Prussia, Normandy, Poland or Lithuania. In the meanwhile, consult a map of the 13th century to see what France then was, a map of the 17th to compare little Prussia with the large Poland and Lithuania. It was people of a different calibre than Boulanger,[10] Déroulède, Maurras or Barrès who made France. This does not take away anything from the merit of the last two in singing its praises and glorifying it. In chronological order, patriots follow the fatherlands; they never precede them. The unifying action in France or the unifying action in Spain were made AGAINST the will of contemporaries or without their interest. Their acquiescence is rare, it is reserved for an avant-garde political elite. Similarly, Mazzini was very far from being understood and followed in Italy in 1840. Only an elite prepared the steps. Thirty years later, the Italian unification was accomplished. Today, the schoolchildren recite monotonously from Naples to Venice the virtues and merits of Garibaldi and Mazzini. But in 1840 rare were those who envisioned modern Italy.

When France was given to the French, the latter refused or showed no interest in it for a long time.

It was not otherwise twenty centuries ago, when Caesar had to force Rome to the imperial vocation. Power belonged at that time to the republicans, that is to say, to the conservatives. The latter did not want to — politically — enlarge the city-state Rome.

The Roman Empire was at the time of Caesar inconceivable for the majority of the inhabitants of Rome as a city. Tyrannical Caesar

---

10 Georges Boulanger (1837–91) was a French general during the Third Republic, whose nationalism took the form of a strong anti-German *revanchisme* provoked by France's defeat in the Franco-Prussian War of 1870–71.

opposed to the virtuous Cassius is a misleading idealised image in the service of the ministry of 'progressive' public instruction. Cassius, Brutus and all the conspirators were historically pathetic personages. Cicero was politically an imbecile. Stabilised political unity, linguistic unity, a certain ethnic homogeneity are ALWAYS posterior to the will to create a nation expressed by a handful of men.

France did not exist because people spoke French but people speak French because France was decreed. The same with Spain, the same with Great Britain.

A nation is a movement, it is something that 'comes from' and 'goes towards'.

Those who contest Spain in the name of Catalonia, those who contest France in the name of Brittany are mediocre backward-looking people. They forget that in this view and through this dialectic process, Catalonia and Brittany can also be contested exactly in the same way and with arguments of the same sort drawn from prehistory or the historical infancy of these two regions.

What then is the process of the birth of a nation? What is it really?

Originally we find an idea, a concept, or an ambition. Then this concept must find a historical terrain (a COMMON external danger for example) and ensure for itself a constraining force (a revolution, an army, a party). Once the nation is made, it requires still some generations to become stable. It then becomes a custom and only then, but not before, is it the object of the cult of patriots.

Among the general public, or even among the relatively politically cultivated but historically unlearned public, ONLY the last last phase commands attention. The others do not seem to exist in their eyes. They do not retain the other phases because they see the nation only at the moment that it is already a heritage.

I always smile while reading school books on the history of France that speak of a Burgundian danger or an 'English' danger in 1420 (for example) starting from the postulate of a France that HAD TO exist.

VII. HOW UNITARIAN EUROPE WILL BE FORMED

The Burgundians and the 'English' in 1420 were not less French virtually than the inhabitants of Bourges.[11]

We shall say therefore that the objective analysis of the history of the birth of a nation proceeds according to this programme: first concept, then the concept fertilises a historical terrain and manipulates a constraining and centripetal force, finally a force and a duration create a custom. And it is only at the moment when the custom is an acquired and obvious matter that the common man SEES the nation and accepts it. Then begin the discourses and the monuments to the dead. Then one finds multitudes of writers to brilliantly (but of course *a posteriori*) explain the nation that is 'eternally willed by God'. We live in Europe at a passionate moment in the history of the birth of a nation. The concept itself dates already from yesterday. But we have now before us the terrain. This terrain is the common danger, the Russian and American appetites. It is in fact Moscow and Washington that provide, which can seem at first glance a paradox, one of the required psychological conditions.

The terrain exists. It exists negatively, thanks to the common threat, to the Danes as to the Portuguese, of Communism and the imperialism of the dollar. It exists positively, for the men and the people of Europe are today at almost identical levels of maturity, a culture is common to them and geography makes them immediate neighbours. The ideal conditions are there, present, within easy reach.

One thing alone is still lacking, the centripetal force, the constraining force, a European party.

Europe will be first a will towards a nation, then a contractual nation and much later, in ten generations, a nation of heritage. To make a nation a unity of historical destiny is required, and a nation is a shared future. This unity, this future are there before us. Let us seize them.

---

11   A city in central France.

The Danger of Internal Racism in Europe

It is to demonstrate a total lack of understanding of anthropology to say that there are no races, it is to deny science when it contradicts the 'progressive' homilies.

There are races and extremely variable qualities. To maintain that the Celto-Germanic is *'the same man'* as the Bushman of the Kalahari is an imbecility that is part of the programme of brainwashing organised at the moment in our primary schools. All men are not equal and only UNESCO will maintain that a Greek of the Mycenaean epoch was 'no different' than a Jivaro[12] of the Amazon.

One can summarily divide the human races into three categories: the creative races, the races capable of rapid adaptation and the sterile races. Within each group also there exist levels.

We shall place notably the Indo-Europeans among the creative races, the Japanese race among the races capable of adaptation, and the black among the races that are especially sterile.

For four centuries, the Portuguese arrived everywhere in Africa; however, in 1900, the Africans had virtually remained in the Stone Age. They had not been tempted to copy us in what was superior about us.

By contrast, let us observe Japan. In 1853, the American captain Matthew Perry obtained, through force, an agreement in favour of some who had been shipwrecked. In 1856, Townsend Harris[13] was the first Western envoy at Yedo.[14] Nevertheless, up to 1865, the xenophobic Shogun clan persisted in wanting isolation. In 1868, a volte-face

---

12   The Jivaro tribes inhabit Northern Peru and Eastern Ecuador and are headhunters, who shrink the heads of their victims.
13   Townsend Harris (1804–78) was the first Consul General of the United States to Japan.
14   Yedo, or Edo, was the seat of the Tokugawa shogunate, which lasted from 1603 to 1868.

and from then on Japan was westernised at an extraordinary speed. The French engineer Émile Berlin created the Japanese war fleet; the English perfected it and, from the beginning of the 20th century, Japan was a modern power! The Japanese realised in 40 years what the blacks could not realise in 400 years. Inequality of races, there's the explanation!

Let us return to Europe.

Very frequently in the north of Europe, especially in the German nationalist milieus in these sterile little groups of the extreme right, we come up against the anti-Bismarckian thought of objection to mixed Europe, to what they call with disgust miscegenated Europe.

They say, or think, that they do want a Europe but with sexual taboos with regard to Sicilians or Poles. This discrimination is as inadmissible as it is stupid. There are only 'more or less' pure races and basic observation reveals to us that between the Rhine and the Seine the Germanic race dominates while from the Oder the Slavic contribution is marked. Nevertheless, in the romantic circles of German nationalists of the extreme right, they consider a German from the East as a pure German because he speaks German — and an inhabitant of Verviers as a 'Latin' because he speaks French. All that is childish, but nevertheless harmful.

It is impossible to accept within the ranks of an integralist[15] European party Germans who would still have superiority complexes with regard to the Poles or Slavs in general. The racist anti-Czech and pro-Slovak, anti-Slav and pro-Croat manias betray a narrow-minded conduct that renders impossible a healthy conception of Europe. A little while ago I heard a German hero of the 40–45 war suggest a Western Europe at the cost of a gift of European Slavs that we would make to Moscow! That is a heretical and suicidal conception for Europe.

---

15   The peculiar French term *'intégriste'* is derived from Maurras' concept of *'nationalisme intégral'*, which is based on a strong government and a thoroughgoing dedication to the nation.

Is it still necessary to speak of the conduct of the German racists of the extreme right who frown at the mention of the Andalusians but swoon before the Arabs through a taste for exoticism, an exoticism dating back to Wilhelm II and his railway to Baghdad.

In an integralist European movement there cannot be any place for those who still stoke the hatred of the 'Boche' in France or in Germany the contempt for the Pole. This racism is absurd.

To speak of *Mischung*[16] between an Italian man and a German woman or between a Polish woman and a German man is a stupidity. There is an undeniable hybridisation between a negro and a French woman and that we refuse. Besides, in fact, the barrier of repulsion is impassable between blacks and whites. After three centuries of cohabitation, even in the USA, the barrier of races has been maintained. There are many false white man-black woman or black man-white woman couples but the legitimate bi-coloured couples are most rare and subject to the contempt of the two communities. Besides it is the trash of the white race and the trash of the black race that interbreed. In the two communities, the individuals that yield to this real *Mischung* are rejected and despised. There is no real danger in this respect, the instinctive reaction is powerful and healthy. We will never manage to integrate the black races and the white, and that is just as well.

By contrast, one cannot claim interbreeding between Slavs and Germans, between Mediterraneans and Scandinavians. Europe can strictly indulge in an EXTERNAL racism, it cannot indulge in the danger of an INTERNAL racism.

Racism of the narrow nationalist form has no scientific basis. The uneducated who use it know nothing about the Visigoth, Vandal, Burgundian, Swabian, Frank and Dane migrations in the course of the period from the 4th to the 11th centuries. To make Europe around a

---

16 German term for miscegenation.

chosen race, for example, the 'Nordic' race or the 'Germanic' race is to make an impossible and dangerous bet.

We will say that the borders of European racism should coincide with its geopolitical borders. This is not a joke but a historical reality and especially a political necessity.

To make Europe around a race, this was rather the dream of the Chancellor Hitler and it is one of the reasons of his failure, without doubt the principal.

A racism of the North, under the hypocritical mask of a certain 'Europeanism' has already been mortal once for Europe from 39 to 45. It cannot at any cost arise again. Its reactivation would only cause all of Slavic Europe to be thrown to Moscow and would, as a reaction, render all of Mediterranean Europe distrustful.

I speak easily of this, belonging myself to this Nordic group and bearing a purely Gothic name. Believe that I write this sentence smiling even though it reflects reality. Nordic or Germanic Europe would not bother me if this group appears with such a force that it could easily dominate Slavic Europe and Mediterranean Europe. But this is not, and never will be, the case. Consequently, this conception, doomed, by statistics and reality, to failure, should be rejected and fought. Europe has need of the last Andalusian, the last Sicilian, the last Pole. It cannot afford the luxury of rejecting a single one of them. Historical Europe owes very much to those who have held the purely Asiatic tides (and I think of the Poles) and to those who retook the Strait of Gibraltar from the Arabs (and I think of the Spaniards).

The Europe of 'Germanic nationalists' with its sexual taboos is impossible, ridiculous and already belied by facts. It is in the millions that Italians, Spaniards, Greeks and Turks work in the industries of the north of Belgium and in Germany. Inevitably these workers will integrate and will take spouses in the indigenous population of the North. One who deplores such a situation is not capable of becoming a good and sincere militant in an integralist European party.

I repeat for the last time, there is no *Mischung* if a German man marries a Sicilian woman or if an Andalusian man marries a Danish woman.

Those who think otherwise are useless for the formative political struggle of Europe.

Negotiated Europe or Europe of the Ingenuous

By negotiated Europe we mean the supranational Europe of the parliamentarians. The examination of history teaches us that, in the course of centuries, parliamentarians have never been unifiers. Excepting the rump parliamentarians who were there only for decoration. The unifying will is manifested through the perseverance of a dynasty or through the will of a man of power, a man of war, a leader of a party.

But never, in the course of the ages, has one seen installed authorities giving up, spontaneously and without dishonest ulterior motives, a power that they held without contestation. The finest example of this phenomenon is Brussels today, and I wish to take it as model: Brussels, which has a million inhabitants, is divided into 19 communes, which provide 19 mayors, 19 firefighting bodies, 19 networks of communal schools, 19 police regiments, etc. Let us add, with 19 different uniforms for the firefighters and 19 different uniforms for the policemen. This represents an edifying example of inefficiency. It is certain that the management expenses of these 19 communes are at least five times higher than the same management of a million inhabitants by a single commune. But, and here begins my demonstration, in case of a fusion of small communes, 18 mayors would be sacrificed, 18 firefighter chiefs sacrificed, 18 chief commissioners sacrificed. Further, the Socialist Party has, at the moment, an absolute majority in a small commune, a majority that it will no longer have tomorrow in a big city. This is true in the same manner of the Flemish or Francophone communes, for the Catholic or non-Catholic communes. The administrative dispersal of Brussels into 19 communes provides too many small but comfortable honorary positions, too many small but childish satisfactions of the ego, for all these people to benevolently give up their profits and their honorary trifles.

In 'parliamentary Europe', the same exact problems are present but on a bigger level. Have you added up all the present members of parliament and senators, Italian, German, French, Belgian, etc.? One should get about five thousand droolers. It would — of course — be inconceivable, even if it were for the most democratic mind — to imagine a parliament of 2,500 members of parliament and a senate of 2,500 senators. It would therefore be necessary to prune, to filter. There's the rub. Each of these little consumers, in possession of a secure career, would then realise that a European parliament presents — for him — infinitely more chances of being eliminated than of being elected.

Negotiated parliamentary Europe is impossible insofar as it threatens habits, tricks, honorary positions. The Europe of 'engagements' is, in addition, so pleasant to the present parliamentarians. It is only study trips, exchanges, visits, research, meetings, banquets. Tomorrow the precise administrative structures of Europe will not have any need at all of these pilgrims or of these revellers. A simple telephone call between Paris and Milan will regulate in five minutes what two commissions of parliamentarians do not manage to resolve at present in five months of travels …

Obviously, in the parliamentarian world, certain greedy men have imagined that they could conserve the present parliamentarians and to add to them a 'super' in Strasbourg. The hustlers of parliamentarism have even imagined that they could render eligible only the candidates of 'authorised parties' (authorised by them, of course) or designated by the parliaments of the small nations of the present.

A Europe constructed by the slow and scholarly negotiation of parliamentarians is the solution proposed to the ingenuous by the hustlers.

To unify one needs a unifying FORCE, a centripetal FORCE, a new and different force. One should also take into account the fact that elections are conducted with the aid of worn-out clichés and not on new ideas.

One should know and say this, UNITARIAN EUROPE is not an electoral drum of values; the crowds vote for things known for a long time. The little song finds its lasting recipes in a vocabulary of a hundred words: love, always, oath, betrayal, abandon, emotion, heart … An election is conducted with some classic ingredients: liberty, work, anti-Fascism, anti-capitalism, anti-Communism, promises … less taxes and more subsidies (one does not demonstrate this algebraic miracle, of course).

And yet, in the present reality, Europe is par excellence social progress. The Common Market will make, and make ten times faster, the material happiness of the workers ten times more than all the socialist bureaucracy. The expansion of the market — thanks to Europe — improves the concentration of industry and perfects distribution. The sales power of the worker emerges from it considerably grown. A worker should vote ONLY for the party of Europe, he chooses it for his own interest.

One could strictly use the term Europe effectively in an election in cultivated or intellectual milieus but definitely not elsewhere. My remark is valuable in the short term; in ten years it will be different when millions of workers will have peregrinated through Europe, going from the south to the north to find big salaries. The high salaries of Northern Europe for the workers of the south and the paid holidays spent in the Mediterranean for the workers of the north will do more for the concept of Europe, among the masses, than all the European academic clubs. But that is for tomorrow. Nevertheless, a tomorrow that is very close.

At present, the old manipulators of electoral parties prefer to work within local nationalism. They find that more rewarding for the time being. Thus, in Italy, the MSI[17] lives off the exacerbation of Italian chauvinism. All the fake fiddlers of neo-Fascism roll up their racket in the green-white-red tricolour flag. The same in Germany, the same in France.

One should conclude from this that Europe has nothing to expect from professional electoral engineers. Europe is not a formula that makes elections fashionable.

Let us conclude by drawing attention to the fact that free 'elections' would certainly have prevented the birth of France. A broad and peaceful electoral 'competition' would never have led to the foundation of the Soviet Union from 1917 to 1918, to the birth of Communist China, to the birth of Algeria.

It was necessary in all these cases to bypass elections or else to fix them. Besides, what makes the solidity of the electoral institution is that it can be falsified. If not, everybody would reject it. In case of electoral clashes, the meanest, the most immediate passions, the fractionalist tendencies, have infinitely more chance than the unifying and constructive will. The former appeal to rancour, to envy, to inferiority complexes, the second appeal to reason. The competition is therefore too unequal! Man being what he is …

Europe through the Alliance of 'Nationalists': a Paradox

Starting from a pure type of hypothesis of nationalist individuals, one constructs in certain milieus of the extreme right a 'Europe of nationalists'. That is a construct of the mind, and a confused mind. One is a French nationalist or a European nationalist; one is a German

---

17 The *Movimento Sociale Italiano* (Italian Social Movement) was a post-Fascist political party in Italy formed in 1946 by supporters of Mussolini. It gained popularity in the late fifties and early seventies under Giorgio Almirante but was transformed in the nineties by Gianfranco Fini into the more moderate *Alleanza Nazionale* (National Alliance).

nationalist or a European nationalist. It is useless to attempt dialectic acrobatics to prove *'that basically all the nationalists are brothers'* and destined to understand one another. When a woman is pregnant, she is that by someone, she cannot be that by two men at the same time; she can much less be that by no one ...

The dialectic pirouettes effected in recent times by certain classic milieus of local nationalism with the sole aim of catching or drumming up a young clientele that is moving towards the European idea cannot deceive us. These people who claim that they are 'nationalist nationalists' are in fact narrow nationalists who try to pass for European nationalists. As they are afraid of losing their old accustomed clientele of narrow nationalists and would like at the same time to recruit the new wave of European nationalism, they have constructed a sort of political duck-billed platypus: the 'nationalist nationalist'. *One is a nationalist of something, of something old or new, of something small or big.* This noun absolutely needs a qualifying adjective. There is no absolute or abstract type of nationalist, a sort of 'nationalist race'. In fact, with the European concept making implacable progress, all the local small-nationalist reactionary groups try to follow the taste, the fashion of the day. The lemonade is the same as before, but they have changed the bottle or the label.

I have personally frequented the 'nationalists' sufficiently to know their congenital powerlessness to make Europe. In Portugal, I discovered among certain nationalists a vestige of anti-Spanish feeling. Yes, in 1954!

The Flemish nationalists detest France in such an archaic fashion that they still celebrate with splendour their victory at the Battle of the Golden Spurs, which dates from 1302![18]

---

18 The Battle of the Golden Spurs was fought at Kortrijk between the Kingdom of France and the County of Flanders. The efforts of King Philip IV of France to suppress the Belgian rebellion against the French rule were unsuccessful.

The Austrian nationalists are subjugated by South Tyrol, the German nationalists live only on anti-Slavic feelings, the Polish or Czech nationalists exist only in their hatred of Germany.

How to make Europe with these negative and fractionalist forces? Nationalism needs a common external enemy to assert itself. In this regard the USSR and the USA serve magnificently as consolidators of Europe and will do that for a long time yet. The Russian occupation and the Yankee exploitation do, and will do, very much to create European nationalism. This is the repetition of a classic historical phenomenon. This is a present, living phenomenon.

On the contrary, the emotional elements that agitate or move the small nationalists belong to the past, to a DEAD past. The small nationalists have not yet realised that their subjects of hostility do not exist any longer! Their nationalism will be extinguished for lack of real nourishment. The force of French nationalist feeling could depend only on anti-Germanism in Alsace or in Lorraine, and vice versa in Germany. Today, one could not find ten Germans and ten Frenchmen to start a war. This nationalism has thus lost, if I may say so, its steam. At the time of the Common Market to be a French nationalist is in in some way to be a nationalist in a void. Devoid of enemies!

Europe formed by the alliance of nationalists is only a big joke. One should have attended meetings where pseudo-Europeans were engaged in a cat fight about South Tyrol, or the Flemish linguistic border, to know that that Europe is rather an exchange of small photocopied publications.

This is the Europe of political mailboxes. A thousand little nationalist groups, more or less pseudo-Fascist, more or less bureaucratic, more or less racist, exchange mimeographed bulletins of a questionable intellectual quality. They think they have made Europe after having practised a postal exchange. Nourished on Fichte, Maurras or d'Annunzio, they are incapable of understanding Europe, for they are incapable of feeling it and living it.

They conceive a Europe of harlequins resembling the terrible mess that Germany was in the 13th century, each one jealously conserving his type of boots, his flag, his dialect. They of course refuse the supremacy of any one of the existing nationalisms, in which they are right, but they equally refuse the domination of a European supranationality this time because they feel uncomfortable in this large new framework, causing in a way a provincial inferiority complex. *It must be noted, and here the matter is very serious and very condemnable, that all the little nationalists who refuse the European supranationalism (under the pretext of* Mischung *and other excuses) are the most servile in accepting the American supranationality.*

Jealous of one another, they only agree in finding a foreign protector.

That is a phenomenon similar to what was observed in Germany of the 17th century, incapable of unifying itself but, in fact, dominated by the political intrigues of France. Every little German prince ferociously jealous of his brother, ran to Paris often and to Vienna sometimes. The royal houses of France on the one hand and of Austria on the other benefited from the pathetic particularisms of the German princes.

Today, with regard to Europe, all the petty nationalists, who in the final analysis practise Atlanticism, that is to say, the subjection to Washington, not being able to agree among themselves, are as criminal as the little German princes of the 17th century with regard to Germany.

Are these petty nationalists, whose policies end definitely in an appeal to the protection of Washington, proud? All end up in this impasse the moment they have to find a military FORCE to resist Moscow. The Europe of petty nationalists is the Europe of jealousy, of meanness, of particularism.

I have heard Spanish nationalists refusing a Europe 'that would not be Catholic' but they already sponge off the majority Protestant USA. I have heard German nationalists distrusting French supremacy (which is very comical) but suffering servilely the colonisation of Federal Germany by the USA. Not being able still to present their own force, the petty nationalists are forced to beg the protection of a really foreign power, the USA.

The Europe of nationalists? Old leftovers.

The Non-Spontaneity of the Peoples: the Necessity of Consensual Rape

History was not written with good wishes, nor made with desires. Those who expect that Europe will arise spontaneously from a 'revelation' among the masses will wait for this event for a thousand years more. The masses, isolated from all education and deprived of management, are capable of riots but never of revolution. Revolution is the organised level of the riot and organised from the outside and in advance.

There is no revolutionary spontaneity among the working masses. Lenin explained that a long time ago.

This truth, applied to the problem of social revolution, is also applied to that of the problem of nations 'in formation'. *The birth of Europe will not occur in any case through a sort of spontaneous awareness among its peoples, but indeed through the TRANSMISSION of this awareness by a lucid elite to the masses.*

The masses, the peoples, are in fact essentially passive and conservative. The birth of Europe will be positively conducted by a small active minority among an immense indifferent mass and against a solid minority clinging either to memories or to the benefits of the past.

The masses do not wish for the unification of Europe as a purely political fact. As a historical fact, they accept it to the extent that they see in it — and it will be necessary still to make a big demonstration of it — the diminution of the cost of automobiles or the increase of their purchasing power. Which is—happy coincidence—real and easy to explain.

One must be naïve to organise 'referendums' in order to know if the masses wish or do not wish for a united Europe. In fact, the response depends on the question. They will reply yes if one suggests to them that this Europe will bring prosperity and comfort; they will reply no if one brings the commercial competition before the eyes of a small industrialist or the sexual competition of the Neapolitans before the eyes of the Teddy Boys[19] of London.

But in no case do the masses have the least interest in the integralist political fact, in the formal historical future. To count on the birth of a political unity through the realisation of the masses or even of the youth is a totally illusory idea. All these cultural stooges in favour of Europe have no efficacity and their influence does not go beyond the society salons of intellectuals.

At the level of the masses, Europe will in a way be imposed after having been simply and clearly explained and justified (see the cost of automobiles above). Europe will be for the peoples of Europe a sort of rape. But it should be a prepared and a consensual rape.

The Necessity of the Political Eviction of the USA from Europe

European politics has for 19 years resembled a house of cards. The base card being the US military power. Take this out and the house crumbles.

In spite of all the risks that that may entail, one should try at any cost to evict the Americans from Europe.

The tutelary power, the United States, has created in Europe habits of security, comfort and, one thing leading to another, the renunciation of personal initiative and finally subjection. Every time that one

---

19 The British Teddy Boys of the fifties adopted neo-Edwardian sartorial fashions even though they favoured the new American music styles of rock 'n' roll.

corners the bourgeois or the democrats with implacable reasoning, at the edges of their dialectic constructions, one bumps into the American. All of them say, 'Ah, but the Americans will not allow that to happen'.

This being so, they do not realise their error at first, for the Americans have already allowed many things to happen since Yalta; but, further, this situation is humiliating, and that does not disturb the clan of cowards in Europe.

'The Americans' is not really the moral Maginot Line[20], behind which Western Europe wallows in its materialistic pleasures.

This foreign, because American, Maginot Line contributes enormously to the creation of habits of laziness and habits of cowardliness among us.

Imagine, hypothetically, the departure of the Americans and the panic that would follow it. The frightened bourgeois, the weak parliamentary parties faced with Communism without the assistance of the US Air Force or the US Navy or the US Army, what a salutary panic, what an awakening!

Still hypothetically, if this phenomenon is manifested today, the great beneficiary of it will doubtless be de Gaulle, towards whom the political animals of Rome, Madrid and Bonn should run to solicit a guide, nuclear armament and an authoritarian style.

But after de Gaulle? The phenomenon and its immediate consequence remain valuable still. A spineless and weak Europe, deprived of the American support, should search for strong men.

To make Europe aware, it is necessary to awaken it from its American torpor, it is necessary to take away its Yankee tranquilliser from it.

---

20 The Maginot Line, named after the French Foreign Minister André Maginot, was a line of fortifications built by France in the thirties on its borders with Italy, Switzerland, Germany and Luxembourg in order to deter invasion by Germany.

The American departure would create a void. In politics, in history, a void irresistibly calls for a force. Imagine a Europe without Americans, a Europe in the style of Monnerville,[21] of Guy Mollet,[22] of Gilson;[23] imagine all these tricksters, all naked, all alone before the Red subversion … what a meltdown!

I shall not return here to the fact that historically, congenitally, the Americans — exactly as the Russians — are our enemies, but I insist on the fact that the American protection has taken away from Europe the taste for independence and the sense of responsibility.

Atlanticism is an opium for political Europe, Americanism is a morphine which coarsens us and takes away all personality from us.

Atlanticist Europe or the Europe of Imposture

Atlanticist Europe is one of the most massive impostures acted out among the general public.

Some people, some honest, others scoundrels, try to imagine an America with a big heart, which would cause a united, free, independent and strong Europe to arise. What naivety on the part of the former, what imposture on the part of the latter! The United States entered the war in 1941, against Germany — at that time, in fact, representing Europe — not to save the poor people confined in the concentration camps but to prohibit Germany from federating the whole of Europe under Germanic leadership.

The USA is against all of Europe, whether it be English, French, German, socialist or Fascist; the USA — and it is their main interest — is, traditionally, against the real unification of Europe. In every

---

21 Gaston Monnerville (1897–1991) was a French politician and the grandson of a slave in French Guiana.

22 Guy Mollet (1905–75) was a socialist politician, who served as Prime Minister of France from 1956 to 1957.

23 Germain Gilson (1906–65) was a Belgian liberal politician.

European formula containing the USA, the latter is in it only to better ensure its supremacy or to cause the matter to fail.

The confrontation between the American and European imperialisms will tomorrow be economic, diplomatic, political, or subversive, if not one day military. That is in the order of things. Tomorrow this confrontation will thus be that of a continent — a big one, ours, of 440 million men — against a small one, the USA, of 200 million. Continent against continent, the battle will be apparent and clear.

However, the confrontation of these two imperialisms is not absolutely new. The American will to dominate and the European hegemony have clashed with each other for almost a century already. But earlier it was not the USA against Europe but the USA against Spain representing Europe, the USA against England representing Europe, the USA against Germany representing Europe.

The American imperialism is a relatively old phenomenon. The Americans played with their gunboats in China in 1850 (Treaty of Wanghia, 1854), in Japan in 1853 (demonstration of force in the Bay of Yedo), fomented intrigues in Cuba until 1853. The complete enumeration would be too long: theft of Texas from Mexico (1845), theft of Panama from Colombia (1903), forced sale of the Philippines by Spain (1899), new military intervention in Mexico (1914). The great inspirers of this expansionist policy were the Presidents McKinley and Theodore Roosevelt. One does not count their interventions in Haiti (1916), in Saint-Domingue,[24] in Cuba. The American imperialist traditions are more recent than ours, but they do not yield to them in anything as regards the cynical and systematic use of force (the so-called big stick policy). The USA a decolonising power? What black humour!

Under the first Roosevelt, American policy was essentially anti-Spanish; under the second, publicly anti-German but in fact essentially anti-English and anti-French. Between 1939 and 1964 all the

---

24 Saint-Domingue was a French colony on the Caribbean island of Hispaniola that became the independent republic of Haiti in the early nineteenth century.

policy of Washington has tended with perseverance to eliminate the French and English positions in the world, from Bombay to Algiers. The USA has driven us out of Africa between 1950 and 1962. We will drive them out of Latin America before 1975 through local subversion alone. One does not see, therefore, the United States putting back on the saddle a powerful unified Europe when they have done everything to destroy Europe in its English, French or German forms, how much less dangerous.

Europe and the United States are industrial powers, rich nations. It is therefore normal that collisions occur and that they occur also between these two giants, who have similar temptations. One can never insist enough on the fundamental character of the inevitable confrontation between the USA and Europe.

Atlanticist Europe is American Europe. Two well known persons, Spaak[25] and MacMillan,[26] know something of that, they who played, the former the role of a valet, the latter that of a liar.

Do you imagine a European America? Do you imagine Washington, its secretaries of state and its senators accepting the humiliating situation of placing themselves in tow with Europe when, since Monroe, they have rejected this tutelage? It is inconceivable. Then how and why accept that we be towed behind the United States? In its present forms, the American alliance is for us a constant humiliation and exploitation. We offer our soldiers to this fine alliance but in the form of a colonial infantry: the 'noble' weapon, nuclear arms, remains forbidden to us.

In fact, we are allies of the USA — in 1964 — just as Morocco or Madagascar were allies of France in 1915. Other elements argue for

---

25 See above p. 69n.

26 Harold Macmillan (1894–1986) was the Conservative Prime Minister of the United Kingdom from 1957 to 1963. He strove to consolidate Britain's special relationship with the USA and his effort to bring Britain into the European Economic Community in 1963 was blocked by de Gaulle, who believed that Britain was too closely tied to the USA to be part of a European arrangement.

the greatest mistrust with regard to the blind union with the United States.

It is mortally dangerous to be associated with a country — like the USA — that so easily entangled itself in the Cuba affair. May the heavens protect us from such associates. The Colonial Office in London would have regulated this affair — in the past — with a frigate. Mr. Kennedy risked provoking an international conflict!

Other troubles wait for the USA in South Asia. Let them get bogged down there and let us disengage from a bad situation. An Atlanticist Europe would perhaps lead us to a second Dien Bien Phu.[27]

Atlanticist Europe is an imposture. That means an American Europe, a sort of Carthaginian colony. The United States has everything to lose in allowing a really unified and really strong Europe to arise. They know that and they act accordingly.

We should know that equally and play our own game.

Three Possible Axes: Bonn-Washington: Servility; Paris-Algiers: Romanticism: Brest-Bucharest: Realism

Three schools claim to give us an initial orientation to the development of Europe.

We have, first, the American school, that is to say, the adherents of Atlanticist Europe. These people slide coyly over the problems of Eastern Europe since their masters — those of Washington — have already sanctioned the abandon of our Eastern provinces. They maintain that nothing can be hoped for or undertaken 'without the Americans'. We must tirelessly denounce this imposture which keeps

---

27 The Battle of Dien Bien Phu took place in 1954 during the First Indochina War and ended in a major defeat of the French forces fighting the Viet Minh Communist nationalists.

Europe in a state of political vassalage and which produces habits that renounce a personal destiny. The American clan is, fortunately for us, very weak in terms of human quality. In the clique of the partisans of American Europe, one encounters neither an idealist nor a militant. Everything works there by way of the dollar, as it was the case in the past in the China of the Kuo-Min-Tang[28] and as it is the case at the moment in Vietnam. The people certainly take dollars, but nobody is ready to die for Washington in this camp of mercenaries.

The clique of Atlanticist Europe controls hundreds of politicians, members of parliament and journalists. But not one among them is ready to fight for his master. Cocktails, society events, glossy magazines, all that can make one think that this is a numerous and powerful group. It is nothing of the sort. At the first revolutionary puff of wind, this façade will be swept away like dead leaves by a tempest.

Atlanticist Europe must be severely condemned, for it is the sanction of the abandon of our Eastern provinces. The American and Russian politicians are closely connected one to the other, the two occupiers will maintain each other together, or will have to leave together, as it were. The very presence of the American army in Western Europe provides an excellent argument to the Muscovites to maintain themselves in our Eastern provinces. The presence of the Red Army in Eastern Europe constitutes, on the other hand, the justification of the Yankee occupation in the West.

Let us imagine, hypothetically, the withdrawal of the Red Army from Eastern Europe. This withdrawal would bring about that of the American Army from Europe. As Washington does not wish in any case to withdraw its armies from Europe, for it is this presence which guarantees our political subordination, the US Army, which is in Frankfurt, is there under the PRETEXT of the presence of Russian

---

28 The Kuomintang was founded in 1911 as a revolutionary party by Sun Yat-sen and Song Jiaoren and was later led by Chiang Kai-shek. It lost the Chinese Civil War to the Communist Party and retreated to Taiwan, where it remains the major opposition party in the Republic of China (Taiwan).

tanks in Leipzig, but in fact and especially to guarantee the American policy of OCCUPATION of Europe. The American clan, in Europe, is that of the collaborationist bourgeoisie and of the venal political world. A rich group but intrinsically not very powerful.

Then there is the Euro-African group. It is itself divided into two schools. First, that of the dreamers, friends of mankind, especially when it is black. These dream of a bi-colour confederation, a sort of immense progressive brothel. Then, that of the old whites of Africa, Belgians and French in particular, who cherish the hope of a rapid return to Africa. I shall restrict myself to putting the second on trial. The first do not deserve our pausing to consider their case. A weak Europe has no chance of returning to Africa. By weak Europe I mean half a Europe, that of the West. Only a Europe reunited from Brest to Bucharest will possess the indispensable power for intervention in Africa.

One should not invert the order of things and begin with Africa when one should end with it. This tendency is that of the circles influenced by the last survivors of the OAS/CNR or by the old white administrators in Africa. It is the nostalgia of the lost African empire that moves them.

A Euro-Africa — starting from a weak Europe — is an unrealistic and dangerous vision. Euro-Africa will be made beginning from a reconstituted Europe, a strong Europe.

The policy that would consist in wishing us to get lost in the African labyrinths, at the present, would lead us to distracting ourselves from the forces that we need in place in Europe.

We must at any cost avoid the dispersal of effort. Is it necessary to draw attention to the fact that a present attempt of the return of Europe to Africa would be systematically thwarted by the entire world aligned against us? From the Americans to the Russians, by way of the neutralists.

What we can hope for at best, in Africa, is the balkanisation of this continent, while waiting for our return. Here the facts serve us and we can count on the black political chiefs to serve us involuntarily but efficiently. By leaving Africa, democratic Europe has left behind a time bomb: all its defects: parliamentarism, demagogy, particularism, corruption. Paradoxically, we should support the negro chiefs against the Americans today and against the Russians tomorrow. But to support them individually in such a way as to maintain the political functioning of Africa. This is the maximum realisable within our reach, at the moment.

To go further and make 'associations' with a socially backward, politically dishonest, militarily powerless Africa would be to drag a deadweight, entertain idlers, compromise our fight for independence and then that for our expansion. Africa will be for a very long time a 'sick man'. Useless to lug this around behind us.

At no cost can we continue to tolerate in Africa an attempt at an American or Russian hegemony; on the contrary, we can support for a certain time at our side a continent in anarchy.

The thesis of 'African Europeans' is vicious, especially in the sense that it does not realise that the liberation of Eastern Europe will occur with the support of the reserve of 130 million whites, oppressed and determined to free themselves (Poznan, Berlin, Pilsen and Budapest are tests of the vigour of these peoples), while the political reinstallation of Europe in Africa would occur against the immediate will of the locals and, besides, in an atmosphere of international tension.

We shall set foot again in Africa as soon as Washington is embroiled in a Latin American continent in flames, as soon as Moscow finds itself in open conflict with China regarding Siberia.

Let us wait for our enemies to be occupied elsewhere.

Let us wait especially to dispose of the entirety of the possibilities of our Empire. The route to Algiers passes first through Bucharest. The route to Bucharest, on the other hand, does not pass through Algiers. One was able to hope up to 1961. Now everything has been modified. Four pusillanimous generals spoiled everything in 1961. The axis of Europe, of its liberation, of its greatness, is the route to Bucharest.

When we are reunited, when we are more than 400 million men, we can settle certain accounts. Not before!

Institutional Europe

On 25 March 1957, in Rome, an event of great scope took place: the Treaty establishing the European Economic Community was signed at the superior level by Spaak, Adenauer,[29] Pineau,[30] Segni,[31] Bech[32] and Luns,[33] and by Snoy d'Oppuers,[34] Hallstein,[35] Maurice Faure,[36] Martino,[37] Schaus[38] and Linthorst Homan[39] at the administrative level of each of the six signatory powers.

---

29 Konrad Adenauer (1876-1967) was the first Chancellor of the Federal Republic of Germany from 1949 to 1963.

30 Christian Pineau (1904-95) was a socialist politician, who served as French Foreign Minister between 1956 and 1958.

31 Antonio Segni (1891-1972) was a Christian Democratic statesman, who served as Prime Minister of Italy between 1955 and 1960 and President from 1962 to 1964.

32 Joseph Bech (1887-1975) was the Prime Minister of Luxembourg from 1926 to 1937 and again from 1953 to 1958.

33 Joseph Luns (1911-2002) was the Dutch Minister of Foreign Affairs between 1952 and 1971.

34 Jean-Charles, Count Snoy et d'Oppuers, (1907-1991) was a Belgian politician, who served as the Secretary-General of the Belgian Ministry of Economic Affairs.

35 Walter Hallstein (1901-1982) was a German politician, who served as the first president of the Commission of the European Economic Community.

36 Maurice Faure (1922-2014) was a deputy in the French Parliament from 1951 to 1983. He signed the Treaty of Rome as secretary to the French Foreign Minister.

37 Gaetano Martino (1900-1967) was the Italian Minister of Foreign Affairs from 1954 to 1957.

38 Lambert Schaus (1908-1976) was the Minister of Defence of Luxembourg from 1947 to 1948 and served on the Hallstein Commission of the EEC from 1958 to 1967.

39 Johannes Linthorst Homan (1903-1986) was a Dutch politician, who became Director for Integration in the Directorate General of External Economic

The Common Market was born.

This fact is of a historic importance that must have escaped the participants themselves. Very few among them believed personally in the very grand success that this economic unity was to experience in 1964. England sneered with contempt and the USA at that time tolerated 'the thing' with good humour, not being able to foresee that six years later this group would make the Yankee economy tremble across the world.

Even today very few people discern what will emerge politically from this economic operation. In the 19th century, the *Zollverein*[40] had been directed explicity against Austria and it had magnificently prepared the German unity achieved by Bismarck in 1871.

A hundred years later, the Common Market was not at all directed intentionally against the USA but it became that in fact and one begins to realise that only today in 1964. The Common Market provoked the capitalist confrontation between the USA and Europe; it created an economic conflict which will sooner or later degenerate into a political conflict. It has provoked a contradiction within the capitalist world and obliged Europe to become aware of its strength!

I should begin a short parenthesis here to condemn the simplistic attitude of petty nationalists of the right who are repulsed by this work of a 'technocratic Satan'. With perfect unanimity all the imbeciles of the extreme right have condemned this monster born in Rome in 1957 and which was going to break the good old conservative traditions. They have proclaimed the end of 'nations' and announced the reign of the horrible economic technician. It is commonplace in the salons of the 'Europe of nationalists' [sic] to despise this Europe of technocrats.

What nobody has seen yet is that the economic Europe born in Rome, and fathered by the big Spaak, the master of ham actors, is in fact an extraordinary instrument of power, an instrument that is going to be

---

Affairs in 1952.

40 The *Zollverein* was a customs union of German states, which was established by Prussia in 1834. It was taken over by the German Empire in 1871.

lost even to those who caused it to be produced because it is too big for them. Ineluctably, this economic power is going to give birth to a political power. The latter will be too heavy, too imposing to be controlled by weak democratic politicians. In March 1957, some good parliamentarians gave birth to an economic child, which twenty years later, when an adult, will become a political colossus which will disown them. In itself the text of the Treaty is excellent, the measures regarding the free circulation of persons, capitals, services, the rapprochement of the legislations, are remarkable.

Whatever these reactionary detractors say of it, it is an excellent instrument, a remarkable start. The fact that this Treaty bears, for example, the signature of a show-off politician like Spaak does not take away anything from its intrinsical value.

Of all the forms that we have examined in the present chapter, the form of institutional Europe is, obviously, the best or, more exactly, the least bad. But, as the Common Market will be realised, an economic confrontation will arise internally between the American capitalism and knots of political difficulty externally. It is at this moment that the present European politicians will prove themselves to be too weak to face the resistances encountered, and other men of a totally different nature and a totally different determination, in a word, of another calibre, will be necessary. The technocrats who gave birth to the European Economic Community will not accept that their work should remain incomplete; it is therefore within the realm of probability that, exasperated by the hesitations and procrastinations of the professionals of democratism, they will turn one day to other more determined politicians, to other more daring political formulas to complete the European work.

In order to be totally concretised, to flourish, institutional Europe should appeal to a political force which does not yet exist at the moment, or to the embryonic state. An obstruction, a danger nevertheless exists; it is that of the infiltration of these institutions by so-called European industrial representatives. Too many European industrial interests are already infiltrated by American capitalism. Once more we meet the same adversaries, the same enemies on our path: the Americans. At the risk of annoying my reader, I do not hesitate to say that everything makes clear that Europe should act as much against the Americans as against the Muscovites. Their interests are not ours. What is certain and evident is the apparatus designed in March 1957 will fall even from the hands of those who conceived it. Sooner or later, but certainly. *To condemn the Common Market is a manifestation of historic myopia. It is so much more profitable and simpler to inherit it, even if it means forcing events a little to reap its legacy.*

The Hierarchy of Urgencies — When One Cannot See the Forest for the Trees

We should condemn everything that deprives Europe of active forces, everything that disperses them by luring them to diversional conflicts.

The most lamentable example is that of the so-called South Tyrol affair. I have neither the leisure nor the space to examine the basis of it here. Let us say anyway in brief that Italy relies rightly on its right to security — and this right is as valid as any other — to control the Brenner, the classic route of invasion, and of a great part of the population, of which Austria can, for its part, invoke the Germanic character.

Let us recognise that the Austrians cannot instal emigrants to South Tyrol and that Italy does it with its emigrants from the South, but let us specify honestly that it is not a question of a particular case or a concerted policy. The Sicilians do not invade merely South Tyrol but equally Milan and Turin! And, besides, Federal Germany contains already almost a million Italians! It is a matter of a movement from the poor South to the rich North and not of an 'Italian imperialism' [sic]. Tomorrow in Europe, where the free circulation of men will be guaranteed, and where there will not exist any strategic problems in the small scale of the Brenner, the South Tyrol affair will be deflated and will be resolved by itself. There will no longer be an Italian Army to park its artillery on the Alpine passes nor borders to halt the migration of Austrians towards Bolzano.

I apologise for this short digression. But it is indispensable. It is necessary to emphasise the smallness of the problem of South Tyrol in comparison to those of Europe. It is necessary also to declare that almost all the youth of the right in Germany and in Austria, on the one hand, and in Italy, on the other, have been systematically fascinated by this affair; they have been because both the Italian and Austrian governments seek to keep unruly young people occupied.

The Austrian and Italian nationalists, as stupid as bulls, charge at a mule with a red cape, and have a brawl about a very small affair in reality. During this time the youth of the right leave the corrupt regimes in Italy and in Austria in peace. The distraction organised by the regime is remarkably profitable! This is the perfect case of distraction wished for by democratism to dissipate the forces that should historically be hostile to them.

The youth of the right make fools of themselves both in South Tyrol and in Belgium, where they are excited by a question of a linguistic pseudo-frontier.

Every time it is a matter of the trees hiding the forest. The forest is Europe with all its immense problems.

The unruly young people of the extreme right should worry more about the Red Army in Budapest than about the Italian policemen in Bolzano; the Flemish youth should smear the street names written in French a little less and study a little more the colonisation of Flanders and Western Europe by American capitalism.

Linguistic quarrels, religious quarrels, all those will be regulated after the reunification of Europe. Those who today dissipate the forces of the youth in fruitless actions are imbeciles or criminals. To take away combatants from the struggle for liberation and for the reunification of Europe, to waste them in petty local affairs, is a politically absurd act.

The Achilles Heel of Communism

Communist imperialism never managed to assimilate Eastern Europe. For almost twenty years already it has made a permanent indigestion of it. The insurgents of Pilsen, Poznan, Berlin and Budapest have saved the honour of Europe. Subjected to the most bloody police terror, they have fought. During this time, Eastern Europe, chloroformed by a stultifying press, wallowed in immediate material pleasures.

Our historic role will consist in encouraging all the secessions of the Communist bloc, all the new 'Titoisms' that could arise therein.

Our revolutionary mission is to prepare, organise, nourish SYSTEMATICALLY all the anti-Russian rebellions and insurrections in Eastern Europe. The role of the fighting part of captive Europe will be to undermine the entire Soviet apparatus in Eastern Europe.

The day will come when the few arms imprudently confided by Moscow to our brothers of the East will be used against the occupier and oppressor. An amnesty without restrictions will be accorded to the Eastern Europeans who have been misled or misguided in the Communist imperialism of Moscow and who will make amends by participating in the liberation of our Eastern provinces.

Before our flags fly in the wind in the streets of Bucharest, the peoples of the East will have opened the path through popular insurrection. It is probably the popular masses of our Eastern provinces who will free themselves to the degree that hope and encouragement and then effective aid comes from the West.

The Achilles heel of Moscow is the popular masses oppressed by the Red tyranny. Without employing the nuclear bomb, through the means of revolutionary strike and popular insurrection alone the Soviet occupier will be driven out.

Europe will make peace with Russia only on the day that its flag will fly on the west bank of the Dniester.

In this regard the treaties of Moscow of the summer of 1963 and the deliveries of American wheat to Moscow in the course of the winter of 1963–1964 constitute a veritable assault on the morale of our 130 million captive brothers in the East. By discouraging our compatriots of the East by a spineless policy of the West towards Moscow, we deprive ourselves of a terrific and magnificent instrument of combat against the Muscovite oppressor.

The revolutionary potential that the suffering and the anger of 130 million prisoners of Communism represent is considerable. It is capable of confronting at least 50 Russian divisions.

Politicians blinded by stupidity or trembling with cowardice can only calm the USSR.

The development of cordial relations with the USSR, when it still occupies all our Eastern provinces, is a crime against oneself, a suicide. The Achilles heel of Communism is Eastern Europe. Now it is our politicians who wish to deprive themselves of the arrow that could kill the occupier.

Eastern Europe, the prisoner of Moscow, can become a powder keg to the extent that it receives encouragement, moral and later material, from the West.

This policy demands a commentary: it is that Europe should be really European and not, as I have emphasised elsewhere, French or German. In the latter case, that of a 'German Europe', we would be deprived of the possibility of attacking Moscow on its own terrain, for we would render our brothers of the East afraid of a rebirth of a certain Germanism. My German friends should not be offended by my remarks, which contain nothing hurtful for them. There is so much mistrust to be extinguished in all parts of Europe and a German Europe would be a historical catastrophe, for it would cause us to lose our Eastern provinces.

The weak point, one of the rare vulnerable points of the Russian Empire, is Eastern Europe. That is its Achilles heel.

Let us therefore prepare Paris' arrow.

The Necessity of the Simultaneity of the Preparation of the Apparatus and of the Ideology in the East and in the West

The European national revolution could present a breaking point either first in the East or first in West. It is necessary therefore to prepare oneself both in the East and in the West. This preparation demands a synchronisation of ideological work and, within this framework, one should, already now, foresee theoretically the conditions of political and economic fusion of the two halves of Europe torn apart for twenty years. One should, already now, envisage the modalities of the merging of the institutions and structures of our Eastern provinces and of our Western provinces. On the economic level, in Eastern Europe, the industries that are the property of the Communist state will be denationalised and will be returned to the managers and the workers, factory by factory. State capitalism will be broken and will make way for the prosperity of the producers. In the West, the American financier capitalism will be ousted. The domination of the economy of Europe by American finance makes the economic fusion of the two Europes—in its present condition—*a priori* impossible. It is necessary therefore as a precondition to break this domination.

The liberal-plutocratic structures of Western Europe rightly make suspicious many of our brothers of the East. Eastern Europe does not want to fall from Charybdis to Scylla, that is to say, from the exploitation of the Russian state to the exploitation of the American financial capitalism.

To arouse hope, and then the revolutionary will, in our Eastern provinces it is necessary to first instal Communitarian structures in the West.

The Communist world is no longer, since the death of Stalin, impermeable, it is even eager for the currents of ideas coming from the West. We should not underestimate the possibilities of ideological infiltration of our European theses through the Communist delegations, commercial fairs and tourism. Every time that the Communists organise — in a neutral country — one of their ideological fairs, of the 'Festival of Youth' sort, the European Party should be present there with its materials and its activists familiarised with the problems of the occupied countries. There are a hundred other possibilities. In the West, the political refugees coming from our Eastern provinces constitute an ideal terrain for the penetration of our ideas and for the recruitment of resolute men. Tens of thousands of them have personally suffered in Communist jails; for them there is no 'right Communism'. The integrated European Party should therefore pay particular attention to an enrolment from the ranks of refugees from the East.

We will in this way be able to prepare in the East structures and managerial forces, which will be sufficient at the desired moment to place in the liberated countries. The external resistance of our brothers of the East should be prepared by the European Party installed in the West. This external resistance is capable, through its origin, of establishing all the links with the internal resistance of the countries which are at present under the Muscovite yoke. The fusion of the two Europes will constitute a remarkable success from the fact of the complementarity of their economies. Industrial hypertrophied Western Europe and in agricultural undercapacity, for its population, is the perfect and ideal complement of underindustrialised and agricultural Eastern Europe. The Danubian wheat, the Serbian maize, the Hungarian chicken, wait to be exchanged for Swiss watches, French automobiles, German tractors. The raw materials that are lacking in the West are found in the East and wait for our transforming industries: Romanian petrol, raw leather from the Balkans, Yugoslav copper, Polish coal.

It would be erroneous to foresee, *a priori*, the organisation of Western Europe and only then the reconquest of our Eastern provinces. Nothing makes us exclude the possibility that unitarian Europe may arise simultaneously in the East and in the West, *nothing also makes us exclude a priori that the European revolution may begin in the East*. In fact, one will find men of the calibre of rebellious workers from Berlin, Poznan, Pilsen and Budapest — which is difficult to do in a Western Europe debilitated by comfort.

The Modern Party of Combat, after Having Ensured Its Ubiquity and Its Mobility, Will Look for a Local Breaking Point

A second Budapest uprising, a second Pilsen or Poznan revolt, a second East Berlin insurrection, remain possible and even probable. One should, on the basis of this eventuality, prepare, even now, a centralised, structured, hierarchical European Party, that is to say, an apparatus ready for immediate intervention. Historically, it is almost certain that this apparatus will be called on in times of crisis or in times of panic — by the events themselves — to substitute our rulers, who are excessively hesitant, excessively cowardly, excessively compromising, or quite simply excessively subjugated to an extra-European power. The political animal that rules over Europe is certainly clever in behind-the-scenes manoeuvres, in bargaining, in trafficking influence; by contrast, faced with a grave historical event, it is inhibited before the importance of responsibilities.

Made to reign, this animal is incapable of commanding.

In Budapest in 1956, they lacked only 10,000 volunteers from the West, but 10,000 organised ones, arriving in structured groups, with their cadres, their hierarchies. If there had been only 100,000 who had come individually, their intervention would have served nothing but to augment the confusion.

It is in this view that we should be able to align, in a few years, one of these corps of '10,000 organised people', whom we should introduce and rush in, when the first fissure appears in the Communist bloc of Eastern Europe — combatants, cadres, technicians of the press, agitators, and no longer watch as passive spectators the agony of the workers rebelling in Berlin, Poznan, Budapest and Pilsen.

A modern European Party will have the double mission of devoting itself in the West to the legal struggle and of preparing itself in the East for the secret struggle. At the first signal, at the first call from our brothers of the East, we should be able to respond by sending supervised, organised and equipped free corps.

The ridiculous parties of the extreme right are incapable of fulfilling this mission and even of envisaging it. At best their authority does not go beyond the borders of their own petty nationalism and, besides, they do not wish to go beyond them. The extreme right constitutes in this regard the bunch of incapable persons: jealous people, informers, psychopaths, compulsive liars, backward-looking people, anarchists. Their only historical usefulness is to constitute a bogeyman that Communism uses with mastery.

The 'International of nationalists' makes one laugh at their structures based on the obsession of a ferocious national independence. Disloyalty is there a rule and the principle of work consists in talking badly of their 'associates' and trying to rob them of their members. Thus all the agitation, in Europe, in the nationalist circles, consists in modifying the divisions of groups, but the entirety is never modified. Group A robs 10 members from group B, from group C 20 militants slide towards group D. But when one adds up the total of groups A, B, C and D, it has been invariable for 15 years. Authority has only been degraded these fifteen years. One should know that to get 10 members to leave organisation A, group B had to promise a GREATER autonomy to these 10 defectors in order to be sure of them. Thus from abandon to desertion, from felony to perfidy, authority has been frittered away, atomised. The extreme right has voluntarily entered into its Middle Ages. Its only activity derives from the field of slander and calumny. The German federal police has counted more than 500 of these imbecile or vicious groups, who denounce and excommunicate one another through modest photocopied bulletins. Still tolerable if they are not informers paid by the numerous police agencies.

The coordination[41] of these tiny groups of anarchists of the right is fundamentally impossible. Even if one manages it in some way, the coordination would tear apart as soon as its balance becomes precarious. Thus coordination will never occur.

What one should substitute this myth of the 'coordination of anti-Communist forces' (?) with is an integrated, centralised party. Integration is the only solution. Does one imagine a 'coordinated' army? No! Then how does one believe in the efficacy of a 'coordinated' political movement?

One of the characteristics of an integrated party is its ubiquity.

It is present everywhere in Europe. It has ears everywhere, it has eyes everywhere. It spreads an identical doctrine everywhere and applies identical orders. This is a body with a hundred ears, a hundred eyes, but with a single mouth and, especially, a single head.

The Catholic Church, Freemasonry, the Communist Party, have given us concrete and edifying examples of this. The Protestant sects, the intellectuals of the 'left' and the nationalists have presented negative examples and constitute living warnings.

A young Spaniard, not very malicious, told me one day that 'the defence of the Angola position did not interest him because it did not pay (that is, electorally) in his country'. That is a strategy of horse traders at the canton fair.

---

41 The term alludes to the term *Gleichschaltung* used in National Socialist Germany to indicate a totalitarian control, or coordination, of all aspects of society.

The problem is not to know what 'pays' (in the short term) but what can contribute to the large common design.

As long as the French 'nationalists' will not be ready to participate in a revolt in East Berlin, as long as the German 'nationalists' will be incapable of doing anything else but bloody puerilities in South Tyrol, their combative power will remain zero.

The conception of political war of all these impotent people of the right constrains them to being able — and want — only to defend their own little fort. They dig little trenches around their puerile positions and crouch there waiting for the Communist 'attack', which will never come — and for a reason — for it will pass disdainfully around them. All the freaks of Flemish nationalism or of Wallonian nationalism in Belgium, of the morbid anti-Gaullism in France, of the holy war in South Tyrol in Germany and Austria, are combatants without any worth in the GLOBAL struggle against Communism. Can you imagine a German soldier who will fight only on the express and formal condition that he will not be stationed outside Bavaria, can you imagine an Italian soldier whose enrolment would guarantee that he would never be stationed outside Alto Adige?[42] That makes you laugh?

But this is what these jokers of the extreme right, these 'nationalists', these naïve people, these Bismarckians, these Maurrassians, or followers of d'Annunzio, do. Their pathetic forces are not only dispersed but, more seriously, they are UNAVAILABLE outside a local, chauvinist, provincial petty combat.

All the efforts of an integrated European Party will consist in making all these soldiers of little forts, all these little trench armies, come out of their individual holes to make of them a manoeuvrable mass, to 'motorise' them in a way, to transform them into a group of MOBILE combat always available NO MATTER WHERE the need is felt. The hundreds of little groups asleep at their crenellations must be substituted with an integrated combat group extremely

---

42   See above p. 38n.

coherent and extremely mobile. It is a mobile war that we should offer to Communism, given our relative numerical weakness. Mobility alone will be able to compensate for this numerical inferiority.

If tomorrow a new insurrection breaks out in Budapest, an integrated movement will be capable of mobilising 10,000 men between Stockholm and Lisbon, between Naples and Dublin — in the space of a week. Only an integrated party will be able to do that.

By contrast, let us imagine a 'coordinated' group of spouting nationalists, negotiating their intervention, some demanding honours, others demanding counter-parties, the latter declaring that that does not interest them. The Red Army would have once more crushed the revolt in 6 months before the first fifty 'nationalists' are yet in Vienna! No! One should constitute an integrated party capable of mobilising, on order, free corps both in Denmark and in Portugal — for a fight taking place in Italy as well as in Berlin.

The integrated European National Party is to the 'coordination of nationalists' what a mechanised and armoured division is to a small fort army corps. Breaking points we will have many in the next twenty years, we need not worry at all about this.

What is important above all is to create the instrument of mobile intervention.

It is necessary that at a sign. a veritable swarm of wasps strikes our enemies at a place where, the moment before, some isolated wasps could relieve or quieten their vigilance on account of their derisory number.

The Unity of Europe around an Integrated Party

In the past the unity of dozens of nations was constructed around a dynasty, in the past the West of the High Middle Ages survived thanks to the spiritual unity around the Catholic Church. Tomorrow the unity of Europe will be constituted around a party.

This party, the veritable microcosm of the future Europe, should present first the qualities which will later be demanded of our entire Fatherland-Continent. No question of reconstituting, within this party, the present petty national divisions and of encouraging there a 'Spanish section' or tolerating an 'Italian section'. That would be to introduce into the microcosm-party of the future the vices of impotence of present Europe crossed by so many 'annoying' currents. One should tolerate in this integrated European Party only militants of French character, militants of German character, but in no case allow the development of a relative autonomy of a 'French branch' or of a 'German branch'.

The utilisation of 'existing nationalisms' to create the European nationalism is a myth cherished by the timid, the backward-looking, or opportunists, who look for an easy clientele.

European nationalism will arise only after having dissolved or crushed the old nationalisms.

Within the integrated European Party it will be easier to make a young socialist militant a good European nationalist than to transform a French petty nationalist into a European nationalist.

As for 'nationalism in itself', that is a fantasy. Either one speaks of a French nationalism or of European nationalism! The pseudo-ideological salad, which tries to make one believe in an abstract nationalist type of man, in a sort of metaphysical nationalist, in a sort of elf, smacks of political mythology but not of politics.

Let us return to the integrated party around which the whole of Europe should coagulate. This party should offer a living model of the future Europe. Within this party, no more question of feeling oneself French or Portuguese, other than in one's origin or language. When it will be necessary to suppress within the Party the anti-European deviations, the 'provincial' deviations like South Tyrolism, or the Flemish movement or the anti-Neapolitan racism of certain Englishmen, the first volunteers for these tasks of repression will be, in the order, precisely the militants of Austrian origin, the militants of Flemish origin, the militants of English origin.

In this integrated party there is no question of tolerating a qualificatory racism within Europe. I know some young Germans who think that they are combatants for Europe but tremble still at the idea that a Sicilian could marry their sister; I know some young 'European' militants living in France who think in their heart of hearts that they are intrinsically superior to the Belgian militants. The former are inspired by an inadmissible Germanic racism, the latter by a patriotic chauvinism issuing from their subconscious.

It will be very difficult, perhaps very long, for many to bend to such rules of renunciation of the old petty nationalisms. This, however, is the condition *sine qua non* of the cohesion and the dynamism of a real European Party. To the extent to which the practice of languages will permit it, the cadre and the militants should be interchangeable throughout Europe.

Every militant, no matter where he comes from or who he might be, participates in all of Europe, and not only in one 'party' of this Europe.

In this view — within the integrated Party, there cannot be any question of militants of Italian origin — for example — refusing the command of a leader of Danish origin insofar as this leader of Nordic origin can command them in Italian and insofar as he had beforehand been 'de-Danished' and designated by the central apparatus. And vice versa a hundred times in all directions.

A Jesuit obeys the Order and not his country of origin. A European militant will owe fidelity, loyalty and dedication to Europe, and not to his country of origin.

For the Jesuit, the hierarchy of fidelities is the Order, then Catholicity, and then his country of origin.

For the militant of an integrated European Party, the hierarchy of fidelities will be the Party, Europe, and then his country of origin.

A time will come when the Party and Europe will be interchangeable. But at the start, at the risk of suffering the dissolving actions that reign within the present invertebrate Europe, the fidelity to the Party, avantgarde of Europe, must have priority. Thus the European man, the European nationalist will exist beforehand for a long time within the Party before existing in Europe itself. The integrated Party should be the prefiguration of Europe. When the Capetians created unified France, there were no 'French nationalists'. The latter followed the former several centuries later. Just as the Capetians created France, the integrated European Party will create Europe.

Yesterday it was around a House, tomorrow it will be around an avantgarde party. Europe will be able to be joined together only around a party filled with the faith of a religious order and the discipline of a military order.

In Conclusion: Eight Theoretical Paths to Form Europe, of Which Seven Are Bad and One Possible

First path: that of a Europe realised by a preponderant nation.

The unity of Europe will not be formed around a country. France tried it with Bonaparte, Germany failed with Hitler. Gaullist France has fewer chances of succeeding in this operation. This formula contains the mortal seed of the reactivation of all the old petty nationalisms in reaction to the unifying nationalism.

Second path: that of a Europe dominated by a race.

The unity of Europe will not be formed around a race that is privileged within it. We condemn as vicious and dangerous the conception either of a Germanic Europe or a Latin or Mediterranean Europe. All the mystical strength National Socialist Germany had drawn in its racism was largely compensated and cancelled by the distrust and then the hatred aroused among the neighbouring peoples, among the occupied peoples, among other European peoples. Slavs, Latins, Germanic peoples are for us Europeans of equal worth.

Third path: that of a Europe negotiated by the political hucksters.

This is a formula that contains its contradiction in itself. The present politicians draw their influence from the divisions of Europe. These divisions multiply, besides the number of honorary positions. How does one reasonably ask these men to destroy what constitutes their influence, what nourishes them? One cannot create the unity of Europe with people for whom the creation and the maintenance of divisions constitute their professional *raison d'être*.

Fourth path: that of a Europe of petty nationalists.

The unity of Europe will not be formed with the assistance of petty nationalists attached sentimentally — and also through lack of creative imagination — to obsolete ideas of a fatherland of memory, a fatherland of custom, a fatherland of the cemetery. Their egoisms and their meanness cause them to detest and envy their European neighbours so much that they prefer to servilely suffer the American tutelage rather than merge into a unified Europe. They refuse the European supranationality but they accept in fact the American supranationality. Some of these nationalists have covered themselves with European labels and use them to encapsulate old reactionary and petty nationalist conceptions. Europe is a concept that bears a dynamism capable of attracting the youth. Thus the reactionaries of the right have taken possession of it with the sole aim of harvesting a clientele. The insincerity of their European attitude immediately betrays them in the eyes of a man who is somewhat informed and warned.

Fifth path: that of a Europe desired or wished for spontaneously by the masses.

The unity of Europe will not be created from the will of the masses for the very basic reason that the masses do not and will never have a political will when they are not organised. There exists neither a spontaneous revolutionary nor a spontaneous unifier among the masses. An apparatus of organisation is necessary to motivate them. They will

VII. HOW UNITARIAN EUROPE WILL BE FORMED

wish for Europe when they have been organised and directed by an avantgarde party. But the unifying will expressed by the masses will then only be the megaphone of the will of the avantgarde party.

Sixth path: Atlanticist Europe or a Europe duped by the Americans.

The antagonism of the European and American interests does not allow one to contemplate this path for a single instant, except for those who are not repelled by subordination. Europe is not the state of Panama. All of the recent past condemns the policy of a Europe towed by America. The United States has, with a remarkable constancy, acted EVERYWHERE and always against Europe since Yalta: Algeria, Katanga, Indochina, Suez. Everywhere and always, as far as the future is concerned, terrible contradictions between the American and European capitalisms oblige us to say that the United States and we will tomorrow be antagonists, both in Africa and in Latin America. Atlanticist Europe is a colony of exploitation for American finance and American politics. That we reject.

Seventh path: institutional Europe, born of the Treaty of Rome of March 1957.

Of the seven chances just sketched, this is evidently the least bad. The spirit of the Treaty is excellent. It only lacks the political spirit to realise itself. It is not the weak and instable political powers of the present petty nations who will be able to realise the Treaty of Rome to its completion. The Treaty of Rome is an excellent idea, which waits to be fertilised by a force that none of the present democratic regimes is capable of arousing.

Eighth path: that of the integrated European party, of the avantgarde party.

This is the only solution capable of giving to Europe an elite destined to form a cadre. The integrated, centralised, homogeneous European Party — rejecting from within it, through its structures, all the vestiges of petty nationalisms — is the only one with the power, through its ubiquity, its discipline, its monolithic character, to prefigure the European state. This integrated European Party will be the microcosm on which will be traced later the European state.

A long time before the European masses feel integrated, the militants of the Party will have acquired this awareness deeply; much before the present political borders of the petty nations are formally effaced, the Party will have swept them away in its internal structures.

Europe will pre-exist within the integrated European Party. It is around this avantgarde Party that the European masses will be first agglomerated and then organised.

CHAPTER VIII

THOSE WHO WILL CONSTITUTE EUROPE OR THE MODERN PARTY

THAT IS TO SAY, ORGANISATION INTRODUCED INTO POLITICS

In this way power passes continuously from its weakened possessor to the one who merits it more.

Sallust

No revolution produces stable results if it does not give birth to a Caesar. Only he is capable of divining the underground historical current behind the ephemeral clamour of the masses. The masses in general do not understand him and do not grant him any recognition. However, they serve only him.

José Antonio Primo de Rivera (1935)

All great actions, all great thoughts, have a ridiculous beginning.

Albert Camus

They did not hope that the unity of Europe would ever be realised by garrulous politicians, who owe their importance and their fortune to its division. It was, for him, as if one would have confided to the button-maker the publicity of the zip.

Alexis Curvers

It is enough that it has a project of its own existence for a nation to exist.

José Ortega y Gasset

A state is first of all an idea, a historical conception.

Jacques Doriot (Congress of the PPF, 1942)

A movement that would, in the second half of the 20th century, like to mark Europe with its signature would not have to look for nor fear an adjective. And it can rest assured that history, if it wrote some pages about it, would give it a proper name.

François Gaucher

The Need for an Instrument

ALL THE ELEMENTS necessary for the formation of Europe as a large unified state have now come together. The moment is indisputably historic. Before 2000, Europe will have been born, resuming after a break of fifteen centuries the role played by Rome.

All the conditions required for the birth of a nation are before us. The humiliations suffered from Batavia to Léopoldville, through Algiers and Tunis, have shown that our weak and corrupt leaders were not equal to the situation.

The demonstration of their incompetence, their weakness, their spinelessness, is not required to be made any longer. Lucid people have known that since 1945. The present rulers are in fact, both in France and in Belgium, the defeated of 1940 returned in the ammunition trucks of the Anglo-Saxon victors of 1945. But in no case did they have the calibre to be the victors of 1945 — except the small clan of the first resistance fighters of 1940–41. The present Italian and German rulers were born in the collaboration with the Anglo-Saxon occupier and, without the latter, would never have existed.

The European legitimacy of all the politicians is not only contested, it is rejected in advance. Hirelings do not create any aristocracy. Not any more than the Koblenz group[1] could claim to represent France in 1795, the Londoners claim to represent Europe in 1941. Two giants

---

1 Many of the aristocrats who fled Revolutionary France grouped together in Koblenz around Louis XVI's brother, the Comte de Provence and future king

tried to recreate the Roman Empire, in fifteen centuries, moved by the obsession of the unity to be recovered. The Popes caused the first to fail, the nationalists the latter. The Europe of Bonaparte perished because it was too French, essentially French; the Europe of Hitler failed because it was too German, essentially German.

In both cases, the construction was vitiated from the beginning and contained in itself the seeds of its future defeat.

Today the situation has changed. The petty nationalisms are moribund as real powers, and that is the unique historic chance for Europe. Apart from some starchy eccentrics, nobody can seriously believe any more in the 'greatness' of France alone, or in the greatness of 'Germany above all'. Similarly, everybody knows that there will never be any Franco-German war, never a civil war in Europe. I insist on this aspect of the problem. In 1939 — only thirty years ago — France, which possessed an empire, England, which possessed another, and Germany, which possessed illusions (as regards the wheat of the Ukraine), could still, with good logic, and with good accounting, hope to succeed separately in great hegemonic adventures.

Today France has lost Syria, Indochina, Tunisia, Morocco, Algeria, black Africa; today England has lost India and Egypt, today the Germans know — finally — that just an attempt to drive towards the Ukraine would weld together the entire Slavic bloc against them, from Prague to Belgrade.

Thus the English and French Europes that were developed during three centuries, principally in a maritime style, from Virginia to Australia and from the Caribbean to Indochina, are going to, by the force of history, to have to envisage now a continental vocation. To concretise the latter they need the collaboration of all.

The first great principal element of the present situation is thus the disappearance of small nationalisms. In itself it justifies the greatest possibilities. The second element is the permanent humiliation

---

Louis XVIII. One of these aristocrats, the Prince de Condé, even formed an émigré army that assisted foreign powers in their wars against France.

suffered by our peoples under the reign of the weak puppets who rule us for the benefit of the occupiers: American in the West, Russian in the East. An excess of humiliation is a good thing for waking up certain people. The third element is that Europe does not possess any political personality in relation to its remarkable economic power. *The bruised and worn out Europe of 1945 could, in the minds of some, resign itself to a fate of effacement; the Europe in economic expansion of 1964 cannot be satisfied with remaining a political satellite.*

The fourth favourable element to our designs is that our enemies are occupied, preoccupied with problems that will not stop worsening. The yellow man in the East and the black American are going to give a hard time to our occupiers. The Chinese affair is only beginning. Moscow will pay dearly for the blunders of its Panslavic nationalist politics. The latter has awoken the dragon: Chinese nationalism.

The Kremlin will have to reduce its ambitions in the East, in Europe, in exact proportion to Peking's demands. All of European politics will consist in paying for the respite or peace which Moscow needs. All of the present tragedy resides in the fact that Moscow negotiates with Washington instead of negotiating with us. The essential condition for a reversal of this situation unfavourable for us consists in the total eviction of the Americans from Europe. After the Americans are ejected from Europe, Moscow will have to negotiate with us. For the moment, logically, it has discussions with our 'tutor'.

The black problem is going to poison the USA for probably a good half century. It is a problem of an insoluble type. The white population will never accept miscegenation or integration. In this question the reflexes of self-defence of the species will play a role on which all propaganda will have no deep effect. We wish our American 'friends' much fun with their negroes.

The superior races have always tolerated the survival of inferior or defeated races only to the extent that they needed them for a certain form of exploitation. If this exploitation is impossible, and that is the example of the redskins, one proceeds to extermination. If this exploitation is possible, and that WAS the case with the negroes, one accepts their conservation and cohabitation. But the moment that the exploitation is no longer possible, even if it were only on the salarial level, the inferior element is rejected from society. When 20 million blacks considered as inferior by 98% of the white Americans wish to have access to all positions, the reaction will in the first place be organised by the workers' trade unions. The black ulcer adhering to the USA is going to suppurate in the next decades and arouse turmoils such that Washington will have to considerably reduce its claims to dominate the international political game.

Sooner or later, the exacerbation of passions will cause the blacks to receive aid and arms from the Chinese (for China, like Europe, is interested in bringing the USA down). What will the reaction of the white Americans who, since Buffalo Bill, have a rapid Winchester, be?

Not only is the USA going to experience the black problem, but an economic crisis lies in wait and finally Latin America constitutes the best terrain that there is to weaken and threaten Washington at low cost.

In Latin America, everybody will begin to proceed to a 'de-Yankeeisation', the Chinese and Europeans openly, Russians in secret. This is a confirmed fact. It is to the Europeans to draw a benefit from it first for fear of seeing their Communist adversaries profit from it.

It is in Latin America that the dollar imperialism earned its stripes in the second half of the 19th century. It is in Latin America that the Yankees will be confronted with the mistake of their international ambitions. They know that in Peking. They know that in Moscow. We know that also. Thus, to summarise, the conditions are favourable for the flourishing of Europe to the degree that our two occupiers, Russian and American, are going to be led to pay more attention to other theatres of operation. Chinese diversion for the Russians, negro diversion and Latin America for the Yankees. All the passive conditions for forming Europe have been brought together. It remains now to examine the active conditions.

VIII. THOSE WHO WILL CONSTITUTE EUROPE OR THE MODERN PARTY

In spite of the extremely favourable — it has never been so — 'passive' situation, Europe cannot arise through SPONTANEOUS GENERATION![2] One must be naïve to believe that the peoples DEMAND Europe; or to believe that our present rulers WISH it. To the peoples of Europe, we 'THE TEAM' should transmit the awareness of the political Europe that we already possess. As for the present rulers, tied to the occupiers by their betrayals, limited by their small personal statures, they have neither the possibility nor the strength to cause Europe to be born.

The active condition necessary for the birth of a historic Europe resides in the direction of affairs by a determined and homogeneous political team, knowing from the start what they want, determined to sweep away everything that could hinder their design.

The entire present chapter will be devoted to defining some conditions indispensable for the construction of an efficient INSTRUMENT, of a political apparatus: a team at the start, a party finally. Our experience derives principally from the fact that we — sometimes an actor, at other times a spectator in the best boxes[3] — have been able to analyse the drama of the mistake of French Algeria. Almost all the errors that could have been committed were from 1958 to 1962. In fact, French Algeria was constantly the fact of men who followed events. We want that the cause of Europe be that of men who precede, prepare and give birth to the fact. The difference therefore is not only one of degree but of kind.

---

2 Spontaneous generation is an obsolete scientific theory that maintained that living organisms could arise from inanimate matter like dust or dead flesh. The theory was mainly disproven by Louis Pasteur's experiments in the nineteenth century.

3 I.e. the boxes in a theatre.

The Historical Presence of the Conscious and Organised Team in All Seizures of Power

Examples abound. Let us take that of Communist China. Its present leaders are the survivors of the first combatants of the thirties.

Today, in Yugoslavia, the highest dignitaries of the regime met in the underground in 1941 and 1942. The masters of Algeria, similarly, were already a team in 1954, when they were still able only to pay for the murder of one postman or one school teacher every week.

The most influential leaders of the National Socialist Party met one another at the beginning in the beer cellars and in the street fights around 1920.

All those who have been up to the peaks, up to the end, were at first in the grassroots of the recruitment and present at the beginning of the adventure. *The power team emerges in fact from the 'derisory start'.* There is nothing surprising in this phenomenon and can be explained easily. The men who perceive a historic opportunity first are gifted with a greater historic acuity. They see what others cannot yet distinguish. They show in this the quality of a leader. On the other hand, they give evidence of a much greater physical and moral courage by participating in a risky, if not dangerous, enterprise. They are neither short-sighted nor resigned. They see far and never accept submission. It is thus quite logical that the 'first' are the most muscled — in terms of intelligence and character. It is quite JUST that it is the most muscled who take the lead and keep it. The laws of selection have drawn out here a real elite. These men, having lived through the dark and difficult years, once they attain power, are not rulers who are easy to fool or timid. This is the explanation of the Chinese miracle.

China of 1930 was for every objective observer a territory torn apart, plunged into the Middle Ages and its history seemed to have been written only for the sake of the games of imperialistic foreigners, the Japanese first of all. Lamentable economy, total political dispersal, military asthenia. China was prey and a booty, not a nation. Its situation was somewhat analogous to that of Turkey of 1910, but darker. Thirty years later, Peking struck its fists on the table of the international game and everybody began to be worried.

Thus the will of some dozens of men drew out of the void, after a long and often discouraging struggle, six hundred million men. The will of a team forged in adversity.

The odyssey of these exceptional men defies our auguries and the good sense of our dull petty bourgeois. Almost all the conditions for failure were objectively united in 1930.

It was at that time an adventure of desperate men, an attempt of 'madmen'.

A determined team caused the sensed forecasts to be belied, the will defeated calculation.

Today, China has at its disposal an extremely homogeneous and determined ruling elite. The miracle of the rise of China derives essentially from the high quality characteristics of its leaders.

Tomorrow, Europe will be created and directed by the men who believed in it and by those who lived it already, in their hearts and minds, in 1956 and 1962.

For those who do not see Europe are blind cowards and one never makes leaders of those who have a narrow vision or easy fear.

Command Is Not an Effect but a Cause

The image maintained by many weak-willed people, who consider themselves revolutionaries, is that intelligence or indignation, or even the two combined, are capable of coagulating the 'healthy' elements of the nation which, after having 'spontaneously' coalesced together, would designate or elect a leader or leaders.

The procedure is ALWAYS the reverse. In the creation of a nation, command is not a phenomenon that follows but a phenomenon that precedes. Power in itself is not an effect but a cause.

The historical awareness of the revolutionary team precedes, at a great distance, that of the masses. Similarly, the awareness of the future and possible event rises in the mind of the leaders much earlier than in that of the men who constitute their team. That is a quite natural hierarchy of revolutionary chronology.

The event is felt in advance and willed by a man or by a handful of men. Later, it is announced and started by a revolutionary team. In order that men might follow, it is necessary that men precede — this is not a statement of the obvious — and the will to command and guide precedes, in time, the will to follow and obey. The idealised image of valiant soldiers or revolutionaries forcing one of their modest companions to accept the position of leader is stupid and false. The leaders exist before the revolution. It is for this reason that they are leaders.

The will to command is a political factor clearly more active than the will to follow suit, and it is this active character, this vigour, that determines the order of appearance of the phenomena on the stage at first, in the hierarchy later.

William the Conqueror, before being the conqueror, was only from Normandy and it would be absurd to see in him the instrument called forth by a metaphysical England that was looking for a leader and new blood! William created historical England and it was not England that called for him! At first there was the pure will of a single man: William. A little later, this will was surrounded by appetites and other desires for expansion: the team of Normans. From the team of Normans emerged modern England. Born in fact from the will of a single man — who, we may add, was himself probably not able to measure the full scope of his gesture. De Gaulle preceded Gaullism, Hitler National Socialism.

In other chapters we develop in detail the idea that the unifying will created nations, then these nations AFTERWARDS possessed a 'patriotism' or nationalism.

All the intellectuals of the right who make nationalism their livelihood are not of the calibre of those who found nations. They are much more similar to the café owners who today sell postcards at Waterloo. To create is to make something which did not exist — this is not a statement of the obvious either — with disparate elements, which often baulk. The great historic constructions were built by the imposition of a centripetal centralised force, to divided, hesitant and sometimes hostile groups. France was created most of the time against the patriotic 'Frenchmen' of the time. The contemporaries of Philippe Auguste did not know yet Maurras or Déroulède.

The only case where the leader is elective or designated by a formal process is that of the societies of ancient structures, possessing homogeneity, a past and traditions.

Then it is necessary to have deeply integrated communities with a state apparatus accepted by all.

Thus, within the reigning families which shared France among themselves in the 12th or 13th century, the power issued more or less from tradition, from the order of succession. These were limited communities and relatively OLD:

Once it was necessary to WISH to think of a unitarian France and it was necessary to WISH for France, it was made by force, by ruse, but never by consent, rule or election. Never indeed! The greater thing NEVER emerges through consent. Every time that one made something greater, gathered together the duchies to create a kingdom, gathered together kingdoms to create an empire, a will was manifested, was imposed, was translated into facts. But the will existed before the historical operation. A man bore the idea.

The corporations of bakers or the democracies which have for too long had formal statutes or rules elect or designate their 'leaders'. Here the community precedes the leaders.

But when it is necessary to make something greater, when it is necessary to make something new, there is no community, there are no statutes or rules that exist beforehand.

Lenin, Tito, Mao, Ben Bella[4] never published the statutes of their enterprise in the official state register … nor, especially, the modalities of rising to power. It was. That is all.

A nation is first a work of imagination, then of will, only then is it a consensus. The nation is imposed, that then is its genesis. It is more or less accepted, it is the nation as a contract. Finally, when it has been accepted for a long time, it becomes a nation as a heritage, a nation as a collective memory. In 1964, France is a nation as a heritage and Europe is not yet a nation as a contract.

Political power of simple management in stable societies can be elective or successional. The political power of creation in societies in genesis or recently created is never that.

A pure will, a power 'in itself' creates a new nation. Much later, perhaps centuries later, the nation can then designate 'leaders' for itself.

Power in itself is command par excellence, it is CREATIVE POWER. 'Elected' power is management. That demands types of men who are essentially distinct. That is the difference that separates a Philip the Fair[5] from a Louis XVI or a Bonaparte from a Guy Mollet,[6] a leader from a notable.

It is superfluous for us to explain further that, for Europe in gestation, a community to be coagulated, it has need of leaders not of managers.

---

4   Ahmed Ben Bella (1916–2012) was an Algerian socialist and revolutionary who became the first President of Algeria in 1963. At the outbreak of the Algerian War in 1954 Ben Bella was in Cairo as an executive member of the *Front de Libération Nationale* which initiated the armed insurrection against the French colonists.

5   See above p. 37n.

6   See above p. 166n.

The rules that apply to a nation in gestation are applicable to the revolutionary parties. They hardly have to worry about holding their annual congress in Vichy or in Brighton; they have better things to do.

The will to command will be the CAUSE of the European National Revolution and will exist before it.

Searching for the Reasons to Act and not Collecting Excuses for Opposition to Change: 'We do not have a Lenin, we do not have a Hitler'

The member or sympathiser or the militant in whom perseverance is lacking in his character will impute the mistake of his section to all causes imaginable except his incompetence. This being so, he imitates the bad travelling salesman who does not sell because he is lazy — but who will say that he does not sell because the merchandise that he was made to sell is of bad quality or too costly.

We see that in the sections of the same movement, where one is developed admirably and the other lamentably. Why look farther than at the quality of the ruling team of a section itself? The reasons are there and not elsewhere.

There is more: certain people in their conscience would like to be provided not only the idea (and that is evidently quite natural) but also the members. Thus there exist these pretenders to a high managerial post who would be ready to 'accept the direction' of one section. It is always those who would, besides, be incapable of FORMING a section.

Mediocre men but infatuated with themselves, it will be necessary to send them away without losing time. That is the classic phenomenon in almost all the political movements.

One of the excuses most frequently used to mask an incapacity or a discouragement is the fact that a movement does not possess 'its Lenin' or 'its Hitler'.

A worthless argument for one who knows history, and the history of political parties in particular. In 1905, Lenin was a polemicist of great talent among dozens of others. Between 1915 and 1917, he slowly emerged and it was still a personage disputed by a number of his collaborators within his own group on the eve of the October Revolution. When the German authorities organised his transfer — during a time of war — between Switzerland and Russia — with other agitators — they thought they had introduced into Russia an element of disintegration of the imperial Russian state. In Brest-Litovsk, Trotsky was treated by the German imperial representatives with an amused and hardly disguised contempt.

In the spring of 1917, when Kerensky shone with his precarious popularity, Lenin was a little intellectual among fifty others. At that time nobody made him the Moses of applied Marxism. What to say then of Stalin crushed, until 1925, by dozens of Bolshevik heads so much more 'brilliant' than him — but so much more inferior ... But who knew it at that time? Who saw it? It is enough to read the life of the Marxist Russian émigrés in exile between 1906 and 1917 to assess what a nest of vipers it was. Trotsky and Lenin, and so many others, devoted the major part of their time excommunicating and hurling insults against one another. That resembled the Talmudic quarrels between the Rabbi of Krakow and the Rabbi of Warsaw.

No police saw in Lenin or Trotsky in 1914 more than agitators AMONG NUMEROUS others. The idols thus never existed before the event — within the event itself they were still disputed — and it is only *a posteriori*, AFTER the event, that they were made 'undisputed leaders' or 'inspired guides'. During their hard combat, these inspired guides were constantly retarded by the envy or blindness of their own fighting comrades. Who took Mao Tse Tung very seriously in 1947 and who read him in French? Who was afraid of Stalin in 1925? Similarly as regards Hitler in 1924. It is enough to reread the few stupid lines that Malaparte[7] devoted to him to realise how CONTEMPORARIES ARE INCAPABLE OF DISCERNING leaders and future orientations. A very important democratic political man, today aged, once confided to me that in 1929, travelling to Berlin, as an invited foreign deputy, one hardly spoke of Hitler, and always as of Poujade[8] in 1962. Nobody thought that this man would hold Germany in his hands five years later. One saw in him only his moustache, which made one laugh, and his Austrian accent. The 'big' political intellectuals who sat in the Reichstag were not even struck by the idea that this man, an 'agitator without diplomas', could one day rule.

In the anti-Communist milieus, Hitler was particularly disputed and of the numerous German nationalist groups many were at that time — in members — more numerous than the National Socialist Party.

The same people who today disguise their laziness as pseudo-militants, their incapacity as pseudo-politicians, under excuses such as 'we don't have a Hitler' or 'we don't have a Lenin' are the same who in 1923 or in 1913 would have systematically refused to follow Hitler and Lenin under the very excuses that they evoke today. They would have said, 'Ah, if we had a Bismarck' or even 'Ah, if we had an Engels'.

Sterile words that hardly hide the refusal of effort, the refusal of discipline, the refusal of work itself. This animal belongs to the 'one needs only...' and 'if I just had...' species.

The failures and the lazy have an inexhaustible arsenal of excuses. Let us not be fooled.

---

7   Curzio Malaparte (né Kurt Erich Suckert) (1898–1957) was an Italian journalist, filmmaker and diplomat, who claimed to be a champion of Fascism though his main interest was Communism. His book *Technique du coup d´etat* (1931) was a study of Bolshevist and Fascist revolutionary techniques and critical of Hitler.

8   Pierre Poujade (1920–2003) was a populist nationalist politician, who propagated anti-parliamentarian and xenophobic ideas. His movement to mobilise small businessmen against the elites was characterized as 'Poujadism'.

Getting Organised before or during

The method of 'spontaneous' recruitment, at least concerning the CADRE, is catastrophic. It contributes to congesting the movement with an extremely high proportion of human refuse, unstable, degraded people, exhibitionists.

By spontaneous recruitment we mean recruitment in the course of the operation, in the thick of the fight. This error was committed notably during the Spanish Civil War, by the Reds, and in North Africa by the OAS.

Improvised recruitment — when one tries to seize the event (when it is necessary in fact to precede it in a good strategy) congests the subversive apparatuses with abnormal people, psychopaths. The stupidities posed by these abnormal people, congenitally unsuited to command, then compromise the good functioning of the operations: one brings in chaos into one's own ranks and one arouses opprobrium in the public opinion. During the war in Spain, the Reds distinguished themselves in this sort of errors: abuses and murders within their own territory and indiscipline while going to the front.

In Algiers and Oran it was the same. The superior authorities of the OAS never had in their hands more than 25% of the sums kept in the banks. The correct plan is the recruitment of a healthy cadre — in times of peace or in quiet times — and the sporadic addition of the mediocre or fanatic elements to the troops at the moment of decisive action.

It is therefore necessary to establish here a formal distinction between the cadre and the troops. It is a widespread error that one can make excellent revolutionaries with asocial people, with 'hard people'. This myth should be denounced. At least we must emphasise it once again for the cadre. With the failures in life, with the crazies of the social order, from the professional unemployed person to the robber through the pimp, one cannot derive anything good for a long time in an operation of scientific subversion. One who has failed in life will, with extremely few exceptions, fail in the revolution. The most persevering, the most disciplined, the most efficient militants are those who find a position easily or are well positioned. This is not a bourgeois prejudice but the lucid observation of the balance of all revolutions.

The 'hard people' with a criminal record contribute sometimes — in brief moments — to courageous revolutionary actions. But if they are taken, they are the first to negotiate and to denounce their comrades. This fact has been repeated a hundred times. If one stops paying them for three months, they will offer their services to the enemy police. Revolution contains so many moments of depression and adversity, and so so many possibilities of discouragement, that it should necessarily be managed by people inspired by an inner force, by faith in the mission that they must accomplish.

Spontaneous recruitment is an easy solution. The smell of gunpowder and the sound of the clarion, the gallantry attract very many people and arouse too many ephemeral vocations. By contrast, cool-headed recruitment is terribly thankless: the candidates are rare.

But the quality of these candidates is so superior. They are inspired by a foreknowledge of the event, by faith in the necessity of the fight and are capable of working without obligatory support of fanaticism.

The preparation of a revolution is anything but fanaticism in the common sense of the word.

This type of men, recruited cool-headedly, calmly, are similar to people who fill their cellars with coal already in August. Those who much later join at the sound of the clarion are similar to the improvident who try to find a coal merchant at the end of November. To the vulgar mind, it seems in fact unthinkable, in the middle of the holidays, that there might still be a winter; it seems unthinkable, in the midst of the present prosperity, that there might be an economic crisis in three years; it seems unthinkable that there might be tomorrow 25% unemployment instead of the present full employment economy.

It was the same people who, in 1946, pontified on the solidity of the regime of Chiang Kai-shek 'aided by the invincible Americans'; it was the same who, in 1953, proclaimed that 'Algeria is not Indochina. It is not the same thing. We shall never [sic] leave one of our provinces'.

Thus the cool-headed recruitment in times of peace, in times of euphoric calm, is quantitatively very difficult. But this recruitment nevertheless constitutes an imperative necessity. Sheltered from the legality of the adversary, under the incredulous smiles of friends, under the amused sarcasm of the regime that thinks it is indestructible, one should patiently and systematically put into place, educate and train the apparatus of the Party. From the very fact of the 'non-fanatic' surrounding psychological conditions, one can hope to arrive only at qualitative results and can never count on quantitative results.

The parties of scientific subversion are then parties of cadre just as the Reichswehr in 1925 was essentially an army of cadre — which in fact camouflaged its officers in the ranks of simple soldiers of the Army of a hundred thousand men, authorised by the Versailles Treaty.

The conclusion is that it is absolutely necessary to be organised BEFORE and especially not during, that it is necessary to establish a precise hierarchy already in peacetime.

An organisation should confront the event with all its hierarchy having been in place for a long time. To wish to improvise a revolution, as the OAS did, is to rush to failure. The OAS was born after the event and tried to engage in it without succeeding. It tackled the Algerian affair 1. without structured cadres, 2. without any doctrine. One should even add that it ended its failed revolution without any doctrine, in the confusion of the sterile democratism of Bidault[9] and the naïve mysticism of Chateau-Jobert.[10]

---

9 Georges-Augustin Bidault (1899–1983) was a French politician, who served as Foreign Minister three times between 1944 and 1954. In 1961 he joined the OAS and was accused of conspiracy and forced into exile in Brazil and Belgium. He returned to France only in 1968 after he was granted amnesty.

10 Pierre Chateau-Jobert (1912–2005) was a colonel of the French Army. In 1962 he was given charge of the OAS in Constantinois, in northern Algeria, by General Salan. In 1965 he was condemned to death for his activities in the OAS but was granted amnesty in 1968.

It would not occur to any ship-owner to take to sea in a ship without having designated, first, its captain or the navigation officers and its equipment. The loose corrective that consists in wishing to use ANOTHER hierarchy, social or military, is ineffective. The OAS wanted to reintroduce quite simply the hierarchy of the French Army into the political hierarchy. It thus gave command 'by right' to generals — because they were generals — when colonels and captains were infinitely more competent to take the subversive operation into their hands.

One should also guard, as against the plague, against opportunists who jump onto a bus that is moving. The same people, who in peacetime thought a revolution or an insurrection impossible and who refused to participate in their preparations, then rise to act as 'leaders'. On the least whim, these people will fail and leave.

The task seems ridiculous. It seems even sometimes aimless, for sure. So much the better, it is that which will notably allow the selection of deep vocations, the characters with foresight and perseverance.

The time of preparation is the 'ridiculous' time. But ridiculous for those who have eyes and cannot see, for those who have a mind and cannot foresee.

The ridiculous time? Ridiculous only for the common people.

We Shall Not Wait for Notables

We despise men who still think, faced with any situation, 'that it is still too early' or 'that it is already too late'.

They try to place themselves in strategic goals in order to disguise their opposition to change, their fear of risk and their lack of appetite for the spirit of enterprise.

All the phraseology with which they surround themselves might sometimes deceive those who have not been warned. Those who have militated a certain time are, by contrast, capable of smelling out these pretentious weak-willed persons. In fact, these pseudo-sage wise people always look for excuses to undertake nothing. The revolution, as soon as it goes beyond intellectual speculation, does not correspond any longer to their inner desires. In which they resemble a little those old gentlemen who dress up, take out and exhibit a pretty woman — reputed to be their mistress — but who return her every evening to her mother without having had any carnal relations with her.

Other bourgeois, so-called sympathisers of the cause, when they are asked to open their purse, baulk, quibble and make demands so ridiculous that they presuppose a desire not to attain them. These people would indeed help the revolution on condition of this and on condition of that. In fact, they would like to buy at a low price shares that are rising and most covered by mortgage security.

It is obviously illusory because where the profit is great, the risk is at least as great. To get rich it was necessary to buy securities of the Mining Union in 1905 and not in 1955. But as soon as a revolution begins its triumph, they are seen returning at a gallop. They are then sometimes surprised that their offers are no longer of interest. It is useless to receive what one can take. *To measure the chances of a revolutionary movement by the yardstick of the attitude of the bourgeois with regard to it, would falsify all serious appreciation. They have a flair for earning money. They singularly lack clairvoyance to discern a revolution that is under way.*

Another classic error that one should denounce, because it is very widespread, is that of those who think that a revolution is signalled by the assembling of notables, chiefs, mandarins or monks of the united society that one wishes to sweep away. The major part of the elite of a society, either through lack of character or quite simply through a short-term interest, is NEUTRAL. This neutral elite '*does not engage in politics*' and is content to be passive but with 'governmental' stability. Certain magistrates served successively Louis XVI, the Revolution, the Empire and the Restoration.[11] With the same diligence, besides. One should not be surprised or angered by that. This neutral elite, more or less fattened, would have everything to lose in compromising itself in a revolutionary enterprise. A revolution that rises to the attack cannot count on it; a revolution installed in its victory should not even call for it; it will itself spontaneously offer its services.

Welfare associations, the Red Cross, or the Blue Cross can solicit the patronage of notables, not a revolutionary organisation.

In reality, in fact, every revolution brings with it a new ruling elite — an elite selected by the rigour of combat that it has just finished after years of struggle and persecution. *Your attention is attracted by the difference between a ruling elite that COMMANDS and a neutral elite that manages*, that administers according to a general guideline received from the former.

The neutral elite takes its place in society in donkey skins;[12] the ruling elite does that by dint of hard work, and that is a euphemism.

In conclusion, we shall say that those who procrastinate, those who wait for the more than improbable rallying round of bourgeois notables, are either seriously mistaken or disguise their wishful thinking or their laziness with falsely rational appearances.

A revolution starts without notables. It buys them afterwards.

---

11 The Bourbon Restoration lasted from the fall of Napoleon in 1814 until the July Revolution of 1830. The two Bourbon Kings who reigned in this period were Louis XVIII and Charles X.

12 Donkey skin is a term derived from the fairy tale "Peau d'Âne" by Charles Perrault (1628–1703). The tale recounts the story of a king who wishes to marry his daughter, who escapes him disguised in the skin of a donkey, which provided the king and his country with gold. A prince later finds her and falls in love with her, despite her unseemly garments.

Beginning Alone and Counting on Oneself

There are people who, placed in the presence of a revolution, in its beginnings, act exactly like boys before the door of a brothel; nudging one another, they say: 'If you go in, I'll go'. Finally none of them goes in.

Similarly, before the idea of a 'long political march', they equivocate with the excuse that 'the others are not yet present'. Being prisoners of gregarious behaviour, they do only what 'the others' do. This as regards men taken individually.

When one observes the conduct of supposedly competing political groups — in fact they are not that because they have different objectives — they can also find an excuse to not disclose their attitude and procrastinate because of the fact that 'they do not rally together'. The selection of a small number occurs with a large number in the beginning.

It is the same for herrings, of which very few reach adult age. It is the same for the human elites, and in particular for the revolutionary elites. It is the same for the revolutionary groups or little groups. A revolutionary group has always been — by necessity — a small group at the start. And it is also an obligation to begin 'alone'. To wait for others, to wait for 'allies', is to act as a follower, not as a precursor. It is especially when a troop gets in gear that it sees its ranks increase. It is like a village fanfare: as long as it is shining its brass, it polarises the attention of some onlookers, but when it gets going and blows into its instruments, the onlookers become, one by one, followers.

Drawing a lesson from this, we shall say that one should not wait to possess an orchestra in full force to get started. Once the march has started, a clarinet, which was missing, will join in and a flautist, who was absent, will join in.

Thus, in one's recruitment technique — this is not valid for combat — the movement should be manifested even with its numbers visibly incomplete, even with its objectives disproportionate and apparently grotesque in relation to its volume.

To defer the start on the excuse that one does not have enough numbers yet is to condemn oneself to definite inaction. Those who are discouraged by the small number do not possess the quality indispensable to real leaders, the capacity to act as 'a desperate number' and that of *doing something not because it has a chance of succeeding but indeed because it must be done.*

The difference between the two sorts of men is easily observable, even in daily life. A man will defend his wife against two rascals without worrying about his numerical inferiority. He will do that because '*it must be done*'.

Similarly, in midwinter, an adult will throw himself into cold water to pull out a friend without waiting for the help of firefighters or an ambulance because '*it must be done*'. It is the sense of active duty.

The enterprise of the European National Revolution is an action that will succeed. It is inscribed in the significance of the life of the nations. But never mind, the moment that a man joins our phalanx, let him know that it bears victory in itself. We do not doubt that the way to this victory will be marked by tombs.

For the man of duty, his engagement should not be determined by the certitude of victory, even when it is for others; his engagement should be an act of faith, an act of duty and his conduct a mission.

Whether he is the second or the 2,000[th] or even the 200,000[th] that joins the formation has no intrinsic significance for men of value. He joins as soon as he knows, he joins as soon as the means of engaging are proposed to him for the first time.

When a courageous man climbs on all fours into a building on fire to pull out a child, he does not worry about knowing if the firefighters, who have been called, are already one kilometre or ten kilometres from the place of the accident.

It is by this conduct that one detects the human elites and the revolutionary elites. *By themselves they do 'what must be done'.*

Irresolute people frequently prove their inertia by speculating on a certain 'burst of honour' of the Army or on a certain vigilance of the Church.

They say then: 'The Army will never allow that to happen', or again: 'The thousand-year-old Church will, in its wisdom and its power, press the brakes in time'.

These are still pseudo-justifications of cowardice and laziness. The Army that 'does not allow this to happen' is a myth. Military people are today — and in particular in the highest ranks — closer to the pension of civil servants, and their sense of honour does not go as far as making them risk their advancement.

The Church is full of progressives and mentally weak people at a political level.

The Army and the Church are quite as corrupted as the rest of our society. The leprosy of weakness has not spared them.

We should begin alone, terribly alone. In any case, one should never think that the counter-current to the present stream of cowardice and surrender will be begun by constituted bodies, either the military, the church or the magistrates. With one little cowardice after the other they will allow things to happen, they will allow everything to happen. With rare exceptions. The rebirth of civic courage in Europe will be begun by a very small avantgarde group: that to which we appeal here.

Then AFTERWARDS, elements of the Army, elements of the Church and elements of the magistrates will regain courage and help us. But the first people will be ALONE, terribly alone.

Passing Rapidly from Order in Ideas to Action: of the 'Byzantines' and the Hydrocephalic Party

A revolutionary movement, at the risk of losing all DYNAMISM, must present as soon as possible to its militants a dialectic sum that is almost definitely fixed. Nothing is more harmful than a fluctuating ideology. The movement must, for example, present some points of dogma related to its action: the territorial integrity of Europe, a unitarian political character, the refusal of the Atlanticist concept, a Communitarian economy, strong power. The rallying of the militant presupposes then the knowledge of these points and his unconditional rallying to these. In order that a militant might rally UNCONDITIONALLY in this way—and this is a condition of the cohesion of the political phalanx—it is necessary that he abandon numerous points considered as emerging from a free personal option. Thus the revolutionary party demands from its men an unconditional rallying to some very important and precise points; in exchange for which it allows them a number of personal options regarding points considered as merely secondary for the planned historic realisation. These permitted personal options constitute in fact the neurological safety-valve, thanks to which one could set the troop in a maximum tension for the action supporting the political dogma.

The specification of the dogma is important. It exists in order to prevent actions of personal ambition from disguising themselves as ideological controversies. From custom we know that no opponent, no ambitious person within a party apparatus, will have the effrontery to dispute a leader by declaring in good humour that he is aspiring to a position; no, he will attack him on points of ideology. One sees here all the danger for a party: conflicts presented as ideological to the troop of militants can sow confusion or division in them. It is advisable thus to fix in advance the entry of the party into the fray, the points of dogma, and to hold on to these without discussions. With rare exceptions, this dogma can be amended only by the leader.

If, on the other hand, one wishes to avoid falling into a rut, into which a number of quality movements have fallen, after having traversed a very small corner of the political path, one should defend oneself vigorously from the temptation of the Byzantinism that leads directly to the hydrocephalic party.

A man who wishes to become a militant does not have to discuss the ideological programme. He enters a movement similar to a religious order. The rule of the order is defined before his engagement. In political organisations that are disciplined and destined to action, there is no place for endless debates, for petty bourgeois scruples, for personal moral torment, for aesthetic hesitation. Either one accepts the menu or one does not eat. There is no choice of dishes.

Otherwise one condemns oneself to become an academy for fine minds. In a French journal of high literary quality (ah, how the excess of talent is contrary to the practical political sense!), I was able to read, on page after page, a brilliant and courteous controversy between two leaders of this organisation. What a shameful spectacle, what a dissipating action for the troops. In this way, two years after its creation, an organisation displays in broad daylight its differences (and in this case they were relatively slight) and its hesitations. How to hope that the troops might have trust in their leaders when the latter exhaust themselves in Byzantine refinements, in a concern to perfect their thought. In our age, what is lacking everywhere, and that to which the true youth, from which combatants will emerge, aspire is a clear, simple, monolithic faith. The unexperienced political leaders frequently allow themselves to be deceived by what we shall call 'letters from readers', that is to say, by observations originating from professional pedants or from elements tormented by an ideal perfection, in search of a sort of political Grail. Command presupposes a deafness with regard to certain bickering. These observations, these doubts, these critiques, do not correspond to the feelings of the large mass of the best militants. For the latter, a rule of life is necessary, a line of conduct, and Talmudic debate is not their aim.

To the young people who have approached me many times to obtain from me what I refuse to write, because it would be sterile — minute details of the future society that we wish to construct, in particular those on institutional problems (how many young Montesquieus have I encountered!) -, I have always replied that things are what men are and institutions have never resolved by their qualities alone things which the nature of men did not permit or would never permit. There have existed easy-going monarchies and ferocious republics, peaceful empires and aggressive cities. Therefore, is it necessary to worry much, now, about the institutions of the future Empire? No, I replied to them, everything will depend on the number of elite men that we will have been able to select, and the institutions will acquire the most efficient form ACCORDING TO the maturity of the masses to be governed. I say, indeed, according to. That is where the whole problem lies.

One thing is certain, that is that the first two or three generations of legal Europe that we will make will be of the same style as that of the revolutionaries who will have brought it to birth. Thus the most important thing is to watch over the morality and the intelligence of these revolutionaries. The rest will follow from that. Once the points of dogma are defined, once what belongs to the domain of intellectual obedience (don't protest) and what belongs to the domain of free opinion are specified, one can move on to action.

This discipline-freedom duality is the key to our intellectual and moral method. An obedience, a discipline without reserve on some points, on some precise objectives: a very large freedom on the other chapters which occupy the mind or the heart. The militant is a soldier who obeys, he is a man to whom a broad and deep inner life is certain, from the cultural to the sentimental and religious. Once order is put into the ideas, and the present book is the result of four years of practical confrontations with my best and closest companions, one moves on to action. Then the vivifying epic of the revolutionary work will begin.

Those who have experienced militant organisations know the intellectual simplicity that prevails there and all the human warmth that animates them. One will never again discuss ideology between comrades. On the contrary, every day one will discuss work and technical methods. One will work together, fight together, but one will never quibble. When one has reached this stage with a human group, one experiences then a mutation, the transition of a political club to the formation of political combat. Then everything becomes so simple, so clear. And how surprised and amused we are when the neophytes come forth with their hesitations, scruples, torments, worries, complexes and sins of complication. Action unifies. Intellectual speculation weakens and divides.

All the amateurs in the science of ruling men will talk to you with a feigned authority of the necessity of 'decentralising', of the necessity of 'autonomy'. They confuse congestion and centralisation. Paris is an example of congestion. The human brain is an example of centralisation. These are federalists, confederalists, autonomists.

First remark for them: feeling in themselves too little capacity to hope for supreme positions, they wish to create the MAXIMUM of minor positions, by proliferation of the latter. Everything that Montesquieu or Rousseau were able to say about the management of states of large area has become totally baseless. A letter took several days from Paris to Marseilles. Today teleprinters crackle between Tokyo and Berlin, between Paris and Stockholm, in a few minutes. Supersonic aviation will carry a PACKAGE in two hours between Paris and New York.

That is a revolutionary fact in the science of government. One fact has disappeared: distance. This overturns all of political science and obliges one to revise numerous concepts.

The modern party should be organised in the image of organic unity, it should be the replica of the hierarchy of the human body. One head, one brain, precise and multiple organs of information, one will, one command. Neither hydrocephaly nor gigantism of certain organs, but a fine balance as that realised by nature in man. Life is organisation and the psychosomatically balanced man is the most complex and finest specimen in it.

Quite naturally, centrifugal forces inhabit every political organisation. These forces are strong and frequent in groups. These forces are rare and occasional in teams.

One of the major worries in the formation of a strong party will be about the structure of such a sort that it allows the centrifugal forces only very few possibilities and opportunities to harm. The Church fathers, in their wisdom, teach us that sin is often a question of opportunity. One must therefore diminish the opportunities and in a party these are the opportunities to leave it, to tear it apart, to leave dissenting, to act as autonomous units.

A centralised, homogeneous party offers few possibilities of betrayal: the militant who might have this intention, the militant who might have a moment of discouragement, would find it impossible to undertake an 'impulsive action', at the risk of finding himself all alone, without the slightest bit of authority, without any means.

From the Group to the Homogeneous — Unitarian — Centralised — Party Team

A political group is extremely different from a political team. The latter follows — when it follows — the first several years later. The former is heterogeneous, the latter is homogeneous. In the former case, that of the group, a resentment, a fear or a calculation brings men together: it is then the OAS, the Popular Front[13] or the 'Independents'. In the

---

13 The *Front Populaire* was an alliance of socialist parties, including the French Communist Party. Founded in 1936 it won the legislative election that year, which led to the formation of a government by the socialist leader Léon Blum.

latter case, that of the team, the aspect is infinitely more positive: men know one another closely, they have already fought together for years, and have decided to create, to construct, to advance.

The group has a precarious character. The team has a definite and permanent character. A team is, for example, the Chinese ruling class, the Yugoslav ruling class, the Nasserist ruling class. The men who compose it have known one another for a long time and the original group, after having suffered turmoil, shake-ups, purges, desertions, persecutions, sorted themselves out at first, rejecting in this way the weak or excessively differentiated elements, than coagulated and finally became a team. The OAS in 1961 and 1962 was a group, a sort of extremely unstable mixture. At the end of 1963, it appears as a team. But bad luck wishes that this team be reduced to fifteen officers without troops, without means, and more seriously, with the timid and delayed start of an Atlanticist — thus fundamentally vitiated — European doctrine. A group is improvised, sometimes fortunately, but rarely; on the contrary, the team is organised. To move from the improvised, that is to say, from the 'meeting' to the organised, one needs many months at least (resistance networks) or many years (hard political parties). If in 1960 a hard and homogeneous political team had existed in France, the Algerian affair could have been taken into hand seriously.

Here appears all the importance of forming, in peacetime, this team, when everything is so calm that even the apparatus of the powers that be cannot imagine a future that is critical for it. Prepare, organise BEFORE and, in particular, never during.

The group is regularly encumbered with unstable and curious elements, which is a phenomenon known by political leaders. A new movement attracts in its beginnings — irresistibly — all the pathological curiosities of politics. It is a little like a new café, which attracts, on its opening day, all the drunkards of the area. These unstable people, a little like those employees who constantly change their employer, and who do not realise that their dissatisfaction is due to themselves, to a mediocrity or to a laziness that they do not wish to admit, give strong advice, debate, quibble, criticise and then lose interest. At no point have they aided the growing party positively.

That is a stage through which every growing party must pass. It should have its childhood diseases and overcome them. I have said it elsewhere, discussions lead to nothing but to divisions. Working together, fighting together, solidly, unites. Here one cannot draw the attention of the neophytes too much to the capital importance of administrative work without show; a party should be managed with the financial orthodoxy of a bank. It should have an administration equal to that of the best commercial businesses. The young recruits are regularly vexed when they are enrolled in a party of order and method. Their political career begins with a can of paint, to whitewash in the night, or with a pot of glue for the work of delivering subscriptions. It is necessary to go through this stage of a soldier of the second class. One method that should absolutely be banned from a party of organisation is the canker of internal elections. One does not vote on actions or on ideas, one votes on persons. This system has a fundamental defect, it is to lead men to count themselves, to divide themselves. In many cases, within a group, points of view differ (later it is no longer the case, when the group has become a team), and at the beginning of the existence of a still very unstable community it is a common thing.

Therefore, one should never count on the group. For those defeated in a vote retain scars of wounded self-love and will only wait for the first opportunity to get revenge. It is the leader's task to cut off in a sovereign manner, after having been broadly advised. His decision will sometimes be unpopular: what does it matter, he is there in his role. *One bears more easily the injustice — or what one thinks is the injustice — of the action of superiors than that of the action of equals.* The unpleasant decision coming from the superior authority is better accepted than the same resulting from the 'electoral victory' of equals. It is one of the attributes of a true leader to hold over them the weight of discontent. At certain moments a true leader will have things done that are unpopular at that very moment but understood and appreciated later. Besides, in itself, the electoral system engenders a pseudo-elite of 'popular leaders' extremely different in character from leaders of command, from leaders of responsibility.

In particular, in a growing party, authority must essentially come from above and the functions and ranks should be designated or appointed.

Much later, when the unstable group has become a homogenous team, the system of vote can be introduced with a series of correctives, that is to say: above all, closed door, then only those who are concerned, competent and responsible vote. Finally, this vote has an indicative, informative, consultative value. Experience then reveals that rarely do divergences appear in teams, while they are frequent and constant in groups.

Those men to whom one would have permitted the destructive game of votes at the beginning of the party would be torn apart, divided, separated. Some years later, the same men may then 'account for' their opinions and views and perceive that they are almost identical.

Unanimity, the cohesion, obtained at the beginning through an authoritarian constraint, within the group, can be continued some years later, but then within the team, through free acquiescence. One sees here that a strong and paternalistic authority at the beginning, imposing itself on a heterogeneous 'gathering', has created a real unified family. That is one of the secrets of command.

The Roots of Historical Legitimacy — The Consent and Then The rights of the Valiant Part

Historical legitimacy takes root and finds objective justification of its mission to the extent that it identifies itself with those who possess an awareness that others do not yet. The possessors of this awareness know the NECESSARY TRANSFORMATION of a people or a nation.

The image of this future, conceived a very long time before the 'public' event or before the accomplished event, by a group or within a group, gives to the latter the leading role. It is the aware avantgarde that, in a regular sense, gives birth to History.

The moment that the organised action of this aware avant-garde begins, legitimacy passes very quickly into its hands. This growing phenomenon escapes the common mortals, and the vulgar continue to confuse legality with legitimacy. A power in place begins to crumble the moment when it does not possess any longer the totality of legitimacy, it loses contact with the historical reality of the people that it claims to rule. It is no longer a state in communion with the destiny of the nation.

For a long time yet, nevertheless, the power using the instrument of legality could abuse sheep-like masses. But the divorce between the power in place and the very near future of the nation is consummated.

Only those who possess legitimacy SEE THE GOAL; they are aware, long before everybody, of the HIGHER COLLECTIVE LIFE of the community, when the factual power, the legality, resembles a myopia that flounders in the immediate present.

Thus, on the eve of great upheavals, the legitimate source of the future legality inhabits some men, the part that is aware, and they can then '*wish for all*', for an entirety that does not yet see what it already conceives very well. From this viewpoint, examples abound in history: the Belgian revolutionaries of 1830 possessed legitimacy much before firing the first shot against the Dutch, the resistant fighters of 1941 or of 1942 possessed a historical legitimacy much before being 'homologous' and 'decorated'. Legitimacy is possessed by a group, it meets the obstruction and often even the distrust of the ruling power, or the hostility of the masses, which it will lead towards their destiny.

But, a revealing phenomenon, the VALIANT PART of the nation, quite rapidly accords its moral encouragement at first, and then its material support later. What is this valiant part of the nation, whose consent is, at a certain moment, the definitive consecration of the legitimacy of the avantgarde?

This valiant part is situated, in the chronological order of the awareness, between the avantgarde that it follows and before the masses that it precedes. It is composed of men capable of courage, or of heroism. It is within it that one finds the combatants who came first on a battlefield and those that one need never call for or mobilise. They are the VOLUNTEERS of History; at the first signal, at the first demand, they emerge from the ranks. What is important thus for the avantgarde is that, at the end of some years of preparation or struggles, it meets this valiant part and communicate its certitudes in exchange for which the latter brings its consent. At this moment, one is already very close to the shock that is going to render public what was known for a long time by the initiated. What essentially distinguishes the avantgarde from the valiant part is that the former alone possesses a lucidity and an acuity that allows them to feel the future and to prepare it, and the latter possesses only rectitude and courage. Much later, after the victory, after the installation of the new power — at the moment when legitimacy has been combined with legality — the problem of the particular rights of the valiant part is posed.

It is natural, and it has always been thus, that only those who have fought for a new social or national order have the right to specify the structures of the new state and to hold all the levers of command of it. This situation, in ancient times, was translated by a large endowment to the combatants — an example, the barons of William the Conqueror — and in modern times by the establishment of the sole Party — witness Ben Bella, Tito and, much earlier, the NSDAP and the Russian Communist Party after 1917. *Right is born from a capacity. That is the reality: there are no other rights, except in the intellectual fogs created by the professors or in the naivety of the petty bourgeois.* One has too often the opportunity to hear everybody bellowing about congenital 'rights' of a really metaphysical nature. As if every newborn had a notebook of the 'savings bank of rights' in his cradle. It is ridiculous. A right is conquered, is merited, is retained. Right is the salary of a service or the appreciation of your strength that an adversary makes of it.

It is therefore equitable that the avantgarde and the valiant part appropriate political privileges during at least a generation. It is, besides, indispensable for ensuring that the revolution of the combatants is not betrayed by the intrigue of procrastinators.

Do those who did not wish to fight to conquer it deserve freedom? Do those who were afraid of taking arms to drive out the occupier deserve independence?

Similarly, those who, in the shelter of a work cabinet in a neutral country, have dispensed advice and woven intrigues should not expect high positions in the new regime.

One of the rare forms of respectable democracy is that of armed men. So were the first free men of Switzerland, the first free men of Rome. One was a citizen who bore arms, who knew to use them, and responded at the first call. That is a healthy morale. One can measure at once the gap that separates our degenerate democracies from their ancient uncouth and virile forms.

Tomorrow, the party card will be given only to those who can prove: 'In 1965 I was in such and such prison, in 1970 in such and such hiding place, in 1975 in such and such army'. Anybody who would like to be something will be asked: 'Where were you yesterday?' The totality of the political and military combatants will constitute the 'valiant part' and when the time of success arrives only they will have a say.

The revolutionary avantgarde, the 'aware part', should not have to be elected except by the 'valiant part'.

As for the others, the former collaborators of the occupier, the cowards, the pusillanimous, the spineless, the procrastinators, the malicious, they can look on, look on, and be silent.

Nothing is more respectable than a free man, but a free man is first a man who fights for his freedom, for his dignity, for his independence. We do not recognise the right of dastards.

Noxiousness of Alliances: the Plagiarisers or the Counterfeiters

The strong person is stronger when he remains alone. That is something that was written before me. It remains valid still.

A homogeneous and dynamic party must always vigorously refuse oganic alliances, that is to say, fusion, but it can, on the contrary, seek tactical alliances of a temporary nature.

The finest champions of political 'regroupments' are in fact those who hope to derive a profit from them. 'I bring one, you bring ten, we form a household and then we share everything', thus is their justification of association cruelly schematised. There are even jokers who propose: 'I bring nobody, then we share', these are the exhibitionists, the show-offs of politics. They exist.

If unfortunately one accepts the process of organic alliance, the new group formed of TWO SMALL AND HOMOGENEOUS TEAMS forms then a new heterogeneous, unstable GROUP, with a disputed hierarchy because it is new, fragile, because it is not proven. All the delicate phenomena of the growth of the group to a team occur again and are repeated. During this period of growth the new expanded group is less strong than one of its parts, from the fact that the latter was already a team. On the other hand, the introduction of groups or teams — even smaller ones — within a specific team, brings about for the latter the danger of seeing feudalism introduced there. The person who has 'rallied' round attaches himself with more or less of a troop and the latter then constitutes a 'clientele' at his disposition within the new group to act there like an unruly and undisciplined feudal lord. The recruitment should always be made person by person and it should avoid collective and organised engagements.

One should hope for alliances, coalitions, but one should wish for them to one's adversaries or one's rivals. A coalition bears within itself the seed of its destruction. Sooner or later, but surely, the crabs are going to move in the basket and pinch one another. Formations structured under the sign of a permanent vote, under the sign of alliances, federations, are defeated in advance by a small homogeneous and unitarian formation. This latter is a hundred times more manageable on the terrain of the action. Its mobility compensates very broadly for its quantitative inferiority.

When one tries to conciliate neighbouring and rival but different companies, one should look for a common denominator. The qualitative level of this common denominator will be so much lower the larger the number of candidates for the fusion present themselves. This is a mathematical law. One ends with an insipid and colourless common denominator. At first the temptation is great among the political novices to make a recruitment at any cost and, in order to do this, proceed to increasing opportunistic ideological concessions. When one begins on this path one finishes by begging, by soliciting recruitment humbly and modestly. One then embarks along with oneself the dregs, but not militants. Plagiarisers are frequent in politics, either they imitate the past, like those jokers who today play at a parody of Fascism or a parody of National Socialism, or they imitate the present.

These are the counterfeiters of politics. They steal an idea, a title, a seal, a list of addresses of members and try then to instal themselves on their account. Very soon they degenerate and collapse. The explanation of this is simple: mediocre within an organisation, they should be that much more outside the support of the organisation that they leave. In fact, most of the time, these plagiarists are in fact former branch managers who have tried to establish themselves on their account: to imitate a 'patron', whose intellectual stature they did not possess. They lack intellectual calibre in general, and much more — real personality. Their action can certainly retard the original group. They remove and weaken something but do not derive anything concrete from it. The stolen water is rapidly poured into the sands of the desert of oblivion.

One test of the value of a revolutionary group is the unanimous hostility that it arouses within groups that are considered to be 'friendly' or 'allied'. Then there is a unanimous clamour about the infamy. They will try everything to defame it: they will say that it is composed of adventurers, provocateurs, double agents, ambitious staff, crazy people, unprincipled and paranoid people. Such a unanimous judgement announces in fact its real value because it is that of jealous and mediocre people who FEEL the superiority of the others but cannot resign themselves to it honestly. When a newcomer, a woman, enters a society, all the local women will form a coalition to diminish, defame, calumniate her. It is that they sense a superior rival.

Similarly, in a circle, when a strong man enters, of those who attract not the look of rejected women but of fortunate women, the 'local' men join together to diminish by their words the dangerous male, in order to slander him.

The same practice is found in the struggle between revolutionary groups. Don't trust 'suitable' groups that do not have any enemies. If they do not have any enemies it is that they do not threaten anybody, the regime in the first place. Around the thirties, the entire democratic mass, short of arguments, presented Hitler as a homosexual. Pretty women are detested by all other women, strong men arouse the hostility of mediocre men and the leaders that are DANGEROUS to a regime provoke a unanimous hatred, calumny and envy. Of those of whom people tell you that they are 'unacceptable', you can be sure that they have a formidable personality.

Victory without Battles: the Work of Termites

The recent campaigns of Indochina and Algeria have taught us that a war could be won without spectacular battles. In the two cases, the French Army was technologically and even numerically superior to its adversaries.

If the ALN[14] had attempted a battle against the French Army, it would have been easily destroyed by the latter. It therefore refused. This is a quite new notion: that of a war won when any pitched battle would have been lost. The paradox is in fact only apparent.

France was defeated because it did not have any longer the determination to defeat; on the left it was divided on the opportunity of this war, and on the right on the means of winning it.

France was defeated because its nerves gave way; the FLN[15] won the war only because its enemy 'no longer wanted any of it'. France was defeated through erosion of morale — it was that in Paris itself — by the progressive and defeatist press.

This phenomenon interests us here to the extent that it can be transposed to the level of political struggle.

One can defeat a regime without spectacular electoral battles, without a civil war, through political attrition, guerrilla warfare, to the extent that this regime is morally exhausted.

Now, the one that we have to combat in the West is that.

A society is in the image of its ruling class. The present ruling class is tired, worn out, pleasure-seeking, spineless.

We know that it is not resolved to die for its privileges. To preserve its sinecures, it will manoeuvre, pay, but it will not fight dangerously.

One of the techniques of political struggle will therefore be that of guerrilla work, a work that is quite underground.

Let us not confuse here underground with clandestine, and much less with illegal.

The regime of moral abdication, the source of the weakness of Europe, should be brought down, but it should be done intelligently.

---

14 The *Armée de libération nationale* (Army of National Liberation) was the armed wing of the FLN (see below).

15 The *Front de Libération Nationale* was a socialist party that led the nationalist movement during the Algerian War (1954–1962).

A big pitched battle in an open terrain would be favourable to it. It has for the latter a heavy resource that we do not have: television, the media, public education.

The big pitched battle would 'provisionally' resolve the centrifugal or contradictory tendencies of the regime.

The regime is an indisputable majority but an unstable, divided, unorganised, Byzantinised majority. *The strength of an organised and disciplined minority is irresistible. It exercises its thrust on every individual isolated from this majority, which thus finds itself always ALONE before the unified and cohesive totality of the minority. Thus a minority of a hundred men 'unitarianised' is stronger than a majority of a thousand diversified men.*

To win battles is a romantic form of combat, to die heroically is another: what counts definitively is to win the peace, that is to say, the END of the war, it is to end alive.

The work of political termites is without gallantry, it demands determination and perseverance. Thus it refutes those whose need of displayed glory betrays a juvenile temperament. The political life of a nation is concentrated in some nerve-centres of information, trade unionism and youth movements. To introduce oneself into these nerve-centres progressively, silently, allows one to organise short circuits there. A regime can seem strong and have muscle, that is to say, many policemen, many newspapers of its own: but what can these muscles serve if the nerve-centres, which determine its movements by giving them impulses, are attacked and disconnected?

The sapping work, the work of termites, should be done not only 'among the masses' (ever since Mao was published, this monistic conception obsesses the judgement of many) but also in the heart itself of the nerve-centres of the regime. Nothing is more annoying than a fight against a partially invisible adversary, nothing is more fatiguing. The moment comes when psychoses and self-intoxications arise.

This factor of self-intoxication is extremely important. One who has discovered that ONE wall of his house was eroded by termites imagines easily that ALL the walls are full of tunnels, and then creates by himself his panic, which leads him to a spontaneous evacuation of the building.

The discovery of some complicities around and in the service of a cohesive minority acts as a poison. The regime, of course, has an immense network of conveniences and complicities, but these are diversified, often mutually competitive. By contrast, one finds rarer complicities but in the service of a single aim. The latter are more formidable than the former.

On Adherence and Engagement: Differences

The weakness of the big classical political formations consists in demanding of its troops only adherence. On the other hand, a revolutionary organisation demands total engagement. The former is a passive acquiescence. The latter is an active acquiescence. Experience teaches us that one can count much more on men when one demands something of them than when one offers them something. I shall add that it is the one — and only the one — of whom one has already made many demands that one CAN DEMAND SOMETHING MORE OF.

The big parties offer positions or Byzantine controversies. In the first case, they recruit opportunists who will disperse on the field at the first hard blow, because they do not wish to die for their 'ideas'; in the second case, they attract intellectually unstable persons, numerous in politics. A revolutionary organisation offers certainties. Big parliamentary parties wave uncertainties.

The French call all these men incapable of stabilising themselves in their search for a satisfaction, which is indispensable for their neuroses, 'intriguers'. I call them debauchees. In fact, many are those men who need uncertainty, rather like the depressed neurotic needs anxieties to nourish his pathological pessimism.

A revolutionary organisation cannot be satisfied with membership. It is of little importance to it that its ideas arouse a sympathetic response.

What is important is that this sympathy is concretised, materialised. Then one passes from membership to engagement. This concretisation which makes the difference between membership and engagement is first of all the undertaking of risk — I mean by that having the courage to display one's ideas publicly — and then financial contribution, the volunteer work.

The member, at best, votes in the secrecy of the polling booth.

An engaged person begins by paying — the regularity and the spontaneity of the act of contributing is a very important sign — then by militating, that is to say, by sacrificing the major part of the time taken by his private life and offer it to his political life.

The member can be one at several neighbouring groups. The importance given to discussions and sterile speculations in the big political formations contributes to augment the fundamental instability. In fact, all these men are infected by changism, the need to question everything, at every moment. This is, for example, the spectacle presented by the French progressive left, the most Byzantine, most sterile, the most promiscuous that there is. The member goes from one group to another, according to the fashions; he is never stationary, he never takes root. If one opens a new group, he goes there, somewhat like a drunkard tries every new bar.

There is reason to distrust people who demand to be convinced. In fact, dialogue with these people is without any interest, they do not wish to be convinced but solely to discuss, and they apprehend nothing more than the possibility of being convinced one day. That is how the member is; he possesses a drawer full of so-called ethical reluctances in order not to have to be engaged. The pseudo-scruple is most of the time an excuse for refusal of engagement.

A marked difference between membership and engagement is that the former can be adapted to many groups, whereas the latter is unique and total.

One is engaged in a single movement, one can be the member of several 'tendencies'. A revolutionary party must do its best to recruit and *enrol only engaged people; each of the latter will devote all his time, all his energy, to the Party He will not dissipate himself as the member does in many, in general 'intellectual', activities. Intellectual because they are neither dangerous nor tiring.*

Having a Past or Having a Future? The Mummies in Politics

The easy solution to launch a party of the democratic parliamentary style is to unearth some heroes from yesteryear to weave a fine tapestry and attract the clientele.

One then discovers who was a general in retreat and who an ancient hero of war.

In fact, one should distrust heroes who did not die a violent death.

Conformism makes the bourgeois ask a new party to show them people having an 'eloquent past'.

But this is a contradiction. For, what should one think of someone who is guaranteed by a brilliant past and who, twenty years later, is forced to offer his services to an opposition organisation?

One should mistrust persons who have been ambitious ... for 20 years.

A valuable hero, an efficient hero, must either die or succeed, that is to say, work his way into the ruling class.

When one examines every man of the team of a revolutionary movement, one should never ask the question, 'Does he have a past (a good one evidently)?' but rather, 'Does he have a future?'

For, if one wishes to count on the past, one should strictly grant a favourable preference to the one who has a bad past and not to one who has a brilliant (in the sense of the regime) one.

In fact, for the one who has a bad (according to the canons of bourgeois and conformist morality) past, there is the excuse and the explanation of his non-accession to the ruling class; this man has been ostracised.

The one who has a good past must explain why, in spite of his extremely favourable factors, he is forced to agitate outside the existing power. The explanation is generally humiliating. Or else he was too mediocre, or else he was too naïve and was duped.

A revolutionary party measures its strength by the ambitious youngsters that it counts in its ranks, youngsters who have a 'future', and not on its rheumatic old eagles who have a 'past'. The temptation to inexperienced leaders is great to drum up, for publicity reasons, political cadavers or ideological mummies.

The post-war years have thus seen dozens of organisations launched on the exploitation of the cadavers of Fascism or National Socialism. The calculation was that there was a clientele for this merchandise and that it was therefore necessary to offer it.

What these people did not see is, first, that this clientele drove out the others and, secondly, that it was composed of ageing people.

The neo-Fascists of 1960 will join the White Russians of 1925 in the museum. For both, there was never the possibility of a return.

CHAPTER IX

FOR A LUCID MORALITY AND AGAINST A DEBILITATING MORALITY

It is not a question of proclaiming that one does not like peace. It is a matter of being strong enough to impose peace on those who want war. And it is with verbiage that one has debilitated this strength in our country.

Henri de Montherlant

States do not rule with prayer books.

Cosimo de Medici

One who does not wish to prepare himself because it would interrupt his pleasure will soon see that very pleasure taken from him on account of which he did not wish to prepare himself.

Thucydides

The nobility has a significance only if it is capable of placing leaders at the disposal of the people.

Johann Gottlieb Fichte

The nobility is defined by demands, by obligations, and not by rights.

José Ortega y Gasset

Things Are What Men Are

THINGS ARE WHAT MEN ARE. Which means that the best institutions do not go beyond the men if the latter are weak or vicious and that one should guard against illusions of reformism through the legal structures of society alone.

Through the centuries of history, the peoples have had a taste of all the institutions with more or less good luck. What have we not heard, what do we still not hear regularly, affirmed with the faith of naivety: 'When will we have freedom?' — I have heard that in Spain, 'When will we have independence?' — I have heard that in the Congo, 'When will we have prosperity?' — I have heard that in Belgium.

Oh well! Men will waste this freedom just as other men have wasted independence and even prosperity.

The study of history places us before apparent paradoxes, enlightened tyrannies, good-natured dictatorships, oppressive democracies, liberal kings and despotic presidents of republics, libertines and Communist curs. When I was sixteen, I fed myself on Rousseau and Montesquieu. Without wishing to take away anything of merit from these authors — for Rousseau is badly understood — I realise today in the fullness of age — the enormous naïve faith that I had placed, at that time, in the mechanisms of institutions alone and in the belief in their pernicious or beneficial power.

At sixteen, or twenty, just out of university, it is an error that is quite excusable and one cannot cast the first stone at the young revolutionary hotheads, who imagine that they can bring in the Golden

Age with the help of a magic recipe, which is called structural reform or socialism or Communism or anything else.

By contrast, one should not underestimate the importance of legal structures and imagine that the virtues of individuals alone suffice to resolve the problems.

One therefore needs balanced men in an ordered society. A year from now, I hope to write about the structures of unitarian Europe. Nevertheless, already at present, I warn the reader. These structures will be applicable or applied only to the extent that, first, the events and their consequences will permit it and, later, and especially, to the extent to which men will instal them.

For the moment, in this chapter, I shall deal with the problem of European man, his ethics and his style.

What would be the use of grafting patriotism onto cowards or socialism onto lazybones, and similarly the unifying revolution of Europe onto confused and indecisive minds?

Things will be, thus, in most part, what men will be.

Let us first pose the problem of men. How are they today and how should they be tomorrow? It is necessary therefore to destroy here an entire series of commonplaces — overturn idols — laugh at very widespread naiveties. Simultaneously one should propose values, explain that the strong man should limit himself — there is the mark of superiority — and how the will to power duly policed can become a will to superiority. It will be necessary to impose on a society wallowing in comfort, in rackets, a morality of demand.

I am by nature a great sceptic and a great liberal. But scepticism can be for man the excuse of opposition to change; it can also be for some a factor of lucidity.

The tolerant and open liberal mind is indisputably a result of the realised man, of perfected man.

Liberalism can be naivety, can be cowardice, as it can also dwell in the hearts of determined men, whom combat, even if aggressive, does not frighten.

History presents some models of this that merit an enthusiastic interest.

Everybody knows Frederick II of Prussia, eternally occupied with expanding his kingdom or consolidating it, confronting momentary reversals with stoic courage, confronting formidable coalitions. This man, shrewd and tenacious in politics, this man rude in war, was the perfect portrait of the strong monarch. But at the same time, this was one of the most enlightened men of his time, living in the company or in the friendship of the greatest minds, French for the most part. The idealised image that portrays strong men as uncultivated and brutal is false; it has been created by our contemporary intellectuals based on their indisputable personal physical cowardice.

Much earlier in history, we find another Frederick II, of Hohenstaufen,[1] bearing the weight of an immense destiny, conducting incessant battles, confronting the Popes, the formidable Lombard communes, the turbulent German princes, even while creating the very remarkable modern legislation, called *Melfi*.[2] This Hohenstaufen, a warrior, a hard man, an authoritarian man, was in his personal life one of the most cultivated men of his time, passionate about mathematics, writing fluently in Arabic, curious about all the intellectual advancements.

It is this sceptical, agnostic man who organised the thrust of the Germanic Empire into Slavic Europe under the banner of Christianity and confided this task to his friend, the Grand Master of the Order of Teutonic Knights, Hermann von Salza.[3]

---

1   Frederick II (1194-1250) was Holy Roman Emperor, King of the Romans, King of Sicily and King of Jerusalem.
2   Frederick II's legal reforms in the Kingdom of Sicily culminated in the Constitutions of Melfi (1231), which codified laws in a way that supported his absolute monarchy.
3   Hermann von Salza (ca. 1165-1239) was in charge of the campaign to Christianise Prussia, which began in 1230. He was a Grand Master of the military Order of Teutonic Knights already in 1210.

The westernisation and the Christianisation of the Baltic was thus realised by the will of a strong man with little belief, first of all, and very little Nordic, besides.

Our two Fredericks, some centuries apart, were men without illusions about their fellows, minds open to all intellectual speculations.

In them, the liberal spirit — I understand by that the mind open to research and indulgent of errors — had not enervated at all the spirit of enterprise, had not at all weakened a will to power of a refined and superior sort. The European men that I am going to describe, the men of command at least, will be enlightened but determined, cultivated but pugnacious.

The tide of gross and primitive materialism that threatens the world should be opposed by a rock made up of European men in possession of a historical maturity infinitely greater than that of their opponents. *It is the armed mind that we must oppose to the assaults of the barbarians.* The mind cannot hold out unless the arm is strong.

One should read Epictetus certainly, but one should also know how a machine gun works. A complete man will thus know how to do both things and to the fanatic barbarians who attack us we should show that the expansion of the mind does not diminish at all our combatant qualities.

On Optimism and Pessimism

It is from the same human species that either delinquents or heroes emerge. The milieu and circumstances cause such and such a young man to militate in a revolutionary movement or to be a gangster.

Between the taste for sacrifice and wicked vacillation we can see only two paths starting from the same crossroads. Man contains in himself the best potentialities and the lowest instincts. The art of ruling consists in favouring the former and containing the latter.

The majority of men do not have personal conduct but a stereotypical attitude. 'Vices' and 'virtues' are among the masses gregarious values. *It is important therefore that the ruling elite make positive values fashionable.* That is the secret of solid societies.

The best legal institutions, the structures of a state, cannot do anything if they are not supported and reinforced by the existence of a morality, of a lifestyle and a social discipline.

The abundance of laws, in a decadent democracy, shows that only coercion can maintain, for better or worse, this rotting edifice. A very recent legislation punishes, for example, the refusal to bring aid to a person in danger of death. That this law was necessary is the confession of the absence of morality of this decadent society. On the other hand, the accounting and pricing of courage throws a rather sordid light on the patriotism of the masses threatened by democracy.

On the subject of man, one cannot definitively conclude with either optimism or pessimism. But it is possible to influence his conduct as much by a morality of conduct as by limiting coercive or repressive laws. No case is desperate and in less than a generation it is possible to transform our Blackshirts into active citizens, and the little progressive sickly persons into combatants.

No case is desperate, no case is incurable. A man should be taken into hand, especially through the action of moral rules. Living examples of virtue and character must be offered to him.

One cannot hold against the youth that they are weak-willed, since the society born of democratism gives it the example of spinelessness, of vulgarity, of comfort, of claims and irresponsibility.

The revolutionary leaders will therefore have to—from the beginning—give the spectacle of a new lifestyle, a conduct entirely different from those of the puppets who manipulate our decadent regimes. A nation around a party, I wrote above, but also a morality around new leaders.

A Political Right Arises from a Capacity

In the task of cleaning out the brain, there is first need to demystify the notion of congenital right in politics. A right corresponds to a capacity, whether it be positive or negative. A leader has the right to command because it is necessary and he is the proof of it; an enemy has the right to peace because he is strong enough to render our plans of conquest vain.

A man who is no longer inclined to fight to defend his property must not expect to save it. It is the same for nations.

A weak man will allow his goods to be taken, a weak nation its colonies or its possessions.

Life — biology, zoology and finally the history of men that is politics teach us that — is only combat, confrontations and perils, adaptive faculty and constant effort. A right is conquered, a right is maintained. If the capacity which permitted one to conquer this right or to be respected disappears, the right disappears immediately in practice.

Life is the balance of forces; the diminution of one force immediately calls forth the thrust or aggression of another. The privileges accorded by birth in the Middle Ages to warriors, to the nobility of the sword,[4] were completely legitimate: these men had acquired the rights — moral and material advantages — because they ensured order, security, because they rendered justice and supervised the construction of bridges and roads. The king could count on them to defend the land against an invader.

The moment this nobility no longer corresponded to a capacity it doomed itself by itself to lose its 'rights', and the Revolution of 1789 was the sanction of the decrepitude of an old nobility of arms to become a nobility of the court, that is to say, a zero.

---

4   The nobles of the sword (*noblesse d'épée*) were the oldest nobility in France, representing the original knights who served the kings of the Middle Ages.

Nothing is more noble, nothing is more respectable than a free man. But one who is not ready to die, if it be for his freedom, no longer merits it, not any more than the man who is not ready to die for his goods deserves these.

Right, as the democratic speech-makers understand it, is an abstraction, a construction of the mind. It is this abstraction which is at the base of all the misunderstandings which deprive of political or historical judgement all those who naively are its heralds.

Right, you will object, exists nevertheless: there are courts of law and laws. Certainly, but this real right, this formalist right, is only a procedure of force.

If the strong people happen to change, new laws appear, which are favourable to the newcomers.

Political right or law is thus in reality a convention against certain forces: it does not have an existence of its own. If you take away the force, it is only an intellectual speculation.

That is a thing that one cannot repeat enough to the young people who enter politics and whose mind has been falsified by a puerile education.

The workers have conquered their rights by force, which the strike and insurrection are; they conserve this right to the extent only that they show themselves capable of resorting to it anew, if necessary.

One witnesses therefore, in developed societies, a policing of force, and that is law, the codification of the relations between groups possessing force.

This conception of right connected to a capacity was in the past healthily conceived in the little democracies of the Middle Ages.

Thus, in certain little republics, in certain Swiss or Lombard cities, only the men possessing a weapon and capable of bearing and using it well were considered citizens. The weak, the cowardly did not participate in the elections, nor therefore in the government. That was the healthy and logical conception of things. Why would a society protect a man incapable of protecting it? There is a contract between society and man. The latter can ask for assistance and security from an organised society to the extent, and only to the extent, that he participates, in one positive way or another, by virtue of his personal aptitudes, in the active life of this society.

How was law born in society? By virtuous generation? Obviously not.

Men probably confronted one another to rob women and caves; little by little they realised that the association of some men, either to defend themselves against others or to hunt and construct together, or to plunder an island, was extremely profitable and efficient; society was born.

In their turn, those dispossessed of power, or the customarily dispossessed, joined together, grouped and organised themselves and created another society, another tribe or another caste and they did that by force — and not by intellectual speculation on rights.

It is intelligent egoism that created the first societies, it is enlightened egoism that later allowed more extended and complex societies.

Parliamentarism, or Reverse Selection

All the societies of sincerely parliamentarian structure are doomed to end in Bonapartism or Caesarism. The democratic parliamentarian regimes have lasted only to the extent that the mechanism was rigged, that is to say, that hidden artifices ensured its functioning. These artifices are the existence of organised oligarchies, either those of the parallel plutocracy or those of mechanised parties. The moment that parliamentarian democracy is really and truly logical in its principles, one rushes towards anarchy and then immediately afterwards to Bonapartism or Caesarism, an obligatory end and inevitable confirmation: or else, further, to absorption by a foreign power. This last hypothesis is that which has been retained by the Communists and the unconscious or conscious agents of Moscow, who clamour for a

IX. FOR A LUCID MORALITY AND AGAINST A DEBILITATING MORALITY 247

total democracy, that is to say, a perfect anarchy, an anarchy that they think will be the only one to master.

An excessively long practice of parliamentarism leads to the decline of a nation. The innkeeper may have indeed decided to make his clients drink and not to drink himself: his trade leads him nevertheless to have to do it, and cirrhosis of the liver lies in wait for him ...

Machiavelli has taught us that the art of ruling retained at one and the same time the qualities of the fox and of the lion in close association.

Parliamentarism has its style of the fox, but only that of it. We have already mentioned above that freedom can be supported only by force and that peace can be guaranteed only by force; we should now declare that that ruse is ineffective if it is not supported by force.

Parliamentarism has neglected the teachings of history and its febrile agitation has led it to lose contact with reality. By developing in a hypertrophic manner, its qualities of ruse, of hustling, of associating its practices to falsely humanitarian beliefs, it weakens itself and rushes to its defeat.

Parliamentarism practised too long leads to a reverse selection. The elites of this system possess eminent qualities of deceit, but not having conserved at the same time qualities of virility, they scheme in a void. What then dooms the system of parliamentarism is the reverse selection in the recruitment of leading men and teams. They recruit tricksters, shrewd people and — just as the innkeeper, by virtue of selling alcohol, must also drink it — I think here of naïve and false humanitarian beliefs, which bear in themselves the seeds of their disappearance, their destruction.

The parliamentarian system becomes an end in itself, the functioning effaces its mission. Parliamentarism, in its final phase, that which we witness at this very moment, is already OUTSIDE the nation. It is the praetorian guard of the parties. But what a miserable praetorian guard!

The ruling class must possess both a head and arms, and both the qualities of the fox and the qualities of the lion. If it happens to neglect one of the two, it rushes towards its disappearance.

The contemporary prototypes of this almost totally degenerate ruling class are the specimens of the Palais Bourbon[5] before 1958, the Belgian parliamentary specimens of 1960, the Wallaces[6] in 1942, and the Stevensons[7] in 1962. The qualities demanded by the profession of democratic politicians — and as a consequence the qualities demanded for the recruitment of renovating teams — constitute the very elements of the death of this system.

All the political games in parliamentarian democracy are a competition of demagoguery. In the long term, this style of combat must bleed onto those who practise it in the absence of all other forms of combat. The selection issuing from this form of competition is finally toxic.

Parliamentarism committed suicide when it accepted Communism into its game and when it thought it could overcome it through attenuation, through ruse, through corruption. It committed suicide more or less long-term in having renounced the use of force to destroy Communism. The latter would perhaps have been able to be corrupted by the pleasures of life, as socialism was by the pleasures of bourgeois life, if Communism did not have a sanctuary situated away from naïve

---

5 The Palais Bourbon is the seat of the French National Assembly, the lower house of the French Parliament.

6 Henry Agard Wallace (1888–1965) was a Democrat Vice-President of the United States and made a famous speech in 1942 called 'The Price of Free World Victory', in which he hoped that the end of the war would result in a world free of slavery, colonialism and poverty.

7 Adlai Stevenson II (1900–1965) was an American Democrat politician, who served as the US ambassador to the UN from 1961 to 1965. In 1962 he suggested that the US should remove its obsolete Jupiter missiles from Turkey if the Soviets would agree to remove their missiles from Cuba. This was considered a sign of weakness by many of the other members of the Executive Committee of the National Security Council that was formed during the Cuban missile crisis.

and debilitating western tendencies, that is to say, the USSR, where the qualities of force are always healthily appreciated and honoured (cf. the Red Army and the Komsomols).[8]

But parliamentarism has wished to oppose Communism, which associates the qualities of the fox and the lion, with only the virtues of the fox. *The fate of a society is almost always tied to that of its ruling class. The present ruling class of Western Europe is doomed; one must therefore, if we wish to save Europe, liquidate these debilitated elites.* No reform of parliamentarism is possible, it is doomed to disappear due to its obligatory practices of recruitment through 'reverse selection'. It will collapse through an excess of cleverness, through a hypertrophy of deceit.

Today, in the West, the men who combine the virtues of force and intelligence, in other words, *virtu* in the terminology of the 15th century, are outside the ruling class. Which announces imminent changes.

Of the Leader: Genesis and Usefulness — For the Leader: Authority or Popularity?

If there is a word in the language of democratism that has a negative connotation, it is indeed 'leader'.

However, nobody disputes — or very few people do — the notion of a leader of an enterprise, in speaking of a factory, for example. In the latter case, it is generally admitted that it is often the leader who makes the enterprise, and that the qualities of the former ensure the vitality of the latter. The same thing in cuisine, where the word signifies the one who knows better and more than the others. The same thing a thousand metres underground where, instinctively, the miner

---

8   The All-Union Leninist Young Communist League was a political youth organisation for youth up to the age of 28 and was the last of three Soviet youth organisations, beginning with the Little Octobrists (to the age of 9) and the Young Pioneers (to the age of 14).

obeys without difficulty the master miner-leader, for he knows that the experience of the latter guarantees his own life.

If in the private sector of industry one still finds such vitality, it is because the role of the leader can still be realised. In the nationalised sectors — where the decisions of the assembly rule — the vitality and initiative disappear rapidly. We see thus in our plutocracies the political power being weak, for this power is a government of assembly, and the economic power can be powerful for it is still personalised.

If, tomorrow, the system of government of assembly is introduced into the industrial enterprise, its creative expansion is finished.

In fact, in democratism, it is not the leader that one disputes, but the principle of authority itself.

The school manuals try to make us believe in a collective power, in a general sovereignty. Nothing is more false. The essential sign of democratism is the vacuity of authority. The so-called popular sovereignty is only the juxtaposition — and juxtaposition is very different from contract or agreement — of numerous or contradictory interests, which should be integrated. Each of these interests being extremely jealous of a possible authority that could become arbitrary. Democratism gives us, thus, the spectacle of a band of advocates refusing *a priori* the intervention of a judge. The indisputable unanimity that reigns in the professional genre of democratism, against personal authority, derives from the mediocrity that occurs there. Everybody would like, certainly, to 'preside', to be in a certain manner the leader, but nobody dares to assume the responsibilities inherent in the function. Thus, through a sort of spite, not being able to be the leader, one makes sure, especially and mainly, that nobody else might become that or be that really.

Of course it is necessary to complete the edifice of democratism and resolve to designate a chief. One then chooses the man who will have made the most promises or undertakes the most commitments to abstain from all freedom of action in his command. Thus, contrary to the natural order of things, the 'leader' in democratism will be inferior even to those who will designate him. Which is the same as declaring that he will be a mediocrity among mediocrities.

Democratism provides equally another variety of 'leaders'. It is those who arise through popularity. Whereas, in order to be invested as 'leader' by his comrades, in democratism the individual will have to give the most servile proofs of his mediocrity—in order to reassure -; the 'leader' of popularity in his turn will have to show demagoguery and be the demagogue among demagogues if he wishes to succeed.

The 'leader of popularity' will never judge, which means that he will never decide. He knows that decision inevitably creates disappointments, thus rancours, thus enemies; he will take care not to decide. The 'leader of popularity' will reign, but he will not rule.

Parliamentary democratism is afraid of the natural leader, as the cat is of water. What democratism calls a leader, fearing the word 'chief' itself, is only a star drawn from the stock of its celebrities.

Manufacturers of discs know the necessity of presenting regularly new stars in order to revive the interest of the buyers. The democratic racket will thus also create, with regular intervals, political stars to respond to the instinctive need of leaders felt by the masses. *The masses are never against the leaders. It is the intermediaries who are.*

And in democratism, the intermediaries are the political bureaucracy. These false leaders, these stars, they are proposed to us regularly, they are people like Daladier, 'Bull of Vaucluse' [sic],[9] Paul Reynaud

---

9   Édourd Daladier (1884–1970) was a left-wing politician, who served as Prime Minister of France in 1933, 1934 and from 1938 to 1940. Born in Vaucluse, he was called the 'Bull of Vaucluse' on account of his thick neck and broad shoulders. Although he was opposed to the Munich Agreement of 1938, which permitted Germany's annexation of the Sudetenland, he finally gave in to Neville Chamberlain's lenient view of Hitler's territorial ambitions.

'of the railway car',[10] Guy Mollet,[11] Defferre[12] and company. They are recruited even in the Army, with the generals Boulanger[13] or Massu.[14]

All these men are stars for a day, never leaders. Just as the successful singers and ephemeral stars are not the owners of the recording companies or the radio-television chains, the political stars do no command anything or anybody in reality.

Before finishing this negative part of the paragraph, I cannot fail to attract the reader's attention to the forms of combat in democratism, forms that select a reverse elite. In searching for the most mediocre of the mediocre, the most demagogical of demagogues, step by step one arrives at removing the cream of society.

The style itself of democratism leads inexorably to draw out the most spineless among the spineless, the most cowardly among the cowardly, the most dishonest among the liars. The end of this process is the fiction of command and the absolute negation of the notion of an authentic leader.

To be a leader is to often decide against all or to see clearly before others.

---

10 Paul Reynaud (1878–1966) was Prime Minister of France in 1940 and refused to sign an armistice with Germany. He was arrested by the Pétain government and imprisoned in Germany and Austria until 1945. The armistice with Germany was signed in the railway car of Marshal Foch, who had led the Allied forces to victory against Germany in the First World War.

11 See above p. 166n.

12 Gaston Defferre (1910–1986) was a French socialist politician, who served as French Overseas Minister between 1956 and 1957. He sought to end French colonialism in sub-Saharan Africa.

13 See above p. 149n.

14 Jacques Massu (1908–2002) was a French general, who served in the Second World War, the first Indochina War, the Algerian War and the Suez Crisis. He was successful in the Battle of Algiers of 1957 but, along with General Salan (see above p. 145n), threatened a coup if the government of the French Prime Minister, Pierre Pflimlin — which wished to conduct negotiations with Algerian nationalists — did not leave. Pflimlin, in fact, left office and de Gaulle assumed leadership of the country instead.

IX. FOR A LUCID MORALITY AND AGAINST A DEBILITATING MORALITY

The authentic leader, the leader of authority — as opposed to the leader of popularity — is quite different. Let us outline quickly a summary portrait.

The natural leader is a being who possesses qualities of clear vision, of promptitude in decision and imagination. Thus he is one of those frightful lieutenants of paratroopers detested by the troops in the barracks, and obeyed blindly by the same troops in combat. These are true chiefs and when the need is felt, they are no longer disputed. In the barracks, they are hard, demanding, contemptuous and, consequently, detested. On the front, they are obeyed. The soldiers trembling with fear under enemy fire, encircled, thrown off balance, turn their eyes then to the natural leader, the one who has kept his cool, his faculties of initiative.

His superiority is then indisputable and not disputed, and his command is not elective but instinctive. The same soldiers who, in the barracks, called their instructor a bastard, find in him under the fire of the enemy machine guns the miraculous virtues of a protective and powerful father.

The leader is one who believes when everybody is still sceptical, the one who sees farther and sooner, who dares when nobody dares. The leader is also a creative genius, he is an initiator, a founder of religions, ideologies, or nations.

Frequently he fails on a personal level, such as Caesar, Frederick II of Hohenstaufen or Charles V.[15] But the more he fails on a personal and immediate level, the more he succeeds FOR THE OTHERS and on a historic level.

The natural leader is thus the one towards whom the masses turn instinctively at difficult, dangerous moments.

How far we are from the pseudo-leaders of popularity of democratism, who literally disappear before a crisis or danger.

---

15 Charles V (1500–1558) was the ruler of the Spanish Empire as Charles I from 1516, and Holy Roman Emperor as Charles V from 1519. Philip II of Spain was his son.

An objection frequently encountered is that the leader is disputed. This objection is without validity because all the leaders have always been disputed — apart from very short periods of acute crises. Whether it be Caesar or Bonaparte, Hitler or de Gaulle, all have been contested, hated and slandered. All have been either assassinated or victims of assassination attempts.

The genesis of personal power is always the same: ferocious or muffled struggles, competition and a slow rise to authority.

Let us begin a parenthesis to note that the authority by way of succession, in the case of hereditary royalty, economises the period of competition between the new candidates to power; but, on the other hand, this system is doomed irremediably through the very fact of the laws of heredity which reveals to us that the son of a genius, or the son of a hero will not himself be a genius or a hero, except in a very reduced framework of possibilities.

The leader is thus, we said above, always contested at the start. He is that often by his partners, at least at the start of the enterprise.

Let us take two recent examples. Hitler took several years to become the undisputed leader of his own party and it was only after coming out of prison that he affirmed the necessity of it, thus four years after the founding of the NSDAP. At a certain period, Goebbels detached himself totally from Hitler. Others separated themselves definitively from the Party, like the Strassers,[16] who could not accept the authority of a single individual.

Closer to us, we see a Ben Bella emerge in a few weeks from the directorship of a college and send his rivals to oblivion. The Algerian leader in fact took eight years, from 1954 to 1962, to become the

---

16 Gregor Strasser (1892–1934) and his brother Otto Strasser (1897–1974) were staunch socialists within the National Socialist Party and worked for a revolution that would be more mass-oriented and less elitist than the National Socialist regime was. Gregor was killed in 1934 in the National Socialist purge of its members called the 'Night of the Long Knives', and Otto was forced to flee Germany in 1933 for, first, Czechoslovakia and then Canada.

undisputed leader. In 1961, even the journalists most aware of the political game — but also least aware of the laws that prevail in hard parties — showed only a feeble interest in Ben Bella and thought that they saw the future 'president' [sic] in such and such a pharmacist hidden in Rabat or in such and such an advocate seeking refuge in Tunis. A revolution or a state which gives birth in pain and blood does not engender presidents ... it brings forth leaders, and then one leader.

At the start, the leader will be contested. He will be that by capable men who could be that in his place; he will be that equally by a number of incapable candidates who do not realise their mediocrity. Others still, who make very good seconds, imagine that they could be a prime minister. If they have qualities to make lieutenants, they can at the same time have none of the qualities that make a leader. Mark Antony and Murat[17] are of this type.

What a leader needs is therefore to get the support of some thing, which can be the Church, Army, Party, a praetorian guard, a banking group, the nobility, the Mamluks[18] or the Janissaries.[19] There is no 'leader all by himself'. That is an idealised image for a socialist school teacher.

In fact, an intense solidarity must unite the leader to the cohesive minority on whom he has chosen to support himself. Through a sort of osmosis, the leader and his entourage, the leader and his support, will have to to become homogeneous, the former influencing strongly the disciplines of thought of the latter, but having always to take into account the opinion of the latter. The hardest leaders, like Stalin, left behind them loyal people. This sufficiently establishes that they maintained relations of comradery with a certain limited entourage.

---

17 Joachim Murat (1767–1815) was a French marshal and admiral under Napoleon.
18 Mamluks were slave soldiers who, in mediaeval Egypt, formed a military caste and even ruled the country as the Mamluk Sultanate from 1250 to 1517.
19 Janissaries were Christian slaves formed into elite infantry troops of the Ottoman sultans during the reign of Murad I (1362–89).

The image of the autocrat 'all alone' in his Kremlin, or of the paranoid person vociferating in his bunker. is childish.

It is inaccurate to declare that the leader should gather the consensus of the 'great majority of the people'. *In fact, he should gather the consensus of the party apparatus, when it is a matter of a fighting party.*

A popular and loved 'leader', such as Alcibiades,[20] who had obtained the consensus of the great majority of the Athenian people, showed himself to be a tragic joker, whereas a strong Stalin, with little direct contact with the masses, proved himself to be an authentic leader.

The natural leader is a little like a doctor or a priest. As long as a man is full of health, he mocks the doctor. If he becomes ill, he will blindly obey the same doctor. How many there are of those declaiming against the Church who, on their deathbed, through simple fear of death, call fervently for the priest whom they mocked yesterday!

Leaders have the privilege of seeing sooner and farther. Similarly, only an aware avantgarde, a historic elite, possesses the particular intuition which makes them rally the natural leaders much before the masses do that.

At the very moment when the masses see only an adventurer or a juggler of utopias, the avantgarde elite, more aware, sense already the historic political leader.

For the masses, leaders are that always as it were a posteriori, *for the avantgarde elite, more aware, more intuitive, the leader is that* a priori.

The argument according to which the one who is not popular cannot become the leader is without validity and does not stand up to an objective examination of history. Let us take only the example of Philip of Macedon and that of Caesar. The official brilliant and famous

---

20   Alcibiades was a 5th century B.C. Athenian statesman and general, who served Athens, Sparta and even the Persian Empire in turns, though he finally returned to Athens and won some military successes before being defeated in the Battle of Notium (406 B.C.) during the Peloponnesian War.

disputants of these two leaders have passed into posterity — perhaps solely to prove that the finest minds are frequently mistaken.

Every schoolchild knows Demosthenes and Cicero. These two personages were garrulous dwarfs beside men of whom they were in a way professional disputants. Between the history seen by Demosthenes and Cicero and that made by Philip and Caesar, our choice is clear. It is for those who do and not those who speak. Thus, the greater they were, the more contested were the historic leaders before the realisation of their plans. The great leaders have never had help except from history itself and some privileged people of their entourage.

People Privileged by Their Lucidity

History sometimes experiences calm waters, sometimes dangerous waters. Many are those who can direct a tourist boat on a Swiss lake, rare are those who can pass Cape Horn in a sailboat.

The history of a nation encounters, in its course, difficult capes. It then calls for exceptional pilots. These pilots are the authentic leaders.

Difficult, hazardous, risky and dangerous enterprises attract only a few candidates to the command.

But once success starts, the flock of impostors accelerates. They exclaim, 'Why him, why not me? We also want to be leaders.' That will be the last wave of 'disputes', the wave of impostors.

History must reply to them: 'Where were you at the time when the enterprise was derisory? Were you uncertain? Oh well! Stay that way! *Only the one who was already present in the derisory time can be a leader in the end. Only the one who was that already in the fight and in uncertainty can be that in peace and in success.*'

A last objection that is formulated against personal power is that it is arbitrary. In fact, most of the time, personal power is arbitral and integrating and not arbitrary. And precisely personal power, that of the leader, draws all its qualities, all its efficacity, from his arbitral and integrating power.

By integrating power we understand the style of government that allows the one whose suggestion has not been retained to not feel wounded, humiliated and minoritised. The contempt of minorities is one of the poisons that undermine parliamentary democracy. The leader integrates into the community all the men, including those who are — provisionally — 'not in agreement'.

Of course, if he cannot take 'the advice of all' into account, he nevertheless governs for all and not with a majority against a minority.

After the integrating decision taken by the leader, those 'not in agreement' participate as much in its implementation as those who are 'in agreement'.

The key to the personal power — of 'the leader system' — is held in a very broad arbitral authority to be associated with a powerful information network. *'Despotism' is enlightened to the extent that it is informed. The reform of our institutions resides in a very great extension of the informative powers and in a very broad reduction of the deliberative powers.*

In democratism one constructs, on very weak and not very serious information bases, a gigantic deliberating apparatus which is not crowned with any real arbitral power. The formula of the leader is, on the contrary, constituted of a very large information mechanism followed by a small deliberating system and the whole crowned by a powerful and undisputed arbitral power. As much as the arbitrary personal power may be odious and dangerous, as much as depersonalised 'power' may be impotent, so much may the arbitral personal power be fortunate in its consequences. This is valid as much of a party as of a nation.

Peace Must Be an Act of Intelligence and Not an Act of Weakness: Peaceful People and Pacifists.

The difference between violence and strength is essential. The simple man does not establish this fundamental distinction. He confuses a strong regime with a cruel regime and a powerful nation with an aggressive nation.

Violence arises from despair or from disarray; it is sporadic. Strength, on the contrary, contains in itself calm assurance; it is constant, organised and accepted. Only the strong are peaceful; as for the weak, they balance the option of cowardice with the option of desperate violence. These considerations are as valid for nations as they are for combatants.

When one speaks of peace, it can signify diametrically opposed things. In Communist jargon — experienced unconsciously by the gullible liberals of the West — peace signifies quite simply non-resistance to Russian nationalist aggression. Peace can also be the confirmation of the vanity of a conflict, it is then peace as an 'act of intelligence'.

Thus the campaigns of Russia of 1812 and of 1941–43 — after the earlier mistake of Charles XII, King of Sweden[21] — oblige us to appreciate the value of resistance to the Russian nation.

An aggression against Russia thus becomes a costly and hazardous enterprise, and therefore the condition of peace between Russia and Europe is imperative, as much for one as for the other.

This is a reasoned peace.

In European politics, we must demonstrate to the men in the Kremlin that they cannot swallow Europe and, *a fortiori*, digest it. We must first of all respect one another and then peace will come of itself.

---

21   Charles XII (1682–1718) was King of Sweden from 1697. He undertook an invasion of Russia in 1708, which ended in the defeat of the Swedish forces at the Battle of Poltava in July 1709.

The rulers of Moscow will become peaceful with regard to us when we will have demonstrated to them the uselessness of their territorial appetites west of the Dniester. For that we must make life unsustainable for them in Eastern Europe until the moment when they will be forced to give it back to us.

In this regard we possess an indisputable superiority over the Muscovite rulers: it is that we are strong with great historical experience and a greater historical maturity. We know the vanity of certain crusades. The Communist leaders, on the other hand, instead of drawing lessons from history, still seek a personal inspiration in a primitive lesson: Marxist messianism. They underestimate in this way our capacity of resistance. Europe only needs to become aware. Our revolutionary role is to initiate and to educate. Once this is done, Moscow will no longer have the least chance to develop here in Europe its imperialism of a young nation. Communism will be contained and then pushed back, as Islam was — the bearer of a sacralised message that was powerful in other ways in the beginning. Communism is a force to the extent that it is a religion, a hope for naïve oppressed people.

For us who have 25 centuries of history, of schooling, peace is easier to conceive than for a regime relatively young like Russian Communism exalted by its religiosity.

The genesis of the peaceful conception comes from the experience of numerous and uncertain combats. Once again, this statement is as valid as much for individuals as it is for nations. A young man, of around 20 years, will be abnormally aggressive; he has just realised his strength, but he has not yet experienced that of others. Later, he will no longer use his strength imprudently.

Nations exhibit the same behaviour: when they are very young, they give themselves up to an expansionism that is imprudent, though profitable in the short term. Societies are peaceful only after having exhausted all experiences, from uncertain conflicts to alternated victories.

Thus, today, war is psychologically impossible between Germany and France, for the peoples of these two nations have realised — finally — the uselessness, the absurdity of periodic conflict.

Peace is thus an act of intelligence. To base the hope of peace on 'good sentiments' is naivety and ingenuousness. Moscow will give up its territorial ambitions in the West when Europe no longer gives it a spectacle of division and gullibility.

In this regard the tolerance of Communism among us constitutes a real encouragement to aggression for Moscow. By tolerating among ourselves Communist parties, that is to say, Russian parties, we display our imbecility and that can only encourage the Kremlin in its ambitions.

It is our gullibility that nourishes the imperialistic hopes of Moscow. As long as we tolerate among ourselves Communists and pacifists, that is to say, manipulated idiots, or cowards, the Communist general staff will not give up its greed.

Peace as an 'act of weakness' leads in a direct line to subjection. The path of peace between Europe and Russia passes necessarily through the display of our moral and material strength.

When Europe will be strong, peace as an 'act of intelligence' will be proposed by Moscow itself.

The Myth of the Perfect Decision and of the Possible Solution

Ever since the 'pure' intellectuals, I mean by that speculative ones as opposed to scientific ones, have poisoned the judgement of public affairs by the adoration of theories and ideologies, the great majority of people believe — in politics — in the possibility of perfect structures and, by extension, in the possibility of the perfect decision.

This belief is supported by the progress of human justice in the matter of general law (in the matter of political justice, we have had experiences that are little edifying). The justice of general law manifests in fact more and more wisdom, prudence and equity. Measuring in centuries.

But the judicial decision is of a totally different nature from the political decision. The judicial decision is applied to a past fact, to a stationary fact, to a known fact.

Conversely, the political decision is exercised on facts that are to come, on things in movement, necessarily with factors of uncertainty.

The procedure of political command is thus totally different from the procedure of judicial decision.

Men called upon to exercise political responsibilities and those called upon to assume judicial responsibilities will thus be of VERY different temperament and intelligence.

The colonel of an encircled regiment, the firefighter captain before a block of buildings on fire, the head of state of a threatened state, the leader of a persecuted political party must take instantaneous decisions, whereas the president of a circuit court or the jury of a literary competition can take deferred decisions.

I think that one must enlighten the masses on this subject and show them that the best institutions with the most refined controls and the most numerous brakes do not at all guarantee efficacity or results.

Further, it must be emphasised that for most of the time a political decision must be rapid and delay does not conduce to a better decision. Quite the contrary.

That is what one should say about those who must decide. Let us see now the factors on which one must decide. In chemistry, in astronomy, in algebra, there exists one solution to each problem, and only one. There is no Catholic chemistry, Communist astronomy or Fascist algebra. The solution is never discussed because it can be demonstrated scientifically.

In politics it is quite different. We find then several ways of seeing things, and several ways of 'resolving' things. The political problem is not soluble, at most it can be regulated.

IX. FOR A LUCID MORALITY AND AGAINST A DEBILITATING MORALITY

Here, therefore, we come across regulations instead of solutions.

The regulation is either imposed, it is then a dictate, or negotiated, then it is a compromise.

Even a compromise allows a certain rancour to persist, a certain regret, a certain friction.

In order to quickly demonstrate the impossibility of a solution in politics, let us cite some concrete cases.

The Brenner Pass belongs linguistically to the Germanic realm. But geographically it belongs to the Italian peninsula. Further — in the past — the law of conservation demanded of Italy that it control at least the Brenner SUMMIT. The Germanic people will appeal to ethnological and linguistic considerations, the Italians to others informed by geopolitics, the military, art, or history. As for the rights of the first settlers, how can one invoke that? They have been dead a long time … as organised peoples or societies.

The same thing in Cyprus, where the reason of the European state demands that these imbecilic conflicts between 'communities' be silenced. But also where, by invoking the history of Byzantium or the history of the Crusades on the one hand, or the Muslim conquests on the other, each of the two parties can have 'rights' [sic] validated. In the case of Cyprus, there are three regulations, but only one solution. A Greek regulation, a Turkish regulation and a European regulation. The last being the forcing of these people to calm down and live together.

But one will see that whatever regulation adopted — or imposed — there will remain regrets or bitterness.

We arrive therefrom at a realistic conclusion which is that, in order to prevent the offensive return of regret transformed into rebellion, the regulation should be not too humiliating for the 'losing' party but further must be consolidated through force, without which it will exist only in an ephemeral fashion.

One should therefore — at a moral level — confront the problem of politics with a feeling of inevitable imperfection and with a will to the least imperfection.

We must destroy the myth of a possible solution and that of a perfect decision.

Political command does not derive from the prudence of the pharmacist before his scale or from that of the magistrate before his file. It does not derive either from the naivety of ideologues or the virtuism of mystics.

Political command demands character and power, lucidity and rapidity. Virtues that democratism excludes by itself.

The Disappearance of the Instinct of Conservation of Peoples

The instinct of conservation among animals and among men does not need demonstration.

On the other hand, what escapes many observers is that the nations themselves are endowed with this quality and that they can lose it. The instinct of conservation is notably made up of recalled experiences, which teach us mistrust, prudence and the necessity of verification.

It is in this way that the one who is endowed with a solid instinct of conservation will not let himself be deceived by appearances; he will in a way discover the reality behind the appearance. The little fish, at the bottom of the ocean, will be suspicious of appetising but fish-eating vegetation.

Organised societies, nations, are not free of these rules and, if they are endowed with a solid instinct, they will then be guided by a total intuitive realism; conversely, if they are no longer that, they will be lacking in this quality and will be taken in by the intoxication of words and falsely humanitarian and falsely pacifist postulates.

It is principally ideological abstractions that cause nations to be intoxicated by their own dreams. They then degenerate in sentimental mawkishness, make guilt complexes and sink into naïve brotherly love. The relations between nations do not escape the rule of relations of strength, and bad luck to those which forget this lesson.

Thus the belief that the relations between nations can be regulated by morality, a morality deprived of material strength, is one of the suicidal forms of the disappearance of the instinct of conservation.

Tolerance elevated to the rank of a principle of government can proceed with a total naivety. Thus, in the West, we tolerate Communists, a kind of Russian 'Muslims', who do not hide their subordination to a foreign STATE; we tolerate pacifists, when the same are non-existent (because not tolerated) in the USSR. Tolerance is the best of things, and it is the perfection, the maturity of intelligence. But when life is at stake, tolerance can become criminal.

Tolerance demands at the very least reciprocity. Now what do we see? In the West, the conscientious objection raised to a principle and codified, whereas in the USSR the cult of the Army is constantly maintained among the youth. In the West, the party of the foreigner is tolerated — even in the bourgeois salons — whereas in the USSR a 'European party' would not last a week.

Among us, Communist literature submerges the schools and universities. Do you think that the present book — in a Russian version — could circulate in the USSR anywhere, except in the offices of the specialist police?

When societies are vigorous, they are endowed with a solid instinct of conservation. Thus, the French Revolution, one should not be mistaken, cut many heads, but when people tried to touch that which was essential — in the perspective of that time — that is to say, property, there was unanimity. François Noël Babeuf[22] experienced it in 1797, at a time when people had lost the mania of cutting off heads.

---

22 François-Noël Babeuf (1760-1797) was a radical revolutionary who called for the abolition of private property and wished to raise a revolt of the poor against

In the past, when the Cathars threatened the very structures of continuity of society, they were destroyed. Rightly. The obliteration of the instinct of conservation, here in the West, is translated today into the practice of a gullible tolerance, a naïve idealistic liberalism.

The moment that a nation believes words more than realities, it has lost its instinct of conservation by renouncing realism and vigilance.

It is the hypnotism exercised by ideologues, in a society weakened by a proliferation of so-called intellectuals, which prepares disastrous futures.

Those who have constructed nations used ideologies as screens for their appetites. It was then men who manipulated facts and things. The baptism of the Saxons by Charlemagne and the repression of homosexuality by Philip the Fair are in this regard models of moralities or ideologies in the service of realities.

On the other hand, when the heads of state themselves begin to believe in ideologies not as a dressing of crude appetites or moral ornaments but as ends in themselves, it is the beginning of decadence.

History teaches us that ambitions and appetites are less harmful to the peoples than intellectual speculations and humanitarian declamations. In 1797, France cut off Babeuf's head: it had then the instinct of conservation. In 1964, Europe agrees to polemicise, compete in a war of words with Communism and demonstrates thus the obliteration or disappearance of this instinct.

Injustice That Returns

It is common to oppose justice to injustice. On the other hand, very few people realise that in fact the problem really posed is that of one injustice opposed to another injustice. Each camp will proclaim in a loud voice that it represents justice, a sort of moral abstraction to which one gives an absolute character. Let us not be deceived by these appearances, destined to take advantage of the masses.

---

the Directory. He was guillotined in May 1797.

The concrete examples are clearer. I refuse to be a Manichean to the point of acknowledging a totally moral England having waged war against a totally immoral Germany, or vice versa, I refuse to maintain that the French colonisation in Algeria was a model or that, on the contrary, it was a disgrace.

In reality, it was neither the one nor the other. The French committed certain blunders in not managing to assimilate in 130 years the Kabyles[23] and the Berbers, of whom it was tolerably easy to make authentic Frenchmen. The French exploited the local labourers and really provoked the Arab wogs.[24] Yes.

But the problem is not there. The problem was that the French maintained an injustice and that the Algerian nationalists promised another (and they indeed kept their word ...).

The tortures and the dispossessions are to be shared equally between the two camps. But the *Pax Francia* was still a sort of *Pax Romana*, hard certainly but fecund and permitting a more equitable future, whereas the anarchy and balkanisation of 1964 promised only growing misery and pauperisation.

Later, and this is the main point of my report, there was, on the one hand, a French injustice and, on the other, an Algerian injustice, and not one injustice opposed to an Algerian 'justice'. The moment one has to choose between two injustices, one should, without the LEAST hesitation, choose OUR injustice (even if it means correcting it later) and fight the other.

For the problem is there and nowhere else. In Algeria, it was necessary to have the courage to recognise and correct the faults of integration even while not accepting in any case to give up presence and power. First maintain oneself and then correct oneself.

---

23 The Kabyles are Berbers living in the Kabylia region of Northern Algeria.
24 Thiriart here uses the derogatory French colonial term '*bicots*' (goats) for Arabs.

Whether the French cause was intrinsically good or bad is without importance. What is important is that the cause of the French was that of Europe and the other that of the enemies of Europe.

Between equity — let us say 'equity' because the word 'justice' is so clichéd — and injustice, one should without hesitation choose and impose equity. This is, besides, the mission of the strong and the leaders. But between two injustices, hesitation is no longer permitted, one should opt for one's own, through the instinct of conservation and, further, through legitimate defence.

Sacred Cows or Stereotypical Idols

Everybody knows the problem of sacred cows in India, to which everything is permitted and beside which one would even agree to die of hunger. Our decadent societies, here in the West, have some of these depraved minds, in a way perverted by fashion, who are filled with love for the good Iroquois, the good negro, or the good Arab wog.

Through intellectual laziness, through superficiality, everybody has his sacred cows, which is true from the good Christian to the good proletarian. Some even prefer cats to people. Others are moved by the conditions of slaughter in a little town and indifferent to the tortures suffered by the French in Algeria.

This attitude betrays a certain stereotype of morality and a destruction of the critical mind.

The political press is cluttered with these cults.

Thus, between 1918 and 1935, it was enough 'to have been in the trenches' to have the say and to have a formal right to the last word. The cult of the old combatant, a sacred cow after 1918, corresponds to that of the Resistance fighter, a sacred cow after 1945. The courage of the majority of these men is not disputable, or disputed, but the fact that they have been made sacred cows has falsified or prevented any later objective analysis.

Even heroes can be abusive, and courage is not necessarily linked to intelligence.

We should carefully guard against reserving for certain categories of men the exclusivity of the virtues that only some among them possess.

This is a sort of collective virtuism, which causes certain intellectuals to be stirred by the word proletariat, a sacred monster of the 20th century.

Let us therefore guard against collective judgements and stratification of virtues and vices. The hero of the day before yesterday can have become today a bothersome imbecile.

Those who claim to rule men must conserve — at least in themselves — a critical mind, which is always alert, to be exercised on individuals taken in isolation. That a man is decorated with the Legion of Honour insignia, a hero of the Eastern Front, an ex-Resistance fighter or a man from French Algeria does not give him the right to any favourable prejudice in facts related to current affairs. Nor, on the other hand, to any unfavourable prejudice.

One should — in political judgement — consider the man of the present in the present situation, with his present usefulness. A ruling elite — in politics — does not know any 'sacred cows'.

The Anti-Elite, or the Social Rejects of Society

Primitive societies were extremely harsh in their measures of selection of their members. The deformed child was destroyed, the coward or the robber was driven out and banned. It will not be a question here of manifest abnormal beings to whom our laws accord care and protection, nor of euthanasia either. I wish only to pinpoint a particular problem, that of intellectual depravation or of civic inversion.

In every collectivity there are social rejects filled with a profound resentment and ready to get revenge by associating with every enemy of society, by which they feel rejected. Rarely does a man admit his mediocrity; most often he ignores it. With a certain fierce humour, one can say that it is not desirable that *absolute justice* should reign one day on earth — if ever that were possible — for, in this hypothesis, each person would realise what his real place is, could no longer dispute it and would be felled by the lightning flash of this truth. The famous injustice of our societies allows the mediocre to transfer the causes of their personal failure to 'capitalism', to the bourgeoisie, to socialism, to everything but themselves.

To admit injustice is a highly charitable act, for it is much more bearable to suffer in the certitude of being the victim of an injustice than to suffer in the certitude of one's personal incapacity. Thus society inevitably contains a sort of anti-elite composed of bitter, abnormal and badly adapted people. Its membership is ensured by sexual perversions, social resentment, the wounded pride of delayed amnesties, etc.

In the Middle Ages, these heterogeneous elements in society were destroyed by fire, under the pretext of witchcraft or heresy. It is not at all my intention to counsel the restoration of similar practices and to ensure social virtue through the stake. In the last four or five centuries the stake has progressively disappeared, but society defended itself still very well by prohibiting the paths of access to power to those who did not correspond to the average conformism demanded by a given collectivity. Nowadays, universal suffrage, obligatory conscription and the delirious demagogy of a decadent parliamentarism cause these dregs, these rejects, to be CONSTANTLY AND POLITICALLY SOLICITED.

Where the matter becomes more serious is when one discovers a systematic enrolment of these rejects by the Communist parties here in the west. In the USSR, these social rejects are brutally eliminated but the scientific cynicism of the Muscovites is such that they destroy or what they do not neutralise in their country, they use in our country against us. In the USSR, the psychopaths are eliminated from the Party. Here the Communists enrol them. This method is extremely efficient in nations like ours, where one has not taken the precaution of distinguishing between the passive citizen, whom the laws protect socially but who has no active part in the management of the community, and the active citizen, who should, alone, have the right to a positive civic life.

I do not intend to demonstrate or to try to demonstrate that the Communist parties of the 'Trojan Horse' type are composed only of abnormal people, but indeed that they are welcomed there with solicitude and rapidly enrolled with special actions in view, such as espionage, wild riots, pillage, political assassination, and ideally, high treason.

The individual rejected by society — rightly or wrongly — is ulcerated. He has only one idea — to get revenge. He does not have to look far: the Communist Party is waiting for him. The West would be very wrong in underestimating this factor of disintegration, for these rejects, this anti-elite, are a minority of desperation, thus ready for anything.

The utilisation of resentment is one of the techniques of the Communist arsenal. One would be wrong not to be alarmed by it. These embittered, hate-filled people are sometimes found in the machinery of our administrations, our public instruction apparatus, or even in the Army or in the police.

We all know the legendary personage Coriolanus, ulcerated by the ingratitude of the Roman plebs and turning against his own. Here, the personage is tragic. Sordid, mediocre, vicious, Coriolanuses can be recruited in large numbers. Moscow knows how to do that. It is for us to defend ourselves against it.

The psychological phenomenon, one would be tempted to say psychiatric, that is at the base of a part of the recruitment of the Communist parties outside the USSR is that of resentment, justified or not.

This resentment, this bitterness, leads to a kind of nihilism. It is this nihilism of defeated whites or of corrupt whites that has led to the myth of the good negro as opposed to the wicked white.

The corrupt white, through bitterness, wishes to take revenge on the white who is not corrupt, who he knows is superior to him. The corrupt person will look, for his justificatory constructions, for an external ally.

This resentment is found among certain racial groups that still have — wrongly — an inferiority complex. They are equally found among those who have been given a veneer of culture on a foundation of weakness of character. Very numerous are the 'intellectuals' who ruin their private, sentimental and professional lives. They ruin them because they have neither calibre nor character, and a university diploma cannot compensate for these deficiencies. But the misfortune is that bookish knowledge has been given to these weak and mediocre people.

Thus they will quite quickly become resentful and will join the forgiving people of Communism, who are so clever in cynically utilising whatever urge that is exploitable.

We have, in any given society, a ruling elite, either in place or on its way to taking its place: this is the ruling class (beside it there cohabits a neutral apolitical elite that does not concern us here). Then come the masses who only demand to be well governed and who, contrary to what one commonly believes, do not demand to participate in the exercise of power: and, in the last place, the rejects of a society, the scum. The harshness of the social order or of the practice of banishment permitted, in the past, the eviction of this anti-elite. Today, it is no longer the same and, through naïve and imprudent humanitarianism, one allows these toxins to attempt the destruction of the societies that contain them. Thus the nihilism of resentment accomplishes its work of destruction with the unconscious complicity of a debilitated and gullible elite.

When the ruling class has become incapable of employing force in a firm manner, one of the principal conditions of serious upheaval is realised.

We would be wrong to underestimate this noxious anti-elite. The Communists know how to utilise them scientifically, sometimes throwing thugs onto the streets, sometimes — and this is the most dangerous — placing eccentric 'intellectuals' in key posts of education or information.

Every society engenders a certain quantity of anti-elite; this is a constant phenomenon. Nations in decline tolerate it, strong nations reduce it socially.

Power as the Source of Freedom

Freedom is not an original state, a natural state. It is, on the contrary, a state that is conquered, a condition guaranteed by a force. Everything that lives, in nature, is free only to the extent that it makes itself be respected.

Freedom is the thing that is most threatened in the order of nature. Everything that surrounds a freedom is interested to dispute it or to suppress it.

One can, one should even, specify that it is more correct to speak of freedoms in the plural than of freedom in the singular. From molecular physics to the history of man, there is not freedom in the context of a void or indifference, there exist only states of equilibrium born of a force opposed to a repulsion or to a reaction to an action.

Men and nations are free to the extent only that they are capable, through their forces, to make this state be validated and respected. If a man is weak, he will occupy, in the social scale, a position of subjection: if a nation is weak, it will be either satellitised or colonialised, or absorbed by another that is more powerful.

Of course, one can deplore the inexistence of a perfect state of human relations, where freedom would need, in order to be manifested and respected, only the evidence of its existence. But this perfect or almost perfect state, will it ever be accessible to us? Governments respect the freedom of the governed to the degree where the latter, if people wished to deprive them of it, are capable of insurrection.

The path of freedom goes through that of power. One should therefore not forget that, or one should teach it to those who do not know it. The freedom of the weak is a virtuist myth, a naivety for demagogic or electoral use. The weak have never been free and will never be. There exists only a freedom of the strong.

One who wishes to be free must want to be powerful. One who wishes to be free must be capable of arresting other freedoms, for freedom is invasive and has a tendency to encroach on that of weak neighbours.

It is criminal, from the point of view of public education, to tolerate that the masses may be intoxicated by debilitating lies like that which consist in 'declaring peace' to one's neighbours, thinking in this way to be able to conserve one's freedom. Each of our freedoms has been acquired after repeated and bloody combats and each of them will be maintained only if we can display a force likely to discourage those who would wish to deprive us of it.

More than others, we like certain freedoms and reject numerous constraints. But we know how much these freedoms are perpetually threatened. Whether as an individual or as a nation, we know the source of freedom and it is power.

If we wish to conserve the former, we must cultivate the latter. They are inseparable.

The Utility of a Community and the Utility for a Community

We mean by utility of a community everything that contributes to its survival, its capacities of resistance.

The historical life of a nation and the duration of this life depend on factors which involuntarily or consciously contribute to the utility of the community.

Conversely, we see the *utility for* a community. These are the material satisfactions, the territorial benefits, the well-being, the 'happiness' [sic].

Let us establish a concrete parallel with the individual. The *utility of* the individual is to take care of his health through good sleep, a healthy diet, physical exercise in the open air — the practice of sports — through the creation of a stable couple.

Conversely, the *utility for* an individual consists in spending the night in a nightclub, in looking for spicy cuisine, in attending a match of catch-as-catch-can in an overheated and smoke-filled hall, in seeking adulterated sentimental adventures.

On the one hand, effort and self-control, on the other, pleasure and enjoyment.

Statesmen watch over the former values, those that can be classified as the *utility of* a community; the parliamentarian politicians, on the contrary, are forced by the laws of obligatory demagogy, to offer to their clientele solutions which lead to being catalogued as *utility for* a community. It is wrong to oppose daily bread to cannons. Without cannons, the daily bread is not possible.

If a nation is no longer in a condition to survive, it is idle to discuss in the abstract if its political structures constitute an 'ideal society', a 'social' philanthropy. Rome and Byzantium, towards their end, constructed very big circuses and very fine racecourses whereas, at the peak of their power, they organised armies.

Let us imagine, hypothetically, that the Western parliamentarian liberal democracy is the most pleasant form, that it leads to the 'happiness' of society. If it is not determined to defend itself against external appetites, it is, in every way, doomed. This is what happens here in the social-bourgeois West and this is why this world is doomed to disappear, either due to the Russian appetites based on the

Communist myth or due to our ourselves. One must choose. What one must have the courage to say is that the enjoyment of territorial goods is conditioned by the capacity to conserve the latter, and the masses must know that the 'conquests of socialism' must be defended by the gun and not by declamations of cosmic philanthropy.

Our choice has been made. We do not avoid the social values and European National Communitarianism will satisfy them. But these values will be defended not by virtuist words but by instruments of force.

The internal utility of the European nation resides in the economic expansion which conditions social progress: the external utility of the European nation finds its expression in the means of power placed in the service of the will to exist as a nation.

Twenty centuries of history teach us that neglecting the external utility leads to disappearance.

European Communitarianism will therefore be pugnacious; it will be armed. A pacifist nation is a fantasy construction. Europe will be a peaceful nation, that is to say, a strong nation. The world needs this strong nation; the world needs Europe.

Heroes of Sacrifice and the Morality of Demand

The race to 'happiness' is characteristic of the plutocratic institutions in which we live. This happiness is essentially based on claims, and materialistic: it is the race to pleasure. Let us observe with interest the heroes proposed to the masses by our decadence; they have powerful cars, they have a square chin, a low forehead. They are, not well-to-do, but rich. The common theme of these personages: 'they are lucky'.

One has, rightly, mocked the romance novels offered to maids towards 1910 and to typists around 1960, in which a future of 'happiness' was made to shine to them through the corridor of 'love'. The illusions offered to these young women do not differ at all from those that are offered unceasingly to the masses in general and to the youth in particular. Our plutocratic society has constructed for itself a utilitarian morality, a morality of consumers and voters.

Who are the heroes offered to the youth? Open the magazines that are aimed at them: easy wealth through easy success. Always ease. The heroes that are offered earn money quickly by being racing drivers, singers, football players.

In Byzantium, the chariot racers were also offered to the admiration of the crowds. The virility of Byzantium had chosen to reside in the racecourses in order not to have to show itself elsewhere, on the fields of battle. Today, the virility that is offered as a model emerges from the car-racing tracks.

The heroes offered are heroes of pleasure. That goes without saying. The heroes of pleasure consume, whereas the heroes of sacrifice do not consume.

The commercial media, through scientific coarsening of the masses, which it must condition to purchase after having prepared them through the creation of artificial needs, destroy the moral and psychological balance of the men who are its victims.

Dissatisfaction is the condition in which they are to be placed. At the same time, the 'happiness' that is offered to them is always through the acquisition of a bigger car, a more snobbish whiskey, a more 'exclusive' cigarette. The commercial imperatives, in their monstrous hypertrophy, are here in formal opposition to the demands of the moral health of a nation.

Few men reach material satiety. Nevertheless, there are thousands who do. Among the beneficiaries of this condition, the large majority sink into boredom, lack of moderation and permissiveness. One has only to observe the *nouveaux riches*. From among the beneficiaries of material satiety, however, emerge here and there men who overcome this condition, who go beyond it. One must have exhausted many pleasures in order to know their vanity and I have always distrusted the asceticism of the poor because it is subject to failures!

This is valid for the future ruling elite, which will have to present moral qualities essentially different from those that those who are on top of the plutocratic world exhibit.

I evoked above the vanity of the miracle-institutions being able to create the felicity of peoples. Things will be what men will be, I wrote.

One must therefore concern oneself with making these men and giving them an adequate instruction and edifying models.

The history of man will have been, first of all, to dominate nature and the other species. He is close to his goal. It will then be to dominate himself, and there he is still close to Paleolithic man. Ever since Socrates, humankind has made very great advances in its struggle against hunger, cold, ignorance and natural phenomena. One cannot say that in the realm of moral and psychological balance he has made remarkable progress. It still remains to man himself to dominate himself.

We must oppose to the man of 'happiness', who the plutocratic world offers us, a man of balance, of internal balance.

I am very far from the moralisers who think that poverty is the creator of virtues. I do not believe that 'paid holidays' are destroyers of the 'immortal values' of piety. A man who is hungry, thirsty, afraid, is not in the required condition to improve himself. Material progress is thus one of the conditions of the elevation of man, but only one among so many others.

Another condition is the knowledge of the law of effort, a law still present in the reality of things. One must oppose to the morality of ease — a snare — the morality of effort, of demand.

One must teach men — or at least those who claim to lead them — that 'happiness' does not exist, that it is an intellectual construct offered to the simple to dupe them.

The man who will run after 'happiness' will never find it; the man who seeks balance will be able, in the best cases, to attain it. That is the main problem. There is no collective solution for men. The collective religious, social and material structures are only a framework, a support. Work should be accomplished individually. The material 'happiness' of humanity through Communism or the American bourgeois system smacks of duplicity or naivety.

The truth is that, in a favourable political framework (political and social conditions), every man must seek to fulfil himself.

And to do that he is alone, all alone. At most, one can show him some paths. But whatever the path may be, he will have to traverse it alone.

The American materialistic society shows us the impasse into which a community that neglects the moral preparation of its executives and of its masses falls. Material satiety has been reached, but it is at the cost of a generalised psychological imbalance. Rich countries, neurotic countries; countries of pleasure, countries of psychiatrists as well. Communism tends to the same and lamentable end. Only its povery has sheltered it, up to the present, from a similar failure. After having emphasised the relative vanity of the most perfect public institutions we must thus teach that men — or at least necessarily the leaders — have to 'finish', conclude, complete themselves, all alone.

We must substitute the gregarious morality of ease and pleasure with the morality of constant effort and demand accomplished individually, and we shall recall Epictetus:

'*Just as the bad chorists of tragedies cannot sing as soloists but sing in a choir of many, similarly certain people cannot go on a walk alone. Man, if you are somebody, walk by yourself, converse with yourself and do not hide yourself in a choir*'.[25]

How many of us, once we leave the choir, are just mediocre soloists!

Forest prison, cell 161 — March 1962.
Groelstveld, Calevoet — April 1964.

---

25 Epictetus, *Discourses*, Book III, Ch. 14.

OTHER BOOKS PUBLISHED BY ARKTOS

SRI DHARMA PRAVARTAKA ACHARYA	*The Dharma Manifesto*
JOAKIM ANDERSEN	*Rising from the Ruins*
WINSTON C. BANKS	*Excessive Immigration*
ALAIN DE BENOIST	*Beyond Human Rights*
	Carl Schmitt Today
	The Indo-Europeans
	Manifesto for a European Renaissance
	On the Brink of the Abyss
	The Problem of Democracy
	Runes and the Origins of Writing
	View from the Right (vol. 1–3)
ARTHUR MOELLER VAN DEN BRUCK	*Germany's Third Empire*
MATT BATTAGLIOLI	*The Consequences of Equality*
KERRY BOLTON	*Revolution from Above*
	Yockey: A Fascist Odyssey
ISAC BOMAN	*Money Power*
RICARDO DUCHESNE	*Faustian Man in a Multicultural Age*
ALEXANDER DUGIN	*Ethnos and Society*
	Ethnosociology
	Eurasian Mission
	The Fourth Political Theory
	Last War of the World-Island
	Political Platonism
	Putin vs Putin
	The Rise of the Fourth Political Theory
EDWARD DUTTON	*Race Differences in Ethnocentrism*
MARK DYAL	*Hated and Proud*
CLARE ELLIS	*The Blackening of Europe*
KOENRAAD ELST	*Return of the Swastika*
JULIUS EVOLA	*The Bow and the Club*
	Fascism Viewed from the Right
	A Handbook for Right-Wing Youth
	Metaphysics of War
	The Myth of the Blood
	Notes on the Third Reich
	The Path of Cinnabar

OTHER BOOKS PUBLISHED BY ARKTOS

	Recognitions
	A Traditionalist Confronts Fascism
GUILLAUME FAYE	*Archeofuturism*
	Archeofuturism 2.0
	The Colonisation of Europe
	Convergence of Catastrophes
	Ethnic Apocalypse
	A Global Coup
	Sex and Deviance
	Understanding Islam
	Why We Fight
DANIEL S. FORREST	*Suprahumanism*
ANDREW FRASER	*Dissident Dispatches*
	The WASP Question
GÉNÉRATION IDENTITAIRE	*We are Generation Identity*
PETER GOODCHILD	*The Taxi Driver from Baghdad*
PAUL GOTTFRIED	*War and Democracy*
PORUS HOMI HAVEWALA	*The Saga of the Aryan Race*
LARS HOLGER HOLM	*Hiding in Broad Daylight*
	Homo Maximus
	Incidents of Travel in Latin America
	The Owls of Afrasiab
RICHARD HOUCK	*Liberalism Unmasked*
A. J. ILLINGWORTH	*Political Justice*
ALEXANDER JACOB	*De Naturae Natura*
JASON REZA JORJANI	*Faustian Futurist*
	Iranian Leviathan
	Lovers of Sophia
	Novel Folklore
	Prometheism
	Prometheus and Atlas
	World State of Emergency
HENRIK JONASSON	*Sigmund*
VINCENT JOYCE	*The Long Goodbye*
RUUBEN KAALEP & AUGUST MEISTER	*Rebirth of Europe*
RODERICK KAINE	*Smart and SeXy*

OTHER BOOKS PUBLISHED BY ARKTOS

Peter King	Here and Now
	Keeping Things Close
	On Modern Manners
James Kirkpatrick	Conservatism Inc.
Ludwig Klages	The Biocentric Worldview
	Cosmogonic Reflections
Pierre Krebs	Fighting for the Essence
	Guillaume Faye: Truths and Tributes
Julien Langella	Catholic and Identitarian
John Bruce Leonard	The New Prometheans
Stephen Pax Leonard	The Ideology of Failure
	Travels in Cultural Nihilism
William S. Lind	Retroculture
Pentti Linkola	Can Life Prevail?
H. P. Lovecraft	The Conservative
Norman Lowell	Imperium Europa
Charles Maurras	The Future of the Intelligentsia
	& For a French Awakening
John Harmon McElroy	Agitprop in America
Michael O'Meara	Guillaume Faye and the Battle of Europe
	New Culture, New Right
Michael Millerman	Beginning with Heidegger
Brian Anse Patrick	The NRA and the Media
	Rise of the Anti-Media
	The Ten Commandments of Propaganda
	Zombology
Tito Perdue	The Bent Pyramid
	Lee
	Morning Crafts
	Philip
	The Sweet-Scented Manuscript
	William's House (vol. 1–4)
Raido	A Handbook of Traditional Living (vol. 1–2)
Steven J. Rosen	The Agni and the Ecstasy
	The Jedi in the Lotus

OTHER BOOKS PUBLISHED BY ARKTOS

Richard Rudgley	*Barbarians*
	Essential Substances
	Wildest Dreams
Ernst von Salomon	*It Cannot Be Stormed*
	The Outlaws
Piero San Giorgio	*CBRN*
	Giuseppe
Sri Sri Ravi Shankar	*Celebrating Silence*
	Know Your Child
	Management Mantras
	Patanjali Yoga Sutras
	Secrets of Relationships
George T. Shaw (ed.)	*A Fair Hearing*
Fenek Solère	*Kraal*
Oswald Spengler	*Man and Technics*
Richard Storey	*The Uniqueness of Western Law*
Tomislav Sunic	*Against Democracy and Equality*
	Homo Americanus
	Postmortem Report
	Titans are in Town
Askr Svarte	*Gods in the Abyss*
Hans-Jürgen Syberberg	*On the Fortunes and Misfortunes of Art in Post-War Germany*
Abir Taha	*Defining Terrorism*
	The Epic of Arya (2nd ed.)
	Nietzsche's Coming God, or the Redemption of the Divine
	Verses of Light
Bal Gangadhar Tilak	*The Arctic Home in the Vedas*
Dominique Venner	*For a Positive Critique*
	The Shock of History
Markus Willinger	*A Europe of Nations*
	Generation Identity
Alexander Wolfheze	*Alba Rosa*

Printed in Great Britain
by Amazon